CIPS Study Matters

Level 4

Foundation Diploma in Purchasing and Supply

Purchasing Contexts

Second Edition

Ian Thompson
Cordie Ltd

THE
CHARTERED INSTITUTE OF
PURCHASING & SUPPLY®

Published by

The Chartered Institute of Purchasing and Supply
Easton House, Easton on the Hill, Stamford, Lincolnshire PE9 3NZ
Tel: +44 (0) 1780 756 777
Fax: +44 (0) 1780 751 610
Email: info@cips.org
Website: http://www.cips.org

© The Chartered Institute of Purchasing and Supply 2006, 2009

First published June 2006
Second edition published June 2009

While every effort has been made to ensure that references to websites are correct at time of going to press, the world wide web is a constantly changing environment and CIPS cannot accept any responsibility for any changes to addresses.

CIPS acknowledges product, service and company names referred to in this publication, many of which are trade names, service marks, trademarks or registered trademarks.

CIPS, The Chartered Institute of Purchasing & Supply and its logo are all trademarks of the Chartered Institute of Purchasing & Supply.

The right of Ian Thompson to be identified as author of this work has been asserted by him in accordance with the Copyright, Design and Patents Act, 1988 in force or as amended from time to time.

Technical reviewer: Steve Langford, America II Electronics

Instructional design and publishing project management by Wordhouse Ltd, Reading, UK

Content management system, instructional editing and pre-press by Echelon Learning Ltd, London, UK

Index prepared by Indexing Specialists (UK) Ltd, Hove, UK

ISBN 978-1-86124-180-1

Contents

Introduction

This course book has been designed to assist you in studying for the CIPS Purchasing Contexts unit in the Level 4 Foundation Diploma in Purchasing and Supply. The book covers all topics in the official CIPS unit content document, as illustrated in the table beginning on page xi.

Purchasing and supply is a transferable skill. Increasingly, it has been recognised as one of the core business skills required by organisations across every sector of industry, commerce and public service.

To understand the transferability of these principles, you need to understand the context within which you are purchasing, both in terms of the organisation and its surrounding environment. This requires a study of the market sector, the organisation itself and its governance, as well as an understanding of the specific requirements of different forms of purchase.

This is the study of purchasing contexts. This course book has a broad focus that covers a range of subjects including the formation of different organisations, market sector dynamics and regulation, transferable purchasing principles, different types of purchase and a range of different funding options.

The diverse syllabus of this unit reflects the needs of the modern purchasing and supply professional and equips you with a broad business understanding across which you can carry your purchasing skills.

How to use this book

The course book will take you step by step through the unit content in a series of carefully planned 'study sessions' and provides you with learning activities, self-assessment questions and revision questions to help you master the subject matter. The guide should help you organise and carry out your studies in a methodical, logical and effective way, but if you have your own study preferences you will find it a flexible resource too.

Before you begin using this course book, make sure you are familiar with any advice provided by CIPS on such things as study skills, revision techniques or support and how to handle formal assessments.

If you are on a taught course, it will be up to your tutor to explain how to use the book – when to read the study sessions, when to tackle the activities and questions, and so on.

If you are on a self-study course, or studying independently, you can use the course book in the following way:

- Scan the whole book to get a feel for the nature and content of the subject matter.

- Plan your overall study schedule so that you allow enough time to complete all 20 study sessions well before your examinations – in other words, leaving plenty of time for revision.
- For each session, set aside enough time for reading the text, tackling all the learning activities and self-assessment questions, and the revision question at the end of the session, and for the suggested further reading. Guidance on roughly how long you should set aside for studying each session is given at the beginning of the session.

Now let's take a look at the structure and content of the individual study sessions.

Overview of the study sessions

The course book breaks the content down into 20 sessions, which vary from three to six or seven hours' duration each. However, we are not advising you to study for this sort of time without a break! The sessions are simply a convenient way of breaking the syllabus into manageable chunks. Most people would try to study one or two sessions a week, taking one or two breaks within each session. You will quickly find out what suits you best.

Each session begins with a brief **introduction** which sets out the areas of the syllabus being covered and explains, if necessary, how the session fits in with the topics that come before and after.

After the introduction there is a statement of the **session learning objectives**. The objectives are designed to help you understand exactly what you should be able to do after you've studied the session. You might find it helpful to tick them off as you progress through the session. You will also find them useful during revision. There is one session learning objective for each numbered subsection of the session.

After this, there is a brief section reproducing the learning objectives and indicative content from the official **unit content document**. This will help you to understand exactly which part of the syllabus you are studying in the current session.

Following this, there are **prior knowledge** and **resources** sections if necessary. These will let you know if there are any topics you need to be familiar with before tackling each particular session, or any special resources you might need, such as a calculator or graph paper.

Then the main part of the study session begins, with the first of the numbered main subsections. At regular intervals in each study session, we have provided you with **learning activities**, which are designed to get you actively involved in the learning process. You should always try to complete the activities – usually on a separate sheet of your own paper – before reading on. You will learn much more effectively if you are actively involved in doing something as you study, rather than just passively reading the text in front of you. The feedback or answers to the activities are provided at the end of the session. Do not be tempted to skip the activity.

We also provide a number of **self-assessment questions** in each study session. These are to help you to decide for yourself whether or not you have achieved the learning objectives set out at the beginning of the session. As with the activities, you should always tackle them – usually on a separate sheet of paper. Don't be tempted to skip them. The feedback or answers are again at the end of the session. If you still do not understand a topic having attempted the self-assessment question, always try to re-read the relevant passages in the textbook readings or session, or follow the advice on further reading at the end of the session. If this still doesn't work, you should contact the CIPS Membership and Qualification Advice team.

For most of the learning activities and self assessment questions you will need to use separate sheets of paper for your answers or responses. Some of the activities or questions require you to complete a table or form, in which case you could write your response in the course book itself, or photocopy the page.

At the end of the session are three final sections.

The first is the **summary**. Use it to remind yourself or check off what you have just studied, or later on during revision.

Then follows the **suggested further reading** section. This section, if it appears, contains recommendations for further reading which you can follow up if you would like to read alternative treatments of the topics. If for any reason you are having difficulty understanding the course book on a particular topic, try one of the alternative treatments recommended. If you are keen to read around and beyond the syllabus, to help you pick up extra points in the examination for example, you may like to try some of the additional readings recommended. If this section does not appear at the end of a session, it usually means that further reading for the session topics is not necessary.

At the end of the session we direct you to a **revision question**, which you will find in a separate section at the end of the course book. Feedback on the questions is also given.

Reading lists

CIPS produces an official reading list, which recommends essential and desirable texts for augmenting your studies. This reading list is available on the CIPS website or from the CIPS Bookshop. This course book is one of the essential texts for this unit. In this section we describe the main characteristics of the other essential text for this unit, which you are strongly urged to buy and use throughout your course.

The other essential text is:

Purchasing Principles and Management, 9th edition, by P Bailey, D Farmer, D Jessop and D Jones, published by FT Prentice Hall, in 2005.

This is a comprehensive, well-written supporting text book that has been developed and kept up-to-date by four highly respected purchasing authors. It has been recommended as the essential text to support your studies because it has a broad coverage of many different market and industry contexts, whether public or private sector.

You will find that there are several complementary references to the source material of this text and it is hoped that you find this a useful companion to your study of purchasing contexts.

Alan Branch has written an excellent and concise text summarising the specific issues of purchasing in the international context: *International Purchasing and Management*, published by Thomson Learning in 2001. It is a highly recommended supporting text for your studies because of its specialism in international perspectives of purchasing and supply.

Second edition amendments

This second edition brings the course book up to date with the latest version of the unit content document approved by CIPS in spring 2009. This affects the 'Unit content coverage' section on the following pages, and the shorter 'Unit content coverage' extracts which appear at the beginning of each study session. Some terminology in the book has also been amended, where appropriate, to bring it in line with the unit content document.

Unit content coverage

In this section we reproduce the whole of the official CIPS unit content document for this unit. The overall unit characteristics and statements of practice for the unit are given first. Then, in the table that follows, the learning objectives and indicative content are given in the left hand column. In the right hand column are the study sessions in which you will find coverage of the various topics.

Unit characteristics

This unit is designed to consolidate the learning from all four units in the CIPS Foundation Diploma. It is designed to enable students to apply the fundamental principles of purchasing and supply in a variety of different contexts, including a range of private sector organisations, including multi-nationals and small and medium-sized enterprises (SMEs), plus the public sector; national and local government; the NHS; and the third sector. Students will be able to consider the procurement cycle as it applies to a diverse range of purchased products and services including raw materials, commodities, components, utilities and services, both domestically and in an international context.

This unit will tackle the different challenges faced by a wide range of organisations and sectors as they strive to achieve value for money (VFM), quality, effectiveness and competitiveness within the broader supply chain.

Successful students will be able to apply sound principles of purchasing and supply management to a diverse range of sectors and organisations and will be able to employ and develop transferable best practice where appropriate.

Statements of practice

On completion of this unit, students will be able to:

- Identify the procurement cycle as it applies to a variety of different organisations and contexts
- Recognise the transferability of the fundamental principles of purchase and supply management
- Appraise the need for different approaches to purchasing in differing organisations and contexts
- Recognise good practice procurement processes and consider how they can be adapted and transferred to other contexts
- Compare the diverse legal and regulatory environments in which procurement activity takes place
- Discuss the ethical implications of purchasing in different contexts
- Evaluate centralised versus decentralised purchasing structures

- Explain how to implement requisitioning and call-off to end users in decentralised value added e-portals

Learning objectives and indicative content

1.0 Understanding diverse organisations, contexts and situations (Weighting 50%)

1.1 Evaluate the different objectives of public, private and third sector organisations and the different environments in which they operate.
  - Ownership and control
  - Sources of finance, financial structures and governance
  - Resource issues
  - Legal and regulatory environments
  - Contrasting business objectives
  - Importance of corporate social responsibility

Study session 1

1.2 Appraise the different types of private sector organisations and the differing demands that they place on those managing the provision of goods and services including:
  - Different forms, including limited companies, plcs and limited liability partnerships
  - Formation and cessation of private sector firms
  - Regulation of private sector and impact on purchasing
  - Impact of profit motive on purchasing activities
  - Transactional activity such as mergers and acquisitions (M&A) together with the role of Competition Commission
  - Specific types of private sector organisations and influences on purchasing function:
    - Manufacturing
    - Engineering
    - Fast moving consumer goods (FMCG)
    - Retail
    - Technology
    - Services

Study session 2
Study session 3
Study session 20

1.3 Review the different types of public sector organisations and the variety of approaches taken to the purchase and supply of goods and services.
  - Different types of public sector organisation ie central government, local government and government agencies
  - Regulation of public sector and impact on purchasing
  - Concept of value for money, balancing conflicting objectives and priorities
  - Multiple forms of stakeholder and their influences

Study session 4

1.4 Review the different types of voluntary and third sector organisations.
  - Different types of third sector organisations
  - Regulation of third sector organisations and impact on purchasing
  - Importance of corporate social responsibility (CSR)

Study session 5

1.5 Evaluate the context of the purchasing function and different purchasing situations.

Study session 7
Study session 8

- Purchasing as a discrete organisational function within the supply chain
- Relationship between the purchaser and a supply market
- The various functional models for purchasing: including centralised, decentralised, centre-led action network (CLAN), lead buyer/business partnering and matrix structure
- Typical division of roles and responsibilities within purchasing
- The part-time purchaser
- Customers of the purchasing function
- Merits of internal versus external outsourcing of supply
- Role of a strategic sourcing unit (SSU) and how it can be measured for effectiveness
- Merits of consortium buying with other independent organisations

2.0 Recognising the need for different approaches to purchasing different types of goods and services (Weighting 50%)

2.1 Analyse and explain different types of product and customer requirements.

- The difference between customers and consumers
- Contribution of purchasing to customer satisfaction
- How customer feedback is collated and used
- The contrast/difference between consumer products and industrial products
- Key requirements in goods for resale
- Regulatory framework for protection of consumers
- Impact of corporate social responsibility (CSR) on consumer confidence

2.2 Identify and explain different methods of purchasing.

- Classification of supply chains, tiered supply, managed services and the role of an agent
- The purchasing cycle, its key stages and its relative transferability
- Importance of cross-functional teams, varying cross-functional requirements and the impact of this on purchases
- Methods of purchase:
    - Spot-buying and one-off purchases
    - Long-term supply relationships
    - Framework agreements and call-off arrangements
    - Projects: how scoped, purchased and paid for
    - Low value orders including use of purchasing-cards
    - Typical purchase-to-pay (P2P) methods
- Merits of competitive tendering: the key stages, appraisal and evaluation of tenders, and merits of e-tendering
- Good practice and its application to purchasing including benchmarking
- Consumables
- Call-off orders

2.3 Analyse and explain different ways of purchasing raw materials and commodities.

- Recognise the key differences between direct and indirect purchasing
- Methods of purchasing raw materials and commodity items and key considerations including finance and the futures markets
- Contribution of purchasing to the bottom line
- Purchasing for stock
- Purchasing for production
- Key considerations when purchasing perishable items

2.4 Analyse the differences between purchasing services as opposed to purchasing goods.

- Key differences between a product and a service
- A range of services: legal, professional, human resources, advertising and media, facilities management, IT, maintenance repair and operations (MRO) and finance
- Key requirements when specifying a service to be purchased
- Operation and merits of managed services
- Managing service level agreements

2.5 Analyse and explain purchasing and financing capital expenditure items.

- Key differences between operational and capital expenditure
- A range of capital expenditure (CAPEX) items
- Financing considerations, including benefit/cost analysis (BCA), investment, return on investment (ROI), break-even, post project appraisal (PPA) and whole-life costing
- Public and private funding initiatives including private finance initiative (PFI), public private partnership (PPP), build-own-operate-transfer (BOOT)
- A simple budgeting cycle
- Economic factors of financing including inflation and interest rates

2.6 Analyse and evaluate the drivers for international purchasing, factors and organisations that affect international trade and the impact on the purchasing function.

- Key drivers for globalisation and standardisation
- The organisations which affect international trade including the World Trade Organisation, World Bank, International Chamber of Commerce and European Union
- International trade zones, tariffs and international trading agreements
- Modes of transport and shipping regulations
- Incoterms
- Reasons for sourcing internationally, including market expansion and competitiveness
- Key considerations when sourcing from another country
- Impact of international standards
- Relative merits of offshoring

Understanding organisations

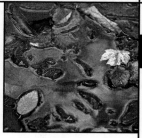

Introduction

The organisation is the single-most defining framework for the purchasing function. It provides the context in which purchasing exists and conducts its activities, as well as defining what those purchasing activities need to be. There are many different types of organisation; this study session introduces their essential characteristics. It provides a foundation for the study sessions that immediately follow by looking at the differences the main types of organisation. These contrasts are drawn through a review of the different sources of ownership, control and regulation of organisations, as well as reviewing the financial and governance structures and the types of business objective within different organisations. This is a fundamentally important study session for this unit, as it starts to define the organisational context for purchasing and helps understand how and why key purchasing activities are performed.

'Organisations, of course, are not objects. They are micro-societies. Those who lead them have to understand the needs and motivations of the people in them.'
Charles Handy, 1998

Session learning objectives

After completing this session you should be able to:

1.1 Describe the different sources of ownership, control and regulation of organisations in all sectors.
1.2 Compare the financial structure and governance of different types of organisation.
1.3 Contrast the business objectives of organisations across different sectors.

Unit content coverage

This study session covers the following topics from the official CIPS unit content document:

Statements of practice

- Appraise the need for different approaches to purchasing in differing organisations and contexts.
- Compare the diverse legal and regulatory environments in which procurement activity takes place.

Learning objective

1.1 Evaluate the different objectives of public, private and third sector organisations and the different environments in which they operate.
  - Ownership and control
  - Sources of finance, financial structures and governance
  - Resource issues
  - Legal and regulatory environments

- Contrasting business objectives
- Importance of corporate social responsibility

Prior knowledge

This is the first study session and provides a basic foundation for many of the following sessions.

Resources

You may wish to access a library for further reading and additional studies, but this is neither compulsory nor essential.

Timing

You should set aside about 4 hours to read and complete this session, including learning activities, self-assessment questions, the suggested further reading (if any) and the revision question.

1.1   Introduction to organisations

Organisations form the core fabric of our society. Everywhere you go and in everything you do, there are organisations. They include government departments, hospitals, companies, shops, religious groups, factories, societies, the police force, charities and internet clubs, among many other examples. In fact it is nearly impossible to live a normal life and not come across an organisation every day.

Although there are many different types of organisation, there are some factors they all share in common. Daft (2003) defines organisations as: '… social entities that are goal-directed, deliberately structured activity systems'.

From this definition we can note several common themes. As a general rule every organisation has the following:

- **People**: organisations are made up of people (two or more) who come together for mutually compatible purposes.
- **Objectives**: organisations share at least one (often more) goal or objective; they have a purpose and a *raison d'être*.
- **Structure**: they have a means of coordinating themselves so that the people can communicate, interact and channel their efforts.
- **Management**: they share a process of directing, controlling, organising and coordinating themselves to achieve their purpose.

In general terms, when people refer to an organisation they are mostly considering a **formal organisation**. That is, they are referring to organisations that have formal structures and fixed physical assets such as buildings, plant or machinery. The formal organisation is deliberately planned, controlled and structured: it is a legal entity in its own right. It has a given modus operandi that is based on a set of governing rules or principles. It exists for a stated purpose or reason and the membership of the organisation is usually clearly understood. Examples of a formal organisation include:

- hospital
- charity
- school
- restaurant
- hotel
- construction company
- government agency
- farm
- software development company
- internet service provider.

The **informal organisation** is equally common, only perhaps slightly less recognised. These types of organisation have a far less predictable and structured existence. They will arise from the social interaction of people who come together with their own relationships and behavioural norms. Typically, informal organisations are flexible and loosely affiliated or structured. The membership tends to be far more spontaneous and less well defined, as are the rules and principles of their behaviour. Some examples of informal organisations include:

- An after-school football team organised by the schoolchildren away from the jurisdiction of the school.
- A book-reading group who meet to share their interest in books.
- A mother-and-baby group who regularly meet to discuss their experiences.
- The members of an internet chat-room who share a particular interest.

It should be noted that none of the above could be considered as a legal entity, nor is there any organised passage of money, goods or services between the members. This helps distinguish these from formal organisations. Although the function of the informal organisation is a very important theme within society, it unfortunately goes beyond the scope of this unit content. For the rest of this study session we will concentrate on the formal organisation. If, however, you would like to know more about informal organisations, you can read about them in Mullins (2005) chapter 4, as detailed at the end of this study session.

In recent times with the revolutionary impact of information technology, much has been made of the **virtual organisation**. The virtual organisation is a concept based on the medium of technology that brings together people and resources, which might otherwise be relatively independent of each other, to undertake specific tasks and objectives. There are many internet companies in the market today that fulfil these criteria, although strictly speaking they are still formal organisations (for example Amazon.com).

Some of the specific features of virtual organisations include:

- Flexibility and spontaneity to work together and respond to market opportunities.
- Few physical assets, such as buildings, if any.
- Mobility and agility that is not tied to a physical location.
- Collaboration based on skill, competence and expertise.

- Usually service related not product related.
- Reliance on computer and mobile technology to communicate and interact.

There are many advantages of the virtual organisation, particularly in the digital age and where there are dynamic, fast-evolving markets. In an environment of change and uncertainty, virtual organisations can offer low cost and yet highly responsive and adaptable solutions. However, there is also often a greater burden of management required to keep virtual organisations working effectively. The independent people and resources making up the membership of the virtual organisation are not likely to work effectively together unless there is a compelling shared vision and a strong element of trust. Even so, contracts are usually required to maintain the bond between members.

Formal organisations are typically divided into two main groups:

- private sector enterprises
- public sector organisations.

The main distinction between these relies on the basis of ownership and control.

Private sector enterprises

The private sector enterprise is an organisation that is owned and financed by individuals. These individuals have control of the private enterprise as a direct result of their ownership, regardless of whether they work or become involved in the day-to-day running of the organisation. The individual owners could comprise an individual owner (sole trader), partners or shareholders. In the case where a private enterprise is owned by another company, its owners will be the individual owners of that (parent) holding company.

We look at the private sector in detail in study sessions 2 and 3 and consider the specifics about how they are formed and the different types of ownership that can occur. One of the key underlying principles of the private sector is the **profit motive**: that is the overriding objective for a private enterprise to make money. For the owners, this is the *raison d'être* of the private sector: a profitable return for the money they have invested in buying their share of the company.

Purchasing in the private sector is heavily influenced by the profit motive. Buying goods and services in a cost-efficient manner will reduce the company's expenditure and therefore support profitability. Where the goods and services are passed on to the company's customers, purchasing has a very important role in supporting the overall proposition and value offered by the company. This context will significantly influence the role fulfilled by the purchasing function.

Public sector organisations

Public sector organisations are established by government to fulfil a form of public service. Unlike the private sector, they are not driven by the profit motive; their *raison d'être* is to serve the public through a political purpose and for the general 'well-being' of society. Public sector organisations include central government, local authorities and various government agencies.

Here are six examples of different forms of public sector organisation in the UK:

- Department for Work and Pensions (central government)
- county councils and district councils (local authority)
- Environment Agency and Highways Agency (government agencies)
- health authorities
- armed forces
- utility organisations.

The distinction between public sector organisations will vary from country to country in line with their national constitution (for example, in the USA there are Federal agencies, State government and local county government, as well as central government) but in essence the principles are the same.

Each of the above type of public sector organisation is publicly owned and publicly funded. By this, we mean that the government has established these organisations and given rules and guidelines under which they are to operate. The government funds the organisations by channelling public money into them to perform their responsibilities.

Purchasing in the public sector is heavily influenced by the type of service offered by the organisation. Cost efficiency of buying goods and services is very important because expenditure relies on taxpayers' funds. However, there is also considerable focus on ensuring the right levels of service are delivered. Purchasing in the public sector also requires a degree of consistency and probity because of the nature of the funds involved; therefore this context has considerable impact on the way purchasing activities are performed. We will consider the public sector in greater detail in study session 4.

Learning activity 1.1

Identify two of each of the following types of public sector organisation and, using table 1.1, describe their principal service:

- central government
- local government
- government agency.

Table 1.1 Types of public sector organisation and their principal services

Name of central government organisation	Description of principal service provided
1.	
2.	
Name of local government organisation	Description of principal service provided
1.	
2.	
Name of government agency organisation	Description of principal service provided
1.	
2.	

Feedback on page 11

1

Third sector organisations

The final group of organisations we consider is those belonging to the third sector. This type of organisation has been set up to fulfil objectives other than profit. Typically this will be some form of public, charitable or social purpose. Examples include charities, museums, sports clubs, religious groups, community ventures and political societies. The Chartered Institute of Purchasing and Supply (CIPS) is a third sector organisation. You can find out more about it from its website: CIPS: http://www.cips.org/.

Third sector organisations are usually owned by either the members (in the case of social organisations) or a charitable trust. They are managed by their own board of directors or trustees who are specially appointed to govern the organisation in accordance with a set of rules and regulations (often called a constitution).

Organisations will market the fact they are voluntary or not-for-profit in order to help their customers understand that they are not making a profit out of the goods or services they sell. This in turn promotes the main objectives of the organisation. For example, an art gallery might rely on volunteers to run its retail shop. It will use all the net revenue from the shop to pay towards the overheads of maintaining the art collection. The shop is a third sector organisation because its sole purpose is to help maintain the art collection.

We consider third sector organisations in greater detail in study session 5. This includes looking at the context and specific impact this has on the purchasing function.

Self-assessment question 1.1

Briefly compare and contrast the different sources of ownership and control between public and private sector organisations.

Feedback on page 11

1.2 Organisational finance and governance

We have already looked at different types of organisation in terms of their ownership and control and noted some significant differences between the private, public and third sectors. Table 1.2 provides a high-level summary of the different ways in which these types of organisation are financed.

Table 1.2 Financing of different types of organisation

Sector	Type of organisation	Source of finance	Use of funds
Private sector	Company, sole trader or partnership	Revenue received from selling goods or services; investment finance	Profitable return to the owners and/or re-investment for future profits
Public sector	Central government	Spending budget is allocated from government funds,	National public services, based on the available budget

(continued on next page)

1

Table 1.2 *(continued)*

Sector	Type of organisation	Source of finance	Use of funds
		which ultimately come from taxation.	
	Local authority	Local taxes and/or community charges	Local public services, based on extent of local budgeting
	Government agency	Spending budget is allocated from government grants and budgets, which ultimately come from taxation	Public services, based on extent of budget
Third sector	Charity	Charitable donations and government grants	Maintaining the work of the charity and/or re-investment
	Third sector	Government grants, sales revenue and/or charitable donations	Maintaining the work of the organisation and/or re-investment

The key distinctions are:

- **Private sector**: exists solely to provide the owners with a profitable return on their investment (the profit motive).
- **Public sector**: relies on public funding (usually obtained from taxes) to provide a public service. The service is therefore operated on the basis of a budget (there is no profit).
- **Third sector**: relies on donations, grants and its own sales to raise money. All revenues are ploughed back into the work of the organisation and there is no profitable return.

Governance

This can be a very complex subject, but in summary there are just two main sources of governing control on an organisation's activities:

- **Legislation**: the governing law that provides a legal framework within which organisations must act. This is laid down in the statutory laws of the country and upheld by the legal system (for example, the laws about employment rights of workers).
- **Regulation**: operating conditions and regulations established by a governing body. This is usually laid down by a specific regulatory body and applies to a specific market sector or activity (for example, a regulator for a utility market such as energy or water).

There are many different forms of regulation placed on an organisation's activities. Governments promote regulation to bring control, stability and a sense of 'fairness' into commercial activities. Here are just a few examples of regulation in the UK:

- Industry regulators, such as Ofcom or Ofgem, which regulate the price and supply standards for the communications and energy generation industries.
- Competition Commission, which regulates levels of competition in key market sectors.

1

- General Medical Council, which regulates the standards and practice of medical care.
- Financial Services Authority, which regulates the provision of financial services.
- Health and Safety Executive, which regulates safety standards.
- Advertising Standards Authority, which regulates the standards and censorship of media advertising.
- Patents Office, which regulates and protects individual rights of ownership in design and innovation.
- Environment Agency, which regulates acceptable levels of commercial waste, gas emission and/or water effluent from premises.

As can be seen from this list, there are many governing rules and regulations about the activities of a company. Each exists to promote good practice standards and a general level of 'well-being' in society. Stop for a moment to consider what might happen if these companies did not exist.

The organisations listed above (and many more besides) are granted special powers by the government to act independently and establish the rules and regulations of acceptable practice. They are also given authority to police these standards, often using summary fines or legislation to enforce them. In study session 2 we will look at this subject in more detail.

Learning activity 1.2

Using table 1.3 below, state the sector and describe the sources of finance and regulation for each of the types of organisation listed (an example is provided to help you get started).

Table 1.3

Organisation	Sector	Financial sources	Regulation
Insurance	Private sector	Revenue from sales of insurance cover	Financial Services Authority and the General Insurance Standards Council
Police			
Food production			
Schools			
Farm			

Feedback on page 11

Self-assessment question 1.2

With examples, describe the two main sources of governing control on an organisation's activities.

Feedback on page 12

1.3 Business objectives

We have already started to review some of the contrasting business objectives of the private, public and third sectors. This subject is reviewed in detail in later units, but for now we are simply talking about the designated purpose of the organisation: what it has been set up to achieve. In summary, so far we have observed the following:

- Private sector enterprises: are driven by the profit motive. Their *raison d'être* is the creation of an acceptable return on the owner's investment.
- Public sector organisations: exist to provide a public service established by the government.
- Third sector organisations: serve a specific social or charitable purpose without making a profit.

Learning activity 1.3

Identify the high-level business objectives of your own workplace and be prepared to compare them with the following text.

Feedback on page 12

From a purchasing perspective, organisational goals provide very distinctive contexts in which to operate. Whereas the private sector is relatively straightforward – the creation of profit as a result of a company's business activities – the public and third sectors have very different and far more complex business objectives.

Andrew Cox has stated: 'It is axiomatic that this [purchasing] process is one that requires that external sourcing and supply is linked at all times with the internal strategic goals of the organisation'. By this, he is arguing that the organisational context and the business objectives will dictate the purchasing activities.

In the case of the private sector, purchasing is concerned with making sure the right goods and services are bought at the lowest cost to the organisation. It is looking to make sure cost savings are achieved and, if appropriate, key suppliers can support the organisation with its customer proposition. The focus is on saving costs and making money.

However, in the public sector (and/or the third sector) the business objectives are not quite as clear-cut. Indeed Andrew Cox has argued that they remain wholly contested.

The recommended text for this unit quotes the following:

'Procurement of equipment, goods and services for the government and the public sector generally is complex. On one hand, there is a need to ensure best value for money on behalf of the taxpayer, and the need to ensure that the processes to achieve this are fair and open to scrutiny. On the other hand there is considerable pressure to make savings (especially in the light

1

of constantly reducing budgets)... This has led to many challenges for those undertaking the procurement action'

Bailey et al (2005, p 75)

Table 1.5 illustrates the point of contested goals.

Table 1.5 Contested goals of public expenditure

Public sector social goals	• Protection of property and law and order
	• National defence of territory
	• Equality of opportunity
	• Minimum levels of social infrastructure
	• Redistribution of wealth
	• Health gain and maintenance
	• Environmental quality
	• Minimum levels of social income and welfare
	• Education
	• Protection against old age and infirmity
Public sector economic goals	• Higher levels of economic growth
	• Protection of infant industries against competition
	• Local or regional economic development
	• Development of specific industries or technologies
	• Investment in industrial or technological transfer
	• Underwriting and subsidising national costs of production and exchange

Source: adapted from Cox and Thompson (1998)

Table 1.5 illustrates a range of just some of the possible 'end-goals' or 'valued outcomes' that public expenditure is trying to achieve. Although there are others that could be added to the list, it is clear that there is no single defining business objective for the public sector, thus making it a far more complex context in which to undertake purchasing activities.

The objective is not to make money, but provide a service to fulfil at least one if not more of the stated social and economic goals. Given that this involves the use of public funds, purchasing still has a responsibility to ensure the right goods and services are bought at the lowest cost to the organisation, while delivering the right levels of service to the public. This is referred to as value for money: or best value when the balance between the level of service and the cost to the taxpayer has been optimised.

We will consider the issues of public sector procurement in study session 4.

Self-assessment question 1.3

Explain in what ways the goals of public sector procurement are contested.

Feedback on page 12

Revision question

There is no revision question for this session.

Summary

In today's mixed economy, there are several different economic sectors. By now you will have been introduced to the different characteristics of organisations in the private, public and third sectors and you will be able to describe the different sources of ownership, control and regulation of organisations within them. You should also be able to compare financial and governance structures, as well as contrasting the business objectives or organisations in each of the different sectors.

In the following four study sessions you will study these in greater detail. This provides an important foundation for the rest of the unit content and an essential guide to the environment in which the purchasing function operates.

Suggested further reading

You could read the relevant sections of Bailey et al (2005), Handy (1999) and Mullins (2005).

Feedback on learning activities and self-assessment questions

Feedback on learning activity 1.1

This should be a relatively easy exercise to complete, but will help bring to life the different types of public sector organisation known to you.

Feedback on self-assessment question 1.1

Public sector organisations are publicly owned and financed by the government with taxpayers' money. Control is divested from central government by statutory powers and authority. In contrast, private sector enterprises are owned by individuals and/or other companies who have invested their money into the business. Directors and management are appointed by the owners to take responsibility for the activities and performance of the company.

Feedback on learning activity 1.2

Here are some examples.

Table 1.4

Organisation	Sector	Financial sources	Regulation
Insurance	Private sector	Revenue from sales of insurance cover	Financial Services Authority and the General Insurance Standards Council
Police	Public sector	Budget allocation from local authority taxes	Her Majesty's Inspectorate of Constabulary and the Independent Police Complaints Committee

(continued on next page)

Table 1.4 *(continued)*

Organisation	Sector	Financial sources	Regulation
Food production	Private sector	Revenue from sales of food products	Food Standards Agency
Schools	Public sector	Budget allocation from local authority taxes	Ofsted
Farm	Private sector	Revenue from sale of products	Defra

Feedback on self-assessment question 1.2

The two main sources of governance comprise the rules and regulations stipulated by:

- The legislative framework
- The regulatory framework

The question requires a description of these frameworks, which should at least be comparable with that supplied in the text. You also should have provided examples with your answers (such as the Disabilities Discrimination Act 2003 for legislation or the Financial Services Authority as a regulator).

Feedback on learning activity 1.3

You should be able to identify several strategic objectives and then in the text that follows identify how they link in.

Feedback on self-assessment question 1.3

The goals of public sector procurement are contested because there is no single over-arching objective. There is more than one goal and these vie for priority at different times and circumstances. One of the principal objectives is the provision of a public service to fulfil a political, social or moral purpose. There is also a need for efficiency with taxpayers' money, probity with public funds and fair competition in the marketplace.

Formation and regulation of the private sector

Introduction

This study session gets 'under the skin' of the private sector enterprise. It is one of the key building blocks of this unit syllabus because of its importance in business and the influential role it plays on the purchasing function. We will consider different types of private sector enterprise and how they are both formed and closed down. Following on from the last study session, we will look in greater detail at the roles of the profit motive and regulation in the private sector.

'The board of directors of a [private sector] business has a responsibility to shareholders to provide them with a reasonable rate of return on their investment'.

Johnson, Scholes and Whittington (2005)

Session learning objectives

After completing this session you should be able to:

2.1 Compare and contrast the different forms of private sector organisation.
2.2 Describe how private sector companies are formed and financed.
2.3 Use appropriate examples to describe how the activities of the private sector are regulated and the impact this has on purchasing.
2.4 Describe how private sector enterprises are terminated and the impact of this in the wider business environment.
2.5 Evaluate the impact of the 'profit motive' on the purchasing function.

Unit content coverage

This study session covers the following topics from the official CIPS unit content document:

Statements of practice

- Appraise the need for different approaches to purchasing in differing organisations and contexts.
- Compare the diverse legal and regulatory environments in which the procurement activity takes place.

Learning objective

1.2 Appraise the different types of private sector organisations and the differing demands that they place on those managing the provision of goods and services.
  - Different forms, including limited companies, plcs and limited liability partnerships
  - Formation and cessation of private sector firms
  - Regulation of private sector and impact on purchasing
  - Impact of profit motive on purchasing activities
  - Transactional activity such as mergers and acquisitions (M&A) together with role of the Competition Commission

2

- Specific types of private sector organisations and influences on purchasing function:
  - Manufacturing
  - Engineering
  - Fast moving consumer goods (FMCG)
  - Retail
  - Technology
  - Services

Prior knowledge

You should work through the preceding study session before attempting this, as it lays a useful foundation to the concepts raised in this study session.

Resources

Internet access is preferable, but not essential. You may also wish to access a library for further reading and additional studies, but this is neither compulsory nor essential.

Timing

You should set aside about 5½ hours to read and complete this session, including learning activities, self-assessment questions, the suggested further reading (if any) and the revision question.

2.1   The private sector enterprise

There are two broad classifications of organisation in the private sector:

- **Unincorporated**: in the form of sole traders or partnerships, where the owners have full responsibility for the affairs of the business. They are fully private in all senses of the word – that is, no accountabilities other than to themselves. In general there are fewer regulations about how they operate, but the owners remain fully liable for any debts, liabilities or claims made against the business.
- **Incorporated**: regularly referred to as companies. There are two types: the private limited company and the public limited company. The owners of an incorporated company are called shareholders and, unlike the unincorporated company, their liability for the debts of the company is limited. The company is a legal entity in its own right and has to be formally registered.

We will now consider each type of private sector enterprise in more detail.

Sole trader (also referred to as Sole Proprietorship):

As the name suggests, this is an organisation with just one owner. The name of the business does not have to be registered and it trades under its own name or that of the owner. However, the business cannot be named the same as another registered company. Therefore if the sole trader business has a unique name, or a name that they want to protect others from using, the business needs to be registered.

Table 2.1 compares and contrasts the relative merits of a sole trader business.

Table 2.1 Merits of a sole trader

Advantages of sole trader	Disadvantages of sole trader
• The business is easy to set up and incurs very low administrative and legal fees • There are very few accounting and book-keeping regulations • The owner has total freedom to make their own decisions in running the business • The owner is fully responsible and therefore receives all the profits from the business	• The business is dependent on the owner's funds which may be limited and it is therefore difficult to borrow large sums of money • Business loans can only be secured through personal guarantees • All financial responsibilities lie with the owner • The owner has to rely on his/her own expertise to run the business

Here are some examples of sole traders:

- painter/decorator
- management consultant
- bookkeeper
- gardener
- website designer
- musician.

In summary the sole-trader business offers freedom and flexibility but it also requires a tremendous amount of commitment and potential personal risk.

Partnerships

Partnerships are owned by two or more people who share the responsibilities, accountability and rewards for owning and running the business. As a general rule there can be up to 20 partners in a partnership, although there are several notable exceptions such as legal firms, accountants and stock-exchange members. As with the sole trader, they trade either under the name of the partners or under a separate business name. The same criteria apply about the protection of the name of a partnership as with sole traders.

Table 2.2 compares and contrasts the relative merits of a partnership.

Table 2.2 Merits of a partnership

Advantages of partnerships	Disadvantages of partnerships
• Responsibility is shared among the partners: the source of expertise is broader • Greater availability to sources of finance than a sole trader • It is probably easier to borrow money as a wider degree of security is available	• Far less freedom than a sole trader because of the need to consult all partners over decisions • Decision-making is therefore slower and more administrative • Profits are shared with the partners • Liabilities are not limited, even though they are shared between the partners

(continued on next page)

Table 2.2 *(continued)*

Advantages of partnerships	Disadvantages of partnerships
• Accountability for debts and liabilities is shared and therefore the individual burden reduced	

Here are some examples of partnerships:

- solicitors
- doctor's surgery
- share club
- independent financial advisers
- management consultancy
- architects.

There is a form of partnership called a **limited liability partnership** where some of the partners have limited liability for any debts or losses accrued. However, in these cases there still has to be at least one partner with unlimited liability.

Partnerships can also have 'sleeping partners' who are partners in that they have a share of the ownership (and share of the profits/liabilities) but they do not take part in the running of the business. Typically sleeping partners are used for financing purposes rather than any skill or capability they can bring to the business.

Learning activity 2.1

Using local library, internet or media resources, identify three sole traders and three partnerships each operating in a different industry. Record the name of the business and their principal activity in the templates below.

Table 2.3 Examples of sole traders

Name of sole trader	Description of activities
1.	
2.	
3.	

Table 2.4 Examples of partnerships

Name of partnership	Description of activities
1.	
2.	
3.	

Feedback on page 27

Limited liability companies

As already noted, limited liability companies are incorporated companies, which means they have been formally registered and are considered as a separate legal entity. We will consider the formation of companies in the next section.

There are two forms of limited liability company:

1 **private limited company**: with the suffix 'Ltd' after the name
2 **public limited company**: with suffix 'plc' after the name

The two forms of limited companies have similarities in that they are owned by two or more shareholders – that is, individuals with a fixed number of 'shares' in the company. Shareholders are owners – they have paid for [invested] their share of the company and expect to receive a return on that investment – but they do not necessarily have to be responsible for the running of the company; directors are employed for that purpose.

The shareholders have limited liability for the company, such that if it gets into financial difficulties with heavy losses or debts their liability is limited only as much as the value of their investment.

Private limited companies are not listed on any stock exchange and so it is not possible for members of the public to trade shares in the company – the ownership is 'closed' or 'private'. Public limited companies however can offer shares to the public via a stock exchange, such as the ones in London, New York or Shanghai.

Generally (although there are many counter-examples) private limited companies tend to be smaller than public limited companies. Most large multi-national companies are publicly listed to attract investment, whereas many medium and smaller enterprises prefer to remain private to avoid the fluctuations of the capital markets.

Table 2.5 compares and contrasts the relative merits of limited companies.

Table 2.5 Merits of limited companies

Advantages of limited companies	Disadvantages of limited companies
• Shareholders have limited liability • The sale of shares of the company allows larger sums of money to be raised • Directors can be brought in as experts to run the company • Trading shares on the stock exchange does not alter the capital base of the company	• There are several regulations and legal formalities required to set up and administer limited companies • Accounting for the companies finances is relatively public because of the annual disclosure of financial reports • Directors need to report to the shareholders on a regular basis • Trading shares can result in changes of ownership which may affect the way the company is governed and directed

There are many examples of limited companies. Your local stock exchange will list the public limited companies for your country.

Self-assessment question 2.1

Describe the key differences between a public limited company and a private limited company.

Feedback on page 27

2

2.2 Company formation and financing

Sole trader

In the previous section we considered the sole trader. It is the easiest form of organisation to set up because of its simplicity. There are no formalities; in fact any adult can claim themselves to be a sole trader. They will have to declare this fact to the tax authorities and probably endure some form of pay-as-you-earn accounting, but apart from this there is no other significant administration.

The sole trader has to find his/her own sources of finances – there are no shares to sell – and so if additional financing is required to set up the business or to expand then some form of business loan is required. Financiers will look to the sole trader to offer their own form of security (for example against the house or some other major asset) such that, if the business fails and the loan cannot be re-paid, the debts can be set off against the value of the sole trader's personal assets.

Partnerships

Financing for partnerships is very similar to that of the sole trader with the exception that the risk of liabilities is spread across all of the partners. Borrowing money occurs in much the same way as the sole trader, albeit that it is often easier to find lenders because of the potentially higher combined worth of the partners.

The partnership is formed by means of a **partnership deed** (or partnership agreement) which is drawn up by an independent solicitor for all partners to sign. The Deed sets out the four essentials of financing partnerships:

- how much capital each partner has invested
- how any profits will be shared
- how any losses/liabilities will be shared
- the nature and amount of salaries to be drawn.

Learning activity 2.2

Describe how unincorporated companies raise and secure finance for their business and the nature of risk associated with this.

Feedback on page 27

Limited liability companies

Limited liability companies are registered in the UK in line with the **Companies Act 1985**. This requires the Company Secretary (or his/her representative) to file a submission to the Registrar of Companies at Companies House.

Companies House is a government agency that maintains current and historical information about companies in the UK. As well as registering newly established companies, it keeps a record of every on-going business through the submission of annual accounts. For a fee, you can submit a request to Companies House to review the account submissions from any company.

To form a limited company in the UK a business needs to submit two key documents:

- the memorandum of association
- the articles of association.

Table 2.6 below stipulates what each document must comprise.

Table 2.6 Founding documents for a limited company

The memorandum of association	• Name of the company and its suffix (Ltd or plc) • Location of the registered office • Capital of the company (referred to as the **authorised share capital**)
The articles of association	• The appointment and powers of the directors • The rules in relation to shareholders' meetings and voting • The types of shares and shareholders' rights attached to each type • The rules and procedures for transferring shares

As seen in the above, the Memorandum of Association is about how the company has been set up. The Articles of Association are about how the company is administered internally. This means the latter can be amended as appropriate, providing at least 75% of the shareholders agree.

These documents are public documents and are available for scrutiny at Companies House for anyone who wishes.

Raising finance by issuing shares

Often when a company wishes to expand, it may find it almost impossible to finance the expansion through internal resources or from the borrowings from financial institutions. One option available in such situations is to bring in new capital from outside sources. This additional investment can be acquired by the company selling shares and spreading the ownership of the business. In this context it is important that we understand the meaning and significance of some commonly used terms:

- **Authorised capital**: this refers to the value of shares that the company is authorised to issue and is included in the capital clause of the memorandum of association of a company.
- **Issued capital**: this is the value of the company's capital that has actually been issued to the shareholders in the form of shares.
- **Paid-up capital**: this is the amount of capital that has actually been paid to the company on the shares issued.
- **Unpaid capital**: if shares that have been issued are not fully paid for, then the amount outstanding is referred to as unpaid capital.

2

Private limited companies are not able to offer shares to the public, which obviously restricts their ability to raise large sums of capital. However, public limited companies are able to increase their issued capital by issuing a prospectus, advertising the opportunity to invest money in the company.

A share prospectus must contain the following information:

- Particulars of all contracts entered into by the company in the past two years that may influence likely investors.
- A report from the company's auditors detailing the assets, liabilities, profits, losses and dividends paid over the past five years.
- If the proceeds of the share issue are to be used to acquire property or any other business, a statement giving all particulars of the prospective vendors and the purchase price.

Self-assessment question 2.2

List the principal contents of both the memorandum of association and the articles of association.

Feedback on page 28

2.3 Regulation in the private sector

Before looking at regulation itself and what this means for purchasing, it is important to understand why we have regulation in the first place. This is very much a philosophical and political question which, depending on your personal views, may give rise to different answers. However, in general the reasons for regulation of the private sector are as follows:

- To offer protection to consumers in terms of service, quality and price.
- To prevent excessive 'profiteering' from private companies providing essential services.
- To offer protection to companies within a market.
- To maintain competitive markets and prevent the development of privately owned monopolies.
- To prevent foreign companies entering and subsuming domestic markets by protecting the interests of domestic companies.
- To maintain national interests and public welfare.

There are many other reasons, but these cover the broad gist of regulation. In short, the objectives of private sector regulation can be summed up in just one word: **protectionism**. In each case above the government has established regulatory structures to protect the interests of either:

- consumers
- domestic markets
- national economy
- public welfare.

Learning activity 2.3

Use the internet to search the websites for three different industry regulators in your country. In each case list the industry, the name of the regulator and the activities that are regulated. If you do not know any regulators by name, use a search engine to help start this exercise.

Feedback on page 28

In recent years, regulatory practice has grown significantly. One of the principal drivers for this has been the **privatisation** of public sector markets. In the UK, Margaret Thatcher led this dynamic throughout the 1980s and it had the effect of revolutionising many domestic markets. Table 2.7 below provides a chronology of the UK industries and organisations that were privatised.

Table 2.7 Chronology of privatisation in the UK

Year	Privatised company
1980	Britoil
1982	Amersham International
1983	British Aerospace; Associated British Ports; Cable & Wireless
1984	British Telecom; Jaguar Cars
1986	British Gas
1987	British Airways; British Petroleum; British Airports Authority; Rolls Royce
1988	British Steel
1989	The water supply industry
1990	The electricity generating industry
1991	The electricity supply industry
1992	The Property Services Agency
1994	British Coal; Railtrack
1995/96	British Rail to rail operating franchises

Privatisation has the effect of de-nationalising an industry into the private sector, in effect by 'floating' its organisations onto the stock market to invite members of the public to invest in them. In the 1980s this was a highly emotive political change – and in many ways it still is today – because of the nature of the industries affected and the 'value' to the national economy or public at large. Although many privatised industries have become more efficient and now offer a better service, there have been several notable failures.

Our place is not to critique privatisation – this as been done in many places elsewhere – but rather to understand why there has been a need for such an extraordinary growth in regulation in recent years.

Some of the responsibilities of a regulator include:

- Issuing and renewing the **licence to operate** for companies that wish to do business in the market.
- Setting standards of good practice including consumer protection, safe practices, quality standards and service levels.
- Handling complaints from the public about any matters concerning the industry, the market, the products or specific companies.
- Monitoring and auditing the activities of companies within the market including compliance to standards, service levels and levels of profit.
- Receiving and reviewing regular company reports, accounts and returns about the company's performance.
- Monitoring levels of competition within the market.
- Communicating and promoting the work of the market to maintain consumer confidence.
- Regulating practice and issuing warnings, controls and levies for repeated non-compliant practice.
- Operating pricing controls through mechanisms such as price-cap formulae.
- Reporting to the government.
- Removal of the licence to operate.

This last responsibility involves the rescinding of a licence to operate and only ever occurs in extreme circumstances. It constitutes the regulator's ultimate sanction and control over the market. The conditions under which a regulator is allowed to remove the licence to operate will vary according to the specific rules, regulations and standards established in the industry: it cannot be an arbitrary decision.

The removal of the licence to operate means that a company is no longer allowed to operate in the market sector: its operational activities in effect become illegal. This sanction results in the cessation of company activities with the effect of potentially closing down or terminating the business.

Such a decision is never taken lightly and will only be for reasons of:

- Significant public risk to health, safety or welfare.
- Repeated non-compliance with regulatory standards.
- Failure to implement appropriate remedies and corrective actions following warnings of non-performance or non-compliance.
- Illegal practices and/or fraudulent behaviour.

As can be seen, acting as the regulator is not an easy task, especially if it involves playing judge and jury to the standards that it has already set.

The regulatory framework established by a regulator has a significant impact on the activities of a company. This includes the purchasing function, which will be impacted in the following ways:

- **Compliance with standards**: purchasing needs to ensure all goods and services relating to the principal activities of the company are compliant with relevant standards and specifications. An example of this is the purchase of pipes or valves in the water industry.
- **Health and safety**: all sourced activities, good and services need to comply with the relevant health and safety standards. For example deliveries by hand need to be packaged safely and must comply with manual handling regulations.
- **Environmental**: similarly, all sourced activities, goods and services need to comply with the relevant environmental regulations. Examples of this include the use of regulated constituent materials and components of products (such as hazardous materials, gases or liquids).
- **Cost**: particularly relevant where the regulator has placed a price-cap on the goods or services produced. Purchasing needs to ensure it delivers cost effective solutions for the company's third party expenditure.
- **Governance**: purchasing may be required to demonstrate that probity, due diligence and due process has been followed when sourcing or outsourcing from third parties. An example of this in the US relates to the provisions of the Sarbanes-Oxley Act.
- **Clear audit trail**: purchasing may be required to maintain files on key transactions to demonstrate they have been fair and acted within the due process and with probity.
- **EU directives**: although usually referring to public sector procurement will also apply for utilities (such as energy, water and telecommunications). These requirements are covered elsewhere in the CIPS content but require purchasing to follow a due process that provides transparency, fairness, audit and competition when purchasing good or services.
- **Appropriate service levels**: particularly relevant when third party suppliers have been sourced to undertake a service that touches the customer (such as call handling, deliveries, inspections or engineering).

This list is not exhaustive and it may be that you are able to add to it from your experience in your own workplace.

Regulation is an increasingly important subject and one of significant political interest. It has an appreciable impact on the purchasing activities of a company and is one context for purchasing that can never be overlooked.

Self-assessment question 2.3

Identify the reasons why an industry regulator might restrict or remove a company's licence to operate.

Feedback on page 28

2

2.4 Termination and closing down

Before we consider how companies are closed down, use the following learning activity to consider some of the broader implications of such an event.

Learning activity 2.4

Reflect on the impact of your own workplace closing (or that of one of your main suppliers). Write down some of the major impacts this would have.

Feedback on page 28

An organisation is similar to a living organism in that it is formed, it grows/matures, it adapts and it can also decline. In the private sector there are usually only two reasons why a company is closed down:

- **Finance**: the company is no longer able to pay its debtors and/or begins to make losses that it cannot pay. In this case the company is wound-up and closed down either as a decision of the owners to cut their losses or, more usually, by a **winding-up order** where the company is legally required to call-in the administrators. In this latter case, the company is placed into a state of administration and the administrators are legally obliged to find ways of re-paying all debts owed. The administrators look to find ways of maintaining the business as a going concern or alternatively of selling it to another interested party. If they are not able to do either option, the administrators have to close down the company.
- **Strategic decision**: the company has fulfilled its objectives and/or the owners no longer want it to continue with its activities. The owners will then usually try to find a way of passing on the ownership to a third party, usually by trying to sell the company.

A company can either continue operating or cease to exist when it is acquired by another company, depending on how the acquisition is merged into the new owner. If the company is dissolved the bought-out company is closed down after transferring any relevant staff or assets into the acquirer (for example in the instance where a competitor buys out a rival company in the hope of utilising its products, assets and market share). Alternatively the acquirer may decide to keep the old company operating under new ownership and possibly a new name (for example in the instance where a competitor makes the acquisition because it wants to sell its rival's products and/or have direct access to the rival's customer-base).

Closing down a company can have significant impact on the surrounding political, economic and social environment. It is not an easy or welcome task, as emotions and attachments to the company may run deep.

Table 2.8 shows some of the potential impacts of closing down a company.

Table 2.8 Impact of an organisational closure

Macroeconomic	• Loss to the national economy • Reduced competition in a marketplace

(continued on next page)

Table 2.8 (continued)

	• Strained industrial relations in other organisations or markets • Lost revenue from taxes • Increased burden on welfare state • Loss of investor confidence in other companies or market sectors
Socioeconomic	• Loss of employment in the area/region • Loss of local employer/sponsor in the community
Personal	• Loss of earnings for the staff • Fear, anxiety and stress among employees and affiliates of the company
Clients and customers	• Loss of a supplier • Threat to the security of supply • Cost of switching supply
Suppliers	• Unpaid bills and invoices • Loss of a customer and future revenue • Risk of potential insolvency if they were dependent on the former client company
Investors and financiers	• Financial losses and unpaid debts • Lost investment/no return on investment

This list is not exhaustive and you can probably add your own thoughts and observations to it, but clearly the closure of a business has a broad impact on the environment.

Self-assessment question 2.4

List three ways in which a private sector company might cease to exist.

Feedback on page 28

2.5 The impact of the profit motive

Mullins (2005) states that there are three primary objectives of a company:

- survival
- growth and development
- profit.

In many ways these three objectives are inextricably linked. Clearly survival is essential, but this requires the creation of a profitable return to the owners and, in turn, growth and development to generate the profits.

In the previous study session we considered the profit motive as being the *raison d'être* of the company, but this is not as completely clear as it seems at first sight. For example, Peter Drucker (1989) has stated:

'To emphasize only profit, for instance, misdirects managers to the point where they may endanger the survival of the business. To obtain profit today they tend to undermine the future… To manage a business is to balance a

2

variety of needs and goals… the very nature of business enterprise requires multiple objectives'.

Clearly, although the profit motive remains the prima facie objective for a company, it is appropriate to take a balanced and measured approach. For example, this balance is needed to ensure short-term profiteering is offset with long-term development and survival.

Learning activity 2.5

Identify four specific ways in which purchasing can influence the profitability of a company.

Feedback on page 29

The principal impact of the profit motive on purchasing will be to cut costs and save money. Where goods and services can be bought more cost effectively, the purchasing function directly supports the profitability of the company with every saving it makes.

However to focus purely on cost savings would be short-sighted. There are several other factors to take into consideration including quality, service and the technical specification. Purchasing on price or cost alone is inappropriate, particularly if there is a detrimental impact to the company's customer or to its operational activities.

Here are some examples where purchasing on price alone could prove detrimental:

- Quality is compromised by purchasing a cheaper product. The product incurs additional wastage and/or re-work and therefore additional costs are incurred which far outweigh the original price saving.
- A lower cost service is purchased thus providing dissatisfaction and/ or additional work internally. The service is not efficient or effective, therefore requiring additional cost to remedy the situation.
- Cheaper but inferior materials are used to make a product and this has a detrimental impact on sales, thus reducing the company's revenue.
- Goods have been priced low because they require expensive maintenance and upgrades. The initial price is beneficial but the full cost to the company is larger than necessary.

There are many other examples than those stated above, but the principle remains. The profit motive does require a focus on cost efficiency, but purchasing on price alone has many risks associated with it.

Self-assessment question 2.5

Explain why purchasing on price alone is usually inappropriate.

Feedback on page 29

Revision question

Now try the revision question for this session on page 281.

Summary

This study session has considered the structure and workings of the private sector in detail. By now you will have a good understanding of the different types of private sector enterprise, how they are formed and financed and how they are closed down. The sections on regulation and the profit motive have provided useful background material and should help understand the environmental context for purchasing in the private sector.

As can be expected, there are many different markets within the private sector and these too have a considerable impact on purchasing activities. The next study session takes a market sector approach to the private sector to consider the differences between various industries.

Suggested further reading

You could read the relevant sections of Bailey et al (2005) and Mullins (2005).

Feedback on learning activities and self-assessment questions

Feedback on learning activity 2.1

This should be a relatively simple activity for you to fulfil. Examples of sole traders might include local tradesmen such as gardeners, bookkeepers, plumbers, and so on. Examples of partnerships might include local professional firms such as accountants, solicitors, independent financial advisers, and so on. By using real-life examples such as local tradesmen or professional partnership practices, it helps bring the text alive and makes it relevant to the everyday business around you. You should note some of the differences between sole traders (being based on the individual) and partnerships (being based on a group).

Feedback on self-assessment question 2.1

As noted in the text, private limited companies are not listed on any stock exchange and so it is not possible for members of the general public to trade shares in the company – the ownership is 'closed' or 'private'. Public limited companies however can offer shares to the public via a stock exchange, such as the ones in London, New York or Shanghai.

Generally, private limited companies tend to be smaller than public limited companies. Most large multi-national companies are publicly listed in order to attract investment, whilst many medium and smaller enterprises prefer to remain private in order to avoid the fluctuations of the capital markets.

Feedback on learning activity 2.2

Unincorporated companies comprise sole traders and partnerships, as explained in the previous section. These types of business rely on personal finance or, in the case of borrowing, securing loans against their personal assets. Because the organisations have unlimited liability, there is the risk that any losses or debts will have to be paid off with personal finance, which could mean the loss of personal assets.

Feedback on self-assessment question 2.2

The memorandum of association	• Name of the company and its suffix (Ltd or plc) • Location of the registered office • Capital of the company (referred to as the authorised share capital)
The articles of association	• The appointment and powers of the directors • The rules in relation to shareholders' meetings and voting • The types of shares and shareholders' rights attached to each type • The rules and procedures for transferring shares

Feedback on learning activity 2.3

Providing you have access to the internet, you should find this exercise relatively easy and informative; a public library will be able to help you get started. In each case, the official website of the regulator should provide specific information about how the industry is regulated and what the rights of the customer/consumer are. You should also be able to find a range of helpful information and documentation about key issues in the industry. One example of an industry regulator in the UK is the Office of Communications http://www.ofcom.org.uk, which regulates the communications industry.

Feedback on self-assessment question 2.3

As in the text provided, it will be for reasons of:

- significant public risk to health, safety or welfare
- repeated non-compliance with regulatory standards
- failure to implement appropriate remedies and corrective actions following warnings of non-performance or non-compliance
- illegal practices and/or fraudulent behaviour.

Feedback on learning activity 2.4

Make the learning activity specific to your own workplace and give specific examples. The purpose is not to identify all the potential impacts, but rather to gather an appreciation of the full scale of a company closure. Make sure you have considered the social impacts as well as the economic and environmental impacts. Later in this text we consider some of the generic types of impact: make a comparison with the list you have just written and add to it where necessary.

Feedback on self-assessment question 2.4

- A company can be given a winding-up order and go into administration.

- A company can be acquired and, once merged into the new owner, it is dissolved.
- A company can be formally closed down by its owners as part of a strategic decision.

Feedback on learning activity 2.5

Here are four specific examples, but there are many others:

- Reduced costs on third party expenditure increases the operating profit.
- Greater compliance to quality standards from bought-in materials reduces wastage and losses.
- Better customer-facing services can be sourced, helping to improve the overall customer proposition, experience and retention.
- Reduced supplier lead times increases the operating efficiency of the company.

Feedback on self-assessment question 2.5

Price is just one factor within the overall cost of purchased goods and services. The cost also needs to be balanced effectively with quality, service and the technical specification. This balance will be dictated by the current strategic direction and objectives of the company, and may vary from time to time. Purchasing on price alone is therefore inappropriate as it only considers one element of the purchasing decision.

2

Types of private sector organisation

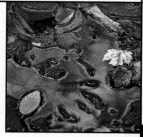

Introduction

This study session looks closely at six different market sectors within the private sector to identify and review their key features. We will also define the market influences and drivers that are characteristic of each of these market sectors and examine what their impact is upon purchasing and supply. The key learning here is to recognise the transferability of some of the fundamental principles of purchasing across these market sectors. We will also note that different approaches to purchasing are required for different contexts.

'No longer can firms afford to keep their staff in ignorance of the external [private sector] pressures which face them if they wish to survive.'
(Cox, 1994)

Session learning objectives

After completing this session you should be able to:

3.1 Compare and contrast the classification of market sectors.
3.2 Describe the characteristics of companies in a range of market sectors.
3.3 Identify key market influences and their impact upon the purchasing function.

Unit content coverage

This study session covers the following topics from the official CIPS unit content document:

Statements of practice

- Recognise the transferability of the fundamental principles of purchase and supply management.
- Appraise the need for different approaches to purchasing in differing organisations and contexts.
- Compare the diverse legal and regulatory environments in which the procurement activity takes place.

Learning objective

1.2 Appraise the different types of private sector organisations and the differing demands that they place on those managing the provision of goods and services.
   - Different forms, including limited companies, plcs and limited liability partnerships
   - Formation and cessation of private sector firms
   - Regulation of private sector and impact on purchasing
   - Impact of profit motive on purchasing activities
   - Transactional activity such as mergers and acquisitions (M&A) together with role of Competition Commission

- Specific types of private sector organisations and influences on purchasing function:
  - Manufacturing
  - Engineering
  - Fast moving consumer goods (FMCG)
  - Retail
  - Technology
  - Services.

Prior knowledge

You should work through study sessions 1 and 2 before attempting this, as they lay an important foundation for the concepts raised in this study session.

Resources

Internet access is preferable, but not essential. You may also wish to access a library for further reading and additional studies, but this is neither compulsory nor essential.

Timing

You should set aside about 4½ hours to read and complete this session, including learning activities, self-assessment questions, the suggested further reading (if any) and the revision question.

3.1 Market sector classification

Learning activity 3.1

Identify well-known examples from each sector of business activity and complete the template below:

Table 3.1

Sector of business activity	Example of organisation
Extractive raw materials	
Manufacturing	
Energy	
Retailing/distribution	
Service industry	
Intellectual production	

Feedback on page 46

There are three main ways of classifying market sectors:

- by ownership and control
- by size
- by business activity.

Classification by ownership

In study session 1 we have already considered how organisations are classified in terms of ownership (that is, private or public sector organisations and the different types within these sectors).

Classification by size

When classifying organisations by size, there are several measures that could be applied:

- number of employees
- annual turnover
- number of premises or sales outlets
- value of the company (that is, amount of capital employed).

Classifying organisations by size has some advantages in that it helps to understand the scale of the organisation and the typical resource-base of the company. This is particularly useful for purchasing to ensure that a potential supplier has the capacity and resources to fulfil an order securely.

One specific classification of organisations is the small–medium enterprise (SME). In the UK, SMEs are defined as having fewer than 250 employees and less than £50million turnover. The UK government is keen to monitor the number of businesses in each sector and to provide economic incentives and competitive protection for SMEs. Many SMEs are new and growing businesses. They do not have the same level of resources as larger organisations and yet many will have innovations of their own. In protecting the interests of SMEs the UK government is maintaining competitive and open markets, whilst also looking to nurture future successful businesses.

An illustration of the importance of SMEs to the national economy can be seen in the UK construction industry. Raftery (1991) notes that there were 350,000 registered companies in the UK of which 180,000 (51%) were construction firms. Over 95% of these firms had seven or fewer employees. Although the precise numbers will have changed since the time of this writing, the main essence of his commentary and the trend in statistics remain the same. The conclusion we can draw from this is that there are many SMEs in the UK economy and, in particular, the UK construction industry.

Further information on the engaging with small businesses and the CIPS position on professional practice is available from the CIPS website (http://www.cips.org).

Classification by business activity

The final classification of market sectors is by business activity. Examples of this include:

- Extractive raw materials: these organisations extract and refine raw materials (such as the mining industry). This sector has also been referred to as the primary sector and includes agriculture and farming.

3

- Manufacturing: these organisations acquire raw materials and, applying technology, using labour and capital, convert the raw material into a product (such as the motor industry). This sector has also been referred to as the secondary sector and includes engineering, production and assembly.
- The following sectors have traditionally been referred to as the tertiary sector, although now given its scale and importance to the world economy the following are legitimate sectors in their own right:
  - Energy: these organisations are involved in converting one type of resource (for example coal) into another (for example electricity).
  - Retailing/distribution: such organisations are involved in delivering finished products to other businesses for resale on to consumers.
  - Service industries: these organisations provide their customers with a service rather than a physical product (for example an accountant). Note: we will consider services and how they differ from products in greater detail in study session 16.
  - Intellectual production: these organisations are engaged in various types of knowledge-intensive work (such as learning, research and development or publishing)

In the 21st century it is now common to find many businesses diversified across several business activity sectors. An example of this is Ford, the American motor-car assembler. Ford now not only manufactures its cars, but it has expanded into servicing and spares replacement as well as owning its own retail showroom 'dealer' network. It offers financing to assist customers purchase its cars and it has a stake in the car rental company Hertz. Ford also has a strong reputation for research and development and has regularly launched innovations onto the market. As such, the company has spread its interests across many sectors of the economy.

Self-assessment question 3.1

Describe how different industrial sectors can be classified.

Feedback on page 46

3.2 Market sectors

The remainder of the study session looks at six specific market sectors in detail. This is only a representative sample of industries in the private sector, but it serves to highlight some of the key differences and similarities between them. You will note that one of the learning outcomes is to recognise the transferability of the fundamental principles of purchasing and supply management, and to do this effectively a general understanding of the main characteristics of some key market sectors is required.

The following six market sectors are considered:

- manufacturing
- engineering

- FMCG
- retail
- technology
- services.

Learning activity 3.2

List well-known examples of companies from each sector and describe what they do using the template below:

Table 3.2

Market sector	Name of example	Description of principal activities
Manufacturing		
Engineering		
FMCG		
Retail		
Technology		
Services		

Feedback on page 47

Manufacturing

Manufacturing has long been the backbone of many national economies. Traditionally, it has been held that domestic production is one of the main measures of economic health. However, in more recent times the effects of globalisation and access to low-cost countries have meant that manufacturing is no longer the mainstay of all national economies, as many now find it most cost effective to source manufactured goods from international markets.

Manufacturing comprises the production and assembly activities required to transfer raw materials into finished goods. Some examples of manufacturing industries include:

- automotive
- electrical goods
- aerospace
- personal computers
- jewellery.

In each example, the finished product has been manufactured from a series of inputs. These inputs include raw materials, processed goods and/or component parts, which are supplied from other sources within the supply chain. Note that in the last example, a distinction needs to be drawn between the manufacture of jewellery and any post-production retailing.

It is relatively easy to understand the supply chain(s) that feed the finished goods producer, as they comprise the tangible flow of goods and materials.

Each tier of the supply chain provides an input to the production of the finished good and, as such with the exception of raw materials producers, they each form part of the manufacturing industry.

We can review this in closer detail by studying a simplified supply chain example from the automotive industry, as shown in the table below:

Table 3.3

Supply chain tier	Example	Comments
Consumer	Members of the public	Not part of the manufacturing industry, but very much the target customer.
Retailer	Car dealership	Part of the retail industry. Responsible for selling the finished gods to the public.
Primary manufacturer	Automotive manufacturer (eg Ford)	Original equipment manufacturer (OEM) and owner of the finished goods 'brand'. Responsible for assembly of the final product.
Component manufacturer	Engine block	Components and parts manufacturer. Responsible for production of components and subassemblies.
Subcomponent manufacturer	Cam-shaft	Subcomponent and parts manufacturer. Responsible for the manufacture of individual elements of the product.
Raw materials producer	Steel producer	Not part of the manufacturing industry, but a supplier to it.

In reality the supply chain is far more complex than that shown above. However, for understanding the production characteristics of the manufacturing industry, this is sufficient. From the above, we note that manufacturing includes: original equipment manufacturers (OEMs), component manufacturers, parts suppliers and subcomponent manufacturers. It does not include retailers or the raw materials suppliers.

In general, manufacturing depends on an efficient transformation process to convert the inputs to finished outputs. This process is referred to as the operations process and will form one of the main focuses of the company if it is to be successful.

There are several key elements to running an effective and efficient operations process and these include:

- Effective use of assets (including plant, machinery, storage, premises and stock). Manufacturing is a capital intensive industry and requires expensive operational plant to undertake the transformation process. Because of the huge expense of these assets, their use needs to be both effective and efficient. This also means that manufacturing is often considered to be a volume-driven business.
- Appropriate use of technology. Technology has the effect of automating processes and increasing efficiency, speed and accuracy. To remain successful in recent times, manufacturing has to optimise the use of technology in its operations process.
- Efficient stock management. Significant sums of money can be held up in stock for manufacturing, particularly as the outputs are a result of

the transformation of the inputs. Stock needs to ordered, transported, stored and quality controlled with efficiency and accuracy.

- Accurate demand management and production forecasting. Predicting sales volumes and production schedules is a critical part of the manufacturing process. If too many goods are produced then there is a danger that they cannot be sold, whereas if there is insufficient production then there are lost sales opportunities. Good production forecasting is critical for efficient supply chain management so that suppliers can deliver the right products at the right time, quality and price.
- Quality management (for both the external supplies and the internal processes). Manufacturing depends on producing quality goods, such that they conform to their specifications with consistency. If this is not the case then there will be unnecessary cost, waste and potential re-work in the manufacturing process.
- Effective purchasing and supply management. Manufacturing is a process that depends on quality inputs at the right time and price. Purchasing and supply needs to maintain an effective feed of supplies to the operations process. By keeping the price down and the quality consistent, manufacturing can be made cost effective.
- Financing of capital equipment and working capital. Manufacturing has two key financing issues to manage: (1) the cost of capital equipment, which as already noted is significant and payback will only occur over a period of many years; and (2) managing the working capital and in particular the cash flow of the company, as suppliers demand payment before customers have paid for the finished goods.

Although there are many other aspects to successful manufacturing, these elements are critical to success, although we do not have the space or scope to study them in further detail here.

Engineering

Engineering is different from manufacturing in that it involves the technical design and production of capital assets. These are often in a one-off capacity, as opposed to the regular operations process of manufacturing. There are several different forms of engineering:

- Civil engineering and building: involving the design and construction of capital works, including buildings, roads, tunnels, railways, groundworks and public infrastructure, etc.
- Mechanical engineering: involving the design and assembly/erection of mechanical equipment and plant. This might include engines, motors, turbines, pistons, generators and other moving parts, etc.
- Electrical engineering: involving the design and assembly of electrical and electronic goods including components, information technology, microchip technology, telecommunications, cabling and transmission, etc.
- Chemical engineering: involving the design, production and processing of chemicals and chemical plants. This might include pharmaceuticals, food processing, agricultural feeds, gases, petrochemicals; the list is very long indeed.

3

- Process and production engineering: involves the design and assembly of operational processes and production plant, for example factory machinery, furnaces, processing and assembly plant, etc.
- Software engineering: involves the design, development and release of software including operating systems, mainframe applications and computer software, etc.

There are of course many other types of engineer such as nuclear, biochemical, marine, aeronautic, etc but the above categories represent the main ones.

One of the obvious points to note is the important role of design in all engineering activities. This is requires the use of intellectual capital (ideas, processes, methodologies and creativity) to create intellectual property. Many engineering solutions will guard their intellectual property closely as it becomes their source of competitive advantage and continued success in the future.

In general the engineering industry is divided into at least two main divisions: those who focus primarily on design (design engineers or consulting engineers) and those who concentrate on the development and assembly aspects (often referred to as engineering contractors). Consulting engineers will charge a professional fee for producing and specifying their design, whereas engineering contractors will charge for the materials, labour and plant required to construct the works.

There are three main applications of engineering work:

- New build: as the name suggests this involves the creation of a new asset (for example the building of a power generator).
- Renewals: this requires a major overhaul of an existing asset usually to improve its current utility or update the asset (for example re-laying track on a railway).
- Maintenance: requiring regular cleaning, servicing and minor repairs to maintain the existing asset in its current condition (for example servicing a factory boiler).

Purchasing engineering works can involve any or all of the above three applications. We will study the procurement of capital items in study session 17; meanwhile if you want more information on the subject, you should read chapter 14 of Bailey *et al* (2005), as detailed at the end of this study session.

Fast moving consumer goods

Fast-moving consumer goods (FMCG) are a specific subsector of manufacturing and production aimed at the volume retail market. In many ways the title speaks for itself: the industry focuses on the production of goods for the consumer mass-market. Although similar in many ways to manufacturing, there are some notable differences concerning the specific requirements of the consumer, retailing and changes in fashion.

Here are some examples of FMCG:

- convenience food
- chocolate bars
- soft drinks
- high-street fashion items (clothing, shoes and accessories)
- training shoes
- hair products
- pharmaceuticals.

Of course, there are many other examples of FMCG items. For our purposes, however, it is important to note that the above each share the following common factors:

- Finished goods are produced for retail to the general public consumer.
- FMCG items are usually aimed at the mass-market.
- To be effective, most FMCG items need to be sold in volume.
- FMCG items are available through a wide variety of retail outlets (supermarkets, high street retailers, convenience stores, on-line shopping, etc).
- There are many associations with fashion and consumer tastes which heavily influence the demand for FMCG.
- Many (but not all) FMCG items have a relatively short product life cycle because of the links with consumer trends (although there are notable exceptions such as Coca-Cola).
- Many FMCG items are heavily branded to create awareness in the consumer market and create customer loyalty to the products.
- There is fierce competition between brands: this can be between similar products and/or between alternative products (eg soft drinks and ice cream).
- Promoting FMCG items is usually supported by heavy advertising and marketing.
- Many branded FMCG are in competition with non-branded 'white labelled' goods produced by low-cost manufacturers for supermarkets and volume retailers.

From the list in this table, we can see that there is a very strong relationship between FMCG, consumer fashions and the retail industry. The supply chain needs to be very responsive and agile to the changing needs and desires of the consumer. We look more closely at these issues in study sessions 13 and 14.

In terms of the manufacture and production of FMCG items, the same issues of managing the operations process exist as in the rest of the manufacturing industry. There is an emphasis on effective use of heavy plant and machinery as well as ensuring an efficient cost-effective supply chain.

Supply chain agility is becoming increasingly important to remain successful in FMCG industries. Consumer trends and fashion changes rapidly and therefore it is essential to develop production plant and machinery that can adapt to the changing manufacturing requirements. Similarly this places additional pressures on purchasing and supply to ensure that the vendor base is equally responsive.

3

Retail

When compared with manufacturing, FMCG or engineering, the retail industry is relatively simple and less technical. That is not to say that retailing is easy or is not as sophisticated; it is just less complex.

Retailers produce very little, if anything. They sell products that are usually made by another company: these are called goods for resale and we will study them in detail in study session 14. In return for offering manufacturers access to consumer markets, they receive a mark up which may vary from +40% to +100% of the price sold by the manufacturer.

Examples of retailers include:

- supermarkets and hypermarkets
- petrol garages
- internet sites
- discount warehouses
- local 'corner' shops
- do-it-yourself (DIY) stores
- duty-free shops at airports and ports
- markets.

Retailing is big business, particularly when associated with branded goods and contemporary fashions. The role of the retailer is to make sure that the goods and products are presented and marketed to customers in the most appealing manner. This includes making sure the location of retail stores suit the profile of potential customers, the goods are packaged and displayed well, and that they are priced attractively (possibly with additional incentives or promotions to win more custom).

Many retailers now concentrate on providing their customers with an 'ambient experience' when shopping so that customers enjoy the experience and are treated well, thus ensuring their loyalty and commitment for future purchases.

As competition on the high street has increased – particularly with out-of-town shopping malls and retail outlets and the recent explosion in internet shopping – retailers have had to find new and innovation methods of promoting their goods.

Securing volume and regular custom is a major objective, with promotional campaigns and customer loyalty schemes now being common features of many retailers. These types of initiative are usually supported by sophisticated technology, market research and customer relationship information. Electronic trading information such as 'electronic point of sale' (EPOS) systems helps retailers to understand the buying behaviours of their customers better and also ensure suppliers are given accurate real-time information about orders.

Although we have only touched upon some of the elements behind retailing, it can be seen that there is a significant level of sophistication to it: it is not just about running a shop.

Technology

The technology market sector has expanded rapidly in recent years and looks continue to grow at significant rates. There are many elements to the technology industry and several ways of classifying its segments; however for this study we will use the following:

- **Hardware** (mainframe, mid-range, personal computing and peripherals). An example of a hardware company is Dell which manufactures predominantly personal computing and peripheral products and retails them over the internet.
- **Software** (applications, web-services, licensed products and operating systems). An example of a software company is Microsoft which develops licensed applications and operating systems.
- **Services** (systems integration, maintenance and programming). An example of an IT Services company is Accenture which provides technology solutions, amongst its other range of services.
- **Telecommunications** (mobile, fixed line, call centre operations, networking and cabling). An example of a telecommunications company is Cable & Wireless which provides a range of fixed line and networking services.

There are also several companies that operate in more than one of these segments, for example IBM.

There are many other distinctions and technological categories that could be noted here, but the purpose is not to delve into the technology itself, as that would be a separate study course in its own right! As far as we are concerned, we need to understand the basic characteristics of the industry and to do that we need to under the key features of each of its main market segments.

The provision of hardware products is principally a manufacturing industry, as described earlier. The technology develops quickly and product life cycles are remarkably short as a result. The industry invests a lot in research and development to ensure it keeps at the competitive leading edge of technology. Within this segment of the technology sector there are also several key component providers, such as Intel, which manufactures processors.

The software industry is very different to hardware in that it does not produce a tangible product. Software applications do exist and they are usually licensed to prevent illegal copying or fraud, but the products cannot be seen or touched. As previously mentioned, software development and maintenance is a form of engineering. Instead of investing in capital equipment and materials to undertake the construction or assembly phase, it employs intellectual capital to complete the development of the product. In general this is a very dynamic and enterprising market which looks set to continue for many years to come.

We will discuss the service sector in the following paragraphs. In general though IT services tend to be solution-orientated and operate similarly to engineering services. Finally, the telecommunications market sector tends to

3

be an extremely diverse sector encompassing hardware, software and service solutions often in the same work activities.

In summary, although technology has a range of applications and the individual segments of the industry appear to be diverse, the industry has broad similarities with engineering in terms of providing a designed solution and manufacturing in terms of producing technology goods and products.

Services

The service sector is perhaps the broadest market sector and the hardest to define. It encompasses the services of management consultancy, accountancy, human relations, banking and finance, insurance, brokerage, legal, research, transportation and many more besides.

A service differs from a product in that it is:

- intangible, it cannot be touched or seen
- unable to be stored or re-sold
- consumed at the point of delivery
- inseparable in that it cannot be broken down into individual elements; and
- heterogeneous in that a service can never be wholly standardised and there will be variations when the service is repeated.

We will look more closely at buying services in study session 16. For now though we need to focus on some of the specific characteristics of the service industries.

Services are delivered primarily through people. They require the skills and intellectual input from people to create and fulfil the service to a customer. Although services are intangible they can still be defined in terms of their performance or outputs. To achieve this, a scope and a specification are required.

Scope refers to the acceptable bounds of practice required to deliver the service. For example when delivering a legal service, the solicitor is required to know the areas he/she is required to act on, how far to take the action and the timescales in which to act.

The specification refers to performance outcome that is required by the service provider. This can be defined in terms of deliverables (the finished solution) and/or service levels (a measure of how the activities are to be conducted). An example of a deliverable would be a broker that is required to find a cost-effective insurance solution. Whereas an example of a service level would be for a transportation company to collect and deliver on-time without damaging freight and with acceptably few complaints.

In these last few pages we reviewed six different market sectors. Each one has comprised its own unique characteristics, whereas at the same time having some similarities with others. Although you will not be expected to know the detailed workings of each of these specific markets, you will need to appreciate some of the key features and to be able to recognise the application of purchasing in different contexts.

The following section considers the influence of the market sector on purchasing activities and some of the key principles that are transferable across industrial sectors.

Self-assessment question 3.2

Compare and contrast the manufacturing and retail sectors in terms of principal activities and added value.

Feedback on page 47

3.3 Market influences on purchasing

As has already been noted, it is more important that you understand the influence of market forces on purchasing than the specifics of each market sector *per se*. One of the learning outcomes of this unit syllabus is to recognise the transferability of the fundamental principles of purchase and supply management.

Learning activity 3.3

Identify (from the list provided below) which purchasing principles are readily transferable across most market sectors.

Table 3.4

Purchasing principles	Transferable across most industries?
Negotiation on cost	Yes/no
Compliance to the EU Public Procurement Directives	Yes/no
Capital investment required to purchase heavy plant and machinery	Yes/no
Electronic trading for cost efficiency	Yes/no
Contract documentation to mitigate commercial risks	Yes/no
Use of competitive tender enquiries to deliver best value	Yes/no
Use of service debit/credit regimes for managing service levels	Yes/no
Just-in-time stockless purchasing	Yes/no
Supplier rationalisation and vendor accreditation	Yes/no
Ethical sourcing and corporate and social responsibility	Yes/no

Feedback on page 47

The following table maps out the key market influences for each of the market sectors you studied in the previous section and then considers what the impact these will have on purchasing activities:

3

Table 3.5

Key market influences and drivers	Impact upon purchasing
Manufacturing	
• Efficient management of the operations process • Effective feed of supplies from the supply chain • Order volumes to create economies of scale • Competition from low cost countries • Efficient stock and supply management • Investment in heavy plant and machinery • Health and safety management • Delivery on quality standards (total quality management)	• Right time, place, price, etc • Lean supply chain • Well-specified product requirements • Quality management of supplies • Supply chain management of suppliers and their supplies • Capital procurement to support investment in operational plant • Challenge on costs to maintain efficient supply chain • Good stock management and/or certain just-in-time deliveries
Engineering	
• Emphasis on technical and quality standards and compliance to specifications • Quality management • Health and safety management • Intellectual property for design and development activities • Innovation for technical solutions • Project management to complete activities • High levels of uncertainty • Risk management for uncertainty • Most engineering project are one-off	• Right time, place, price, etc • Project management skills to ensure materials are sourced for the development phase • Well-specified materials requirements • Contract management skills to manage specialist suppliers and subcontractors • Quality management of materials supplies • Challenge on costs to maintain efficient supply chain • Protection of intellectual property • Insurance provisions for key risks
FMCG	
• Efficient management of the operations process • Effective feed of supplies from the supply chain • Supply chain agility and responsiveness • Order volumes to create economies of scale • Branding to support marketing and product promotion • Efficient stock and supply management • Investment in heavy plant and machinery • Health and safety management • Delivery on quality standards • Response to consumer trends • Speed to market (first mover advantages)	• Right time, place, price, etc • Lean, agile and responsive supply chains • Well-specified product requirements • Quality management of supplies • Supply chain management of suppliers and their supplies • Capital procurement to support investment in operational plant • Challenge on costs to maintain efficient supply chain • Good stock management and/or certain just-in-time deliveries • Protection of intellectual property and brand • Sourcing from low cost countries
Retail	
• Sales volumes to create economies of scale • Branding to support marketing and product promotion • Efficient stock and supply management • Efficient stock turn	• Right time, place, price, etc • Well-specified product requirements • Clear re-sale and returns policies • Quality management of goods

(continued on next page)

Table 3.5 (continued)

Key market influences and drivers	Impact upon purchasing
• Response to consumer trends • Locational dependencies of retail premises • Understanding and targeting customer needs • High competition from many sources, including internet shopping • Speed to market (first mover advantages)	• Contract management of suppliers and their supplies • Challenge on costs to maintain efficient supply chain • Good stock management and/or certain just-in-time deliveries • Ability to switch suppliers rapidly • Electronic point of sale technology to call-off orders
Technology	
• Emphasis on technical standards and compliance to specifications • Quality management • Intellectual property for design and development activities • Innovation for technical solutions • Project management to complete activities • High levels of uncertainty • Risk management for uncertainty • Many IT solution projects are one-off • Speed to market (first mover advantages) • High competition from alternative sources of supply	• Right time, place, price, etc • Project management skills to ensure resources are sourced for the solution phase • Well-specified solution requirements • Contract management skills to manage specialist suppliers and subcontractors • Challenge on costs to maintain efficient supply chain • Protection of intellectual property • Insurance provisions for key risks • Management of key licensing issues
Services	
• Emphasis on service levels and compliance to specifications • Management of scope and resources • Emphasis on differentiation through intellectual capital • Intellectual property for service delivery • Innovation for creative solutions • Project management to complete activities • Good process management for repetitive services (eg recruitment)	• Project management skills to ensure resources are sourced for the service delivery • Well-specified service requirements and service levels • Contract management skills to manage specialist suppliers and subcontractors • Challenge on costs to maintain efficient supply chain • Protection of intellectual property • Insurance provisions for key risks (such as professional indemnity)

The table shows several interesting trends that support the learning outcomes for this unit:

- Firstly, it should be noted that each market sector has its own specific set of market drivers. We know this because of the distinct characteristics described in the previous section.
- Secondly, we can see that the market drivers and influences have a direct impact on purchasing activities and priorities. The key learning is that: purchasing activities and principles can only be defined in the context of the market and its drivers.
- You will note that several of the market sectors share similar drivers (such the need to deliver on quality standards in manufacturing, FMCG and engineering).

3

- Similarly there are several purchasing principles that are shared and transferable across several sectors.

Self-assessment question 3.3

Describe how the purchasing activities in an IT hardware-manufacturing firm might differ from a software development firm.

Feedback on page 47

Revision question

Now try the revision question for this session on page 281.

Summary

This chapter has looked closely at six different market sectors within the private sector to note their key features. In this we have identified the market influences and drivers that are characteristic of each of the market sectors and defined what their impact is upon purchasing and supply. The key learning has been to recognise the transferability of some of the fundamental principles of purchasing across these market sectors. We have also noted that different approaches to purchasing are required for different contexts.

The next study session considers the public sector and the impact of its environment on purchasing activities.

Suggested further reading

You could read the relevant sections of Bailey et al (2005), Raftery (1991) and Slack et al (1998) and also take a look at the CIPS Positions on Practice Note 'Use of Small Suppliers' available to download from the CIPS website CIPS: http://www.cips.org.

Feedback on learning activities and self-assessment questions

Feedback on learning activity 3.1

This should have been a relatively easy task for you. It is worthwhile using well-known names and recording them here for future reference and revision purposes.

Feedback on self-assessment question 3.1

There are three main ways of classifying market sectors:

- by ownership and control
- by size
- by business activity.

Feedback on learning activity 3.2

This should have been a relatively easy task for you. It is worthwhile using well-known names and recording them here for future reference and revision.

Feedback on self-assessment question 3.2

Your answers should reflect the text provided in this section of the study session. Typically retailers do not manufacture any physical goods or products but provide the medium for sales to the public consumer. Manufacturing is focused on providing an efficient operations process to produce goods at the right specification, quality and pricing.

Feedback on learning activity 3.3

The following purchasing principles are transferable across most market sectors:

- negotiation on cost
- electronic trading for cost efficiency
- contract documentation to mitigate commercial risks
- use of competitive tender enquiries to deliver best value
- supplier rationalisation and vendor accreditation
- ethical sourcing and corporate and social responsibility (CSR).

There are of course many more transferable purchasing principles. The purpose of this exercise was to demonstrate that although some purchasing activities and principles are specific to particular sectors of industry, there are many that are equally applicable and transferable across all sectors. You will consider these issues at greater length in the text that follows.

Feedback on self-assessment question 3.3

From the text provided you will have been able to establish that the production of hardware is actually a manufacturing process, similar to any other part of the manufacturing sector. Purchasing will support the manufacturing process with the sourcing of direct materials and components from the supply chain to feed production operations.

Software development however is predominantly a service industry utilising the intellectual capital of its workers. In this instance there is no direct materials supply chain and purchasing's role will focus on ensuring the indirect expenditure of operational support items are procured for the company.

3

Types of public sector organisation

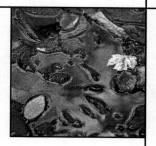

Introduction

By now, you have studied the private sector in detail. In this study session we turn our attention to the public sector. There are several differences to the private sector and, generally, public sector procurement is more complex and procedural. We will consider the different types of public sector organisation that exist as well as looking more closely at regulation of the public sector. Picking up from the study session 1 we take a closer look at claims that the objectives of public sector spending are contested. We also will review the variety of stakeholder interests in public spending and consider what their impact is on purchasing activities.

'Procurement of equipment, goods and services for the government and the public sector generally is complex... This has led to many challenges for those undertaking the procurement action'.
Bailey et al (2005)

Session learning objectives

After completing this session you should be able to:

4.1 Compare different types of public sector organisation and their inter-relationships.
4.2 Describe the role of regulation and its impact on purchasing activities.
4.3 Appraise the objectives of a public sector organisation.
4.4 Analyse the multiple forms of stakeholder in the public sector and their impact on purchasing activities.

Unit content coverage

This study session covers the following topics from the official CIPS unit content document:

Statements of practice

- Recognise the transferability of the fundamental principles of purchase and supply management.
- Appraise the need for different approaches to purchasing in differing organisations and contexts.
- Compare the diverse legal and regulatory environments in which the procurement activity takes place.

Learning objective

1.3 Review the different types of public sector organisations and explain the variety of approaches taken to the purchase and supply of goods and services.
  - Different types of public sector organisation, such as central government, local government and government agencies
  - Regulation of public sector and impact on purchasing

4

- Concept of value for money, balancing conflicting objectives and priorities
- Multiple forms of stakeholder and their influences.

Prior knowledge

You will need to have worked through study session 1 before attempting this, as it lays a useful foundation to the concepts raised in this study session.

Resources

You may wish to access a library for further reading and additional studies, but this is neither compulsory nor essential.

Timing

You should set aside about 5 hours to read and complete this session, including learning activities, self-assessment questions, the suggested further reading (if any) and the revision question.

4.1 Types of public sector organisation

In the study session 1 you were introduced to public sector organisations and provided with an overview of six different types. This section builds on that work with a view to enabling you to contrast the different types.

Table 4.1 outlines the six main types of public sector organisation.

Table 4.1 Types of public sector organisation

Type of public sector organisation	UK example
Central government	Department of Work and Pensions
Local government	New Forest District Council
Government agency	Environment Agency
Health authority	Hampshire and Isle of Wight Strategic Health Authority
Armed forces	Defence Logistics Organisation
Utility organisations	London Transport

Learning activity 4.1

Read the first section of the public sector procurement chapter in the recommended text, Bailey et al (2005). Using the examples above as context, consider the various issues facing managers of public sector expenditure. Write a list of the areas where public sector procurement differs from private sector procurement.

Feedback on page 57

When studying the public sector, the obvious starting place has to be the source of income, or without this, there would be no public services and therefore no public sector. This in itself is a surprisingly complex subject, but in general there are only a few main sources of income for the public sector:

- Company taxation (of employer's contributions and company profits).
- Personal taxes (income tax and/or capital gains/inheritance).
- Local taxation, community charging and rates.
- Sales taxes (such as value added tax in the UK).
- Specific duty (on purchases such as tobacco, petrol, housing, and so on).
- Customs and excise duties (import taxes and the like).
- Fines, fees and ancillary charges.

Put simply, these sources of income boil down to one thing: they come from the tax-paying public.

The government has several means of collecting the income and, although some is collected locally to support local services, most is aggregated nationally for distribution across the public sector as a whole. In the UK the Treasury provides this financing and accounting role and holds the 'purse-strings' of other government budgets and grants.

In the case of central government, all finance is centrally funded by the government using taxpayers' money to provide services nationally. Each government department runs its own complex budgeting process, which is constantly monitored and reviewed on a fiscal basis.

Local government, however, is funded by local taxes paid through community charging to provide a specific service to the locality of the taxpayers. There is also often a complex system of subsidies and/or levies from central government that overlays this.

Local government supports local services such as street lighting, waste disposal and local law and order. It also pays significant grants to local public services such as the police, ambulance and fire services.

In some cases, the government sets up agencies to concentrate on specific issues or areas of responsibility. These agencies are still funded by central government from taxpayers' money but are given the relative freedom to form their own policies and procedures and to act independently of the government.

In the UK, for example, the Health and Safety Executive (HSE) is an independent government agency which has specific emphasis and jurisdiction for health and safety matters. As such, it operates independently of the government and its policies apply equally across both public and private sectors, with only a few minor exceptions for defence purposes. The HSE has powers to inspect and advise on matters of health and safety. It also has the powers to fine an organisation or even temporarily shut down operations if people's health and safety is at significant risk.

Where agencies act as the industry regulator, they are jointly funded by government subsidy and levies on the companies operating in that particular sector.

4

4.2 Regulating public sector procurement

Regulation of the public sector works in many ways like regulation of the private sector. In study session 2, we noted the following responsibilities of a private sector regulator:

- Issuing and renewing the licence to operate for companies who wish to do business in the market.
- Setting standards of good practice including consumer protection, safe practices, quality standards and service levels.
- Handling complaints from the public about any matters concerning the industry, the market, the products or specific companies.
- Monitoring and auditing the activities of companies within the market including compliance to standards, service levels and levels of profit.
- Receiving and reviewing regular company reports, accounts and returns regarding the company's performance.
- Monitoring levels of competition within the market.
- Communicating and promoting the work of the market to maintain consumer confidence.
- Regulating practice and issuing warnings, controls and levies for repeated non-compliant practice.
- Operating pricing controls through mechanisms such as price-cap formulae.
- Reporting to the government.
- Removal of the licence to operate.

You will have observed a strong similarity between regulation of the public and private sectors. In study session 2 we described the role of the private sector regulator as protectionism, and that is exactly what it is in the public sector too. The only difference to note is that they are not regulating openly competitive commercial markets.

The main role of the public sector regulator is therefore to protect national interests, public welfare and institutionalised standards.

Given this, we can therefore review the impact of a regulator on public sector procurement as follows:

- Compliance with standards: purchasing needs to ensure all goods and services relating to the principal activities of the public sector organisation are compliant with relevant standards and specifications. An example of this is the purchase of pharmaceuticals in the health industry.
- Health and safety: all sourced activities, goods and services need to comply with the relevant health and safety standards. For example deliveries by hand need to be packaged safely and must comply with manual handling regulations.
- Environmental: similarly, all sourced activities, goods and services need to comply with the relevant environmental regulations. Examples of this include the use of regulated constituent materials and components of products (such as hazardous materials, gases or liquids).
- Probity and accountability: purchasing is required to demonstrate that probity, due diligence and due process have been followed when sourcing or outsourcing from third parties, and in particular that taxpayers' money has been used appropriately.
- Clear audit trail: purchasing is required to maintain files on key transactions to demonstrate they have been fair and acted within the due process and with probity. This includes demonstrating that the appropriate procedures and regulations have been followed in selecting suppliers and letting of public sector contracts.
- EU Directives: these requirements are covered elsewhere in the CIPS unit content and require purchasers to follow a due process that provides transparency, fairness, audit and competition when buying goods or services.
- Appropriate service levels: particularly relevant when third-party suppliers have been sourced to undertake a service that touches the general public (such as call-handling, deliveries, inspections or engineering).

A final comment needs to be made about the role of the EU and public sector procurement (as mentioned above). All public sector procurement is required to follow the EU's *Good Procurement Practice* guide, which recommends:

1   A set of clear and concise objectives.
2   A full understanding of the market and the law.
3   A clear specification.
4   Good sourcing and careful consideration when choosing suppliers, service providers and contractors.
5   Well-considered contract award criteria.
6   Effective contract management.
7   A sound supplier and contract performance review process.

Public sector procurement and compliance with the EU Procurement Directives are worthy of a whole study session in themselves. You will cover this subject in detail in other units of the CIPS unit content. For now, those who wish to study the subject in detail should review the second section of the public sector procurement chapter in our recommended text, Bailey et al (2005).

Self-assessment question 4.2

Outline the role of the regulator in the public sector. Illustrate your answer with examples.

Feedback on page 58

4.3 Contested public sector objectives

In study session 1 we noted that the private sector has one principal objective (the profit motive), whereas the public sector has multiple objectives. For reflection, these are listed in the following table:

Table 4.2

Public sector social goals	• Protection of property and law and order • National defence of territory • Equality of opportunity • Minimum levels of social infrastructure • Redistribution of wealth • Health gain and maintenance • Environmental quality • Minimum levels of social income and welfare • Education • Protection against old age and infirmity
Public sector economic goals	• Higher levels of economic growth • Protection of infant industries against competition • Local/regional economic development • Development of specific industries/technologies • Investment in industrial/technological transfer • Underwriting and subsidising national costs of production and exchange

Source: Cox and Thompson, 1998

Learning activity 4.3

The following list outlines 13 responsibilities of a local police constabulary. Assuming the constabulary has an annual budget of £100 million, try to rank the objectives in order of priority and then allocate an appropriate proportion of the budget to each cause:

1 Proactive prevention of crime (such as supporting neighbourhood watch schemes).
2 Acting fairly and consistently with all members of the public.
3 Educating the public on risks.
4 Maintaining a visible presence for public confidence and security.

(continued on next page)

Learning activity 4.3 *(continued)*

5 Providing information, such as directions and community advice.
6 Managing lost and stolen property.
7 Investigating crimes and catching criminal suspects.
8 Charitable community service and support.
9 Equal opportunities.
10 Accountability for expenditure.
11 Protection and security of the public and their property.
12 Comforting and counselling victims and the bereaved.
13 Maintaining the peace during crowded events and demonstrations.

Feedback on page 58

4

Professor Andrew Cox has argued that public sector objectives and the values that lie at the heart of the EU Procurement Directives remain wholly contested. In short he has posed five key challenges:

1 What are the end-goals of public spending and what are its 'values'?
2 What are the most appropriate means of delivery and who should decide them?
3 How should performance be measured?
4 Who should play Solomon over allocative scarcity?
5 What is the most appropriate regulatory structure to achieve valued outcomes?

Although we have already observed the multiple numbers of end-goal objectives and the conflict this can cause, some of Cox's other challenges need briefly reviewing. He maintains that the presence of multiple objectives leads to an inevitable management tension within any organisation. Put simply, you cannot achieve everything at once and you need to prioritise, particularly if you only have limited budget or resources, as in the learning objective above. Cox argues that the multiple objectives (economic and/or social goals) of public sector procurement lead to a contested view of which are the most important.

Although this is the role of the government of the day, it does mean that current policy governs many of these decisions and outcomes, and that this will change with changes in public opinion.

The issues associated with making these decisions concern the matter of perspective. The public sector has many interested parties and stakeholders including politicians, civil servants, the media, the electorate, unions and pressure groups. Public affairs need to remain transparent and accountable but if each objective and end-goal has its own set of values and its own measures of success, then it is certain that public sector procurement will continue to be contested.

To help audit public sector organisations and maintain accountability for their public spending and performance, the government uses auditing agencies such as the Audit Commission and the National Audit Office.

These agencies maintain a programme of regular reviews on standards, spending accounts, market conditions and public opinion. They act independently and publish their findings in the form of government reports to help maintain public confidence and accountability. As well as publishing the findings of their reviews, they also publish recommendations for improvement. Government regularly reviews and acts upon the findings of such reports.

For further reading on the contested nature of public spending, please refer to the reading list at the end of this study session.

Self-assessment question 4.3

To what extent do you agree that the goals of public spending are contested?

Feedback on page 59

4.4 Stakeholder management

We have already noted that the public sector comprises many interested parties. This point is brought home in the following learning activity:

Learning activity 4.4

Using the table provided, list six of the key stakeholders for a hospital near you and state what their requirements on the hospital are likely to be:

Table 4.3

Hospital stakeholder	Probable interest(s) in a hospital
1.	
2.	
3.	
4.	
5.	
6.	

Feedback on page 59

The learning activity aptly demonstrates the multiple numbers of stakeholders for a hospital, but the activity could have equally been applied to any other public sector service such as a school, the police, the environment or public transport. There are many different stakeholders, each with their own specific interests and loyalties. These stakeholder interests are often contested, in that they have their own perspectives and views on what is important.

Purchasing in the public sector is impacted by the demands of multiple stakeholders in the following ways:

- need for accountability
- need for probity
- cost effectiveness and efficiency in the use of public funds

- transparent sourcing processes and award criteria
- open, non-discriminatory and fair competition
- compliance to regulations
- appeals and complaints procedures
- policy and procedures.

4

Self-assessment question 4.4

A local school is about to invest £3 million in an extension for its science and technology department by building a brand new networked computer centre for its students and adult education services.

Identify four key stakeholders in the project and describe their specific interests in the purchasing project.

Feedback on page 59

Revision question

Now try the revision question for this session on page 281.

Summary

This study session has focused on the public sector and drawn several key comparisons with that of the private sector. You have observed that public procurement is, as a rule, more complex and procedural. The reasons for this lie in the need for public accountability and probity. Public spending has many more objectives than that of the private sector; it also has a broader range of stakeholders that it needs to take account of.

The following study session takes a closer look at the voluntary and not-for-profit sectors. There are several broad comparisons with the public sector that are worth noting as you work your way through the text and learning activities.

Suggested further reading

You could read the relevant sections of Bailey et al (2005), Cox (1993), Furling and Cox (1995) and Lamming and Cox (1995).

Feedback on learning activities and self-assessment questions

Feedback on learning activity 4.1

Areas where public sector procurement differs from private sector procurement include:

- Need for public accountability and probity.
- Value for money, rather than the profit motive.

- Compliance with EU regulations.
- Use of open and fair competition, as a rule.
- Procurement is likely to be more procedural in the public sector.

Feedback on self-assessment question 4.1

You should find this a relatively easy task. It is useful to research and be familiar with named examples, as this will assist your studies. If you are interested in further study, use the internet to look up these organisations' websites to see how much information you can find out about them.

Feedback on learning activity 4.2

There are several well-known regulators operating in the public sector; for example Ofsted (for education standards) or the General Medical Council (for standards of medical care). Private sector regulation differs from that of the public sector in that it needs to consider the following aspects: monitoring price tariffs, profit levels, reviewing company accounts and maintaining competitive markets. In effect, all other duties of regulation apply, whether in the public or private sectors.

Feedback on self-assessment question 4.2

Your list of roles and responsibilities should compare with that of private sector regulation, but without the need for protection of commercial markets. Typically this might be as follows:

- Setting standards of good practice including consumer protection, safe practices, quality standards and service levels.
- Handling complaints from the public about any matters concerning the industry, the market, the service or specific organisations.
- Monitoring and auditing the activities of organisations within the market including compliance to standards and service levels.
- Receiving and reviewing regular organisational reports and returns about the organisation's performance.
- Communicating and promoting the work of the market to maintain consumer confidence.
- Regulating practice and issuing warnings, controls and levies for repeated non-compliant practice.
- Reporting to the government.
- Closure of non-performing operations (such as a school or hospital).

Feedback on learning activity 4.3

The list is fictitious and serves only to illustrate the point made in the text. However, you should have found this task virtually impossible: even if you were given further information to support your analysis (such as previous years' budget allocations, performance metrics and/or statistics) you would still not have been able to define the absolute priorities.

The point is that everyone has a different perspective on what are the constabulary's most important responsibilities. Furthermore, because budget and resource allocations are limited, not every task can be fulfilled to the degree we would all like. This means that management needs to make some important and yet very difficult decisions: the objectives and their outcomes are contested.

Feedback on self-assessment question 4.3

Public spending goals depend on the achievement of a range of economic and social welfare objectives. Although they are often complementary and there is little conflict between the goals themselves, the issue of limited/finite resources creates an automatic tension between them. Limited budgets lead to the issue of choice which itself depends on prioritisation. This is termed 'allocative scarcity'. The goals of public spending are contested because there are different public views, opinions and political positions as to the allocation of resources for public expenditure.

Feedback on learning activity 4.4

There are many different stakeholders for a hospital, ranging from the medical staff to support staff, patients and their visitors, suppliers of medical equipment, the government, regulating bodies, students and (in the case of privately owned hospitals) the directors, owners and investors. Below is an example of how the table could have been completed.

Table 4.4

Hospital stakeholder:	Probable interest(s) in the hospital:
1. Doctors	Clinical environment to undertake prognosis and treatments, as well as source of personal employment
2. Nursing union	Nursing standards and conditions of employment provided at the hospital
3. Drug supplier	Potential revenue stream and client reference
4. Local media	Public interest and current affairs
5. Counsellor	Supportive environment to provide public service and source of personal employment
6. Local politician	Public spending, standards of care, public opinion, hospital performance ratings and local source of employment

Feedback on self-assessment question 4.4

There are many more than four types of stakeholder in this example, but here are a few answers you could have chosen:

- Science and technology teachers: will want high technology specification and pedagogical aids to assist their teaching and ensure best results for students.
- Head-teacher: will want to ensure budget is adhered to, the building work is completed on time and that the projected revenues from adult education can be achieved.
- Other teachers: will want the noise and disruption of the building site to be minimised so as not to disturb their own lessons. They may also hope that in future years the head-teacher will spend the same amounts of money on their departments!

4

- IT suppliers: will want their preferred specification for the IT equipment.
- Students: will want state-of-the-art technology and access to their preferred internet and software solutions.
- Local builders: will want to win the contract and make money on the job.
- Parents: will want the building work to be undertaken safely and also to ensure that appropriate controls are placed on use of the IT equipment.
- School governors: will want to ensure that vale for money is achieved and that the school can account for the expenditure.

It is worth noting that not everyone's interests can be met and that some difficult decisions will need to be made.

The third sector

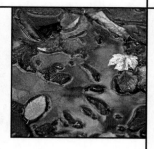

Introduction

This is the final study session on business sectors. It looks at the important contribution from the voluntary and third sector sectors. Although these sectors can often be overlooked, they play an important role in business society, particularly as the distinctions between public and private sector are gradually diminishing.

As with previous study sessions, we examine the key features of these sectors, how charities in particular are regulated and some of the multiple objectives that exist, and the impact this has on purchasing in this sector. We also consider the increasingly important aspect of corporate social responsibility and its role in the third sector.

'The only way to achieve true success is to express yourself completely in service to society.'
Aristotle (384–322 BC)

5

Session learning objectives

After completing this session you should be able to:

5.1 Describe the defining characteristics of third sector organisations.
5.2 Explain with examples how these organisations are regulated and how this influences purchasing decisions.
5.3 Identify the principal strategic objectives of third sector organisations and analyse their impact on purchasing activities.
5.4 Evaluate the importance of CSR for third sector organisations.

Unit content coverage

This study session covers the following topics from the official CIPS unit content document:

Statements of practice

• Recognise the transferability of the fundamental principles of purchase and supply management.
• Appraise the need for different approaches to purchasing in differing organisations and contexts.
• Compare the diverse legal and regulatory environments in which the procurement activity takes place.
• Discuss the ethical implications of purchasing in different contexts.

Learning objective

1.4 Review the different types of third sector organisations.

- Different types of third sector organisations
- Regulation of third sector organisations and impact on purchasing
- Importance of corporate social responsibility (CSR)

Prior knowledge

You will need to have worked through study session 1 before attempting this, as it lays a useful foundation to the concepts raised in this study session.

Resources

You may wish to access a library for further reading and additional studies, but this is neither compulsory nor essential.

Timing

You should set aside about 3½ hours to read and complete this session, including learning activities, self-assessment questions, the suggested further reading (if any) and the revision question.

5.1 Key features of the third sector

Although we will see several broad similarities to the public and private sectors, the third sector has its own distinguishing features. This affects its strategic objectives and management, its employment culture and its activities.

Learning activity 5.1

Identify well-known examples of a third sector organisation, stating what its principal activities are and how it receives funding.

Feedback on page 70

A common feature of third sector organisations is that none of them has been set up to make a profit in the true business sense of the word. You should be able to note this in your above examples. We will look more specifically at motives and objectives later in this study session.

Important distinguishing features of third sector organisations are their strategic management and their employment culture. These are usually driven by the ideologies, values and over-riding objectives of the organisation. Many of the workers within these sectors are volunteers, although there are usually always a small group of people who are employed to undertake management responsibilities and administration of the organisations.

The values and expectations of various stakeholder groups of the organisation play an important role in the development of the organisation's strategic plans and operational activities. The following table highlights some of these characteristics and the likely impact of them.

Table 5.1

Objectives and expectations	
• May be multiple service objectives and expectations • May be multiple influences on policy • The expectations of funding bodies are usually very influential	• Complicates strategic planning • Many incidences of political lobbying • Consultation becomes a major activity • Decision-making can be slow and administrative
Market and users	
• Beneficiaries of service not necessarily contributors of revenue/resources • Multiple stakeholders • Multiple 'customers'	• Service satisfaction is not measured readily in financial terms • Satisfaction has the potential of being subjective to individual perspectives
Resources	
• High proportion from sponsors/donors (could be government) • Received in advance of services, often with an attached expectation • Often there are multiple sources of funding	• Influence from funding bodies may be high • May be emphasis on financial or resources efficiency rather service effectiveness (or sometime vice versa) • Strategies and communications may be addressed as much towards sponsors as clients

Source: Johnson, Scholes and Whittington (2005)

In third sector organisations such as charities, religious groups, private schools, foundations and so on, the sources of funding may well be diverse. It is often the case that the donors and not necessarily the beneficiaries of the service (particularly in the case of many charitable societies). This leads to a complex management operation.

As well as operating within a formal organisational structure of employees and volunteers, the management of third sector organisations has to contend with the variety of interests from stakeholders such as governors, donors, beneficiaries, regulators, the media and the general public.

As such decision making and direction setting can be a complex time-consuming task. It is also possible that some stakeholders with the 'loudest voice' (such as a major financial sponsor) will divert and change the course of activities planned by the organisation. Examples include the influence of a major financial sponsor in the leadership elections of a political party, or the influence of a financial sponsor on how the societies' premises are used (as in the case of football clubs selling their grounds).

To avoid undue influence or loss of direction, third sector organisations establish a **constitution**, which defines the objectives, rules and regulations

5

of the organisation. The constitution also defines many of the financial activities and the rules of membership.

As well as a constitution, third sector organisations establish clear and transparent **governance structures**, which define the roles, responsibilities, accountabilities and authorities of individual members of the organisation. The combination of the governance structures and constitution helps provide clarity, accountability and social responsibility.

Finally, one form of organisation that needs mention is the **company limited by guarantee**. This type of company is usually established by charities that wish to protect the extent of liability of their membership. The liability of members is limited to the extent to which they individually guarantee the debts of the company, but not through shareholding. Most companies established in this way set a maximum amount of guarantee at £1. The advantage of this arrangement is that the institution or charity receives all the advantages of being set up as a company, without the administrative burden and cost of issuing and managing shares.

Self-assessment question 5.1

Identify three different ways in which a third sector organisation can be funded.

Feedback on page 70

5.2 Regulation of the third sector

We have already considered extensively the role of regulators in the public and private sectors. In this section we will therefore concentrate specifically on the regulation of charities and the work of the Charity Commission.

Learning activity 5.2

Identify what is meant by the terms 'charity' and 'charitable work' and develop a working definition of both terms. Use the internet to help your studies – or, if you do not have access, ask your local library resources. You may find the Charity Commission website a helpful starting point The Charity Commission: http://www.charity-commission.gov.uk.

Feedback on page 71

You should have found this learning activity helpful in understanding more about the third sectors. We will now look more closely at the role of the Charity Commission by asking ourselves why charities need regulation.

To quote from the Charity Commission website:

'Charities are free and independent organisations whose work is essential to society. But we need a charity regulator which regulates on behalf of those who give to and benefit from charities, and on behalf of wider society:

- to ensure that charities meet the legal requirements for being a charity, and are equipped to operate properly and within the law;
- to check that charities are run for public benefit, and not for private advantage;
- to ensure that charities are independent and that their trustees take their decisions free of control or undue influence from outside; and
- to detect and remedy serious mismanagement or deliberate abuse by or within charities.

'Our work, our partnerships with other regulators, and charities' own work to manage their affairs, should result in public confidence in charities and the work they do.'

Charities clearly need regulating because of the huge degree of public interest, trust and benefit we place in them. As members of the public, we all trust charities to use our donations wisely, appropriately and definitely for the purposes they state.

You will note from the above that there is a wholly different emphasis in regulating charities than the activities of companies in the private sector. The Charity Commission has been established by law as the regulator and registrar of charities in England and Wales. This role is fulfilled by:

- securing compliance with charity law, and dealing with abuse and poor practice
- enabling charities to work better within an effective legal, accounting and governance framework, keeping pace with developments in society, the economy and the law; and
- promoting sound governance and accountability.

Here are some of the specific responsibilities of the Charity Commission:

- **Gathering and maintaining information about charities**: this is achieved by acting as the registrar of charities (much like the registrar of companies at Companies House) and making this information accessible (and accountable) to the public;
- **Offering advice and guidance to charities**: to run more effectively and efficiently. This is done through a call centre helpline and also by ad hoc visits on site;
- **Promoting legal compliance**: by publishing information, reports and books on legal guidance and also through direct advice;
- **Intervention and enforcement of the law**: by maintaining accurate records, monitoring complaints, auditing and investigating key issues.

The following table summarises the seven key operating principles which govern the activities of the Charity Commission when undertaking their responsibilities:

Table 5.2

Principles of the Charity Commission	What it means
1. Accountability	The commission is accountable to the Public Affairs Committee in government and is audited annually by the National Audit Office
2. Independence	The Commission acts in the public interest but is not beholden to any one organisation or particular motive. It is independent of government and other public sector bodies, although working alongside them.
3. Proportionality	The Commission acts with proportionality to the scale of the issues at hand. Significant issues or complaints will receive significant resources, input and effort.
4. Fairness	In exercising its legal power, the Commission acts with impartiality, fairness, independence and honesty.
5. Consistency	Actions and decisions are taken with accuracy and a consistent interpretation of the law.
6. Diversity and equality	The Commission is compliant with all laws about diversity and equality and acts proactively to promote diversity and equality in the workplace.
7. Transparency	The Commission openly sets out the criteria upon which they make decisions and they publish their own guidance on charities' legislation and regulations.

Self-assessment question 5.2

Describe the principal roles of the Charity Commission in England and Wales.

Feedback on page 71

5.3 Strategic objective and impact on purchasing

When studying the objectives of private and public sector organisations, we noted the impact that these had on the operational aspects of purchasing. In a similar manner, the overarching strategic objectives of organisations in the third sector have a direct impact on purchasing.

Learning activity 5.3

Identify and record the strategic objectives of the Chartered Institute of Purchasing and Supply (CIPS). You may find the website (www.cips.org) a helpful resource.

Feedback on page 71

The strategic objectives of third sector organisations are defined in their governing documents. These can be in the form of a constitution, a trust deed or (like in the private sector) the memorandum and articles of association.

In the case of charities, these documents need to state the following:

- what the charity is set up to do
- how the charity will do those things
- who will run it (the charity trustees)
- what happens if changes to the administrative provisions need to be made
- what happens if the charity wishes to cease operating.

Like public sector organisations, third sector organisations rarely have a singular motive. They exist to provide a service and/or public benefit.

Given the nature of charitable purposes, the operation of a charity's activities will also be governed by their strategic objectives. For example, a charity promoting environmental protection will ensure that all of its purchasing activities adhere to a well-defined environmental procurement policy. Purchasing is not the lead activity of the charity but it needs to support the overarching objectives in a complementary manner.

Here is a list of some of the ways in which purchasing activities will be influenced by the strategic objectives of the third sector organisation:

- Cost-effective and efficient use of the organisation's resources and spending budgets.
- Accountability to the members, trustees and, in turn, to the regulators.
- Need for probity in all financial transactions.
- Pursuit of ethical, environmental and corporate social responsibility policies in line with the organisation's objectives.
- Transparent accounting and transactions.
- Compliance to legislation and regulations.
- Acting in alignment with the values and culture of the organisation.

Like the nature of public sector spending, the objectives of third sector organisations are often contested, not least because of the number of parties and stakeholders maintaining an interest in the organisations' activities. This has its effect on the management of the purchasing activities, just like any other functional responsibility.

Self-assessment question 5.3

Describe the impact of a charity's objectives on its purchasing activities.

Feedback on page 71

5.4 Importance of corporate social responsibility

Corporate social responsibility (CSR) has become the broadly accepted concept to describe a collection of related disciplines, all of which combine to represent an organisation's overall ethos, its personality, philosophy and character in regard to its role in the world in the widest possible sense.

Among the increasing number of issues raised under the overall banner of CSR, the following are perhaps the most common factors present when considering purchasing and supply chains:

- environmental responsibility
- human rights
- equal opportunities
- diversity
- corporate governance
- sustainability
- impact on society
- ethics and ethical trading
- biodiversity
- community involvement.

The following table outlines the response of CIPS to the increasing awareness and profile given to these issues. It comprises eight principles advocated by the Institute for all purchasing and supply management professionals to observe in their activities.

Table 5.3

Environmental responsibility

We must consider the obligations we have to our surroundings, from local to global.

Human rights

We will honour and observe and not exploit fundamental human entitlements.

Equality and diversity

In our purchasing activities we will commit to improve our organisation's performance in relation to fairness to all.

Corporate governance

Our system of internal and external reporting and responsibility matches our espoused values.

Sustainability

We will proactively promote sustainable practices and products throughout the supply chain without jeopardising future security.

Impact on society

We will add value to the communities and societies upon which our organisation has an influence, either directly or indirectly.

Ethics and ethical trading

(continued on next page)

Table 5.3 (continued)

All out purchasing activities will be transacted with due regard to the needs and challenges of all involved parties.

Biodiversity

Through our purchasing activities we will proactively avoid reducing the number of interdependent species around us.

Let us now stop to consider some of these principles in action. In themselves, the principles represent high-level aspirations without specific direction or policy. However, when placed in a specific organisational context they begin to take sharp relief. This can be observed most clearly in the third sector.

Learning activity 5.4

Examine a local charity and its approach to CSR. Make a record of your observations.

Feedback on page 72

The impact on purchasing is considerable, not least of all because, in this sector, these commercial activities and practices can strike at the very heart of the organisation.

Imagine the impact of any of the following:

1 An environmental lobby group buying stationery and furniture from non-sustainable sources.
2 A human rights activist group buying cheap products from suppliers employing child labour in low-cost countries.
3 A political party found with accounting irregularities and accused of fraud.
4 A charity buying inappropriately expensive luxury items for its trustees.
5 A religious community forming a long-term supply relationship with a group espousing the complete antithesis of their beliefs and values.

These matters simply would not happen, or at least if they did there would be some form of public outcry. The credibility of the third sector organisation would be significantly jeopardised. Thus, from a purchasing perspective, CSR offers clear guiding advice on how funding and third-party expenditure needs to be managed.

Self-assessment question 5.4

Explain why it is important for a charity to adhere to an ethical purchasing policy.

Feedback on page 72

5

5

Revision question

There is no revision question for this session.

Summary

This final study session on the business sectors looked at the important contribution from the third sector. Although this sector is often overlooked, it does play an important role in business society. We have examined the key features of this sector, how charities are regulated, some of the multiple objectives that exist, and the impact this has on purchasing in this sector. We also considered the increasingly significant aspect of corporate and social responsibility and its role in the third sector.

We build on the knowledge and understanding you have gained in these first five study sessions by going on in the next study session to consider some of the key financing issues and decisions that have an impact on purchasing activities.

Suggested further reading

Further reading about ethical business practices and CSR in the purchasing context is available on the CIPS website: http://www.cips.org.

Further information about the work and regulation of charities is available on the Charity Commission website: The Charity Commission: http://www.charity-commission.gov.uk.

Feedback on learning activities and self-assessment questions

Feedback on learning activity 5.1

Examples of third sector organisations could include large-scale international charities such as Oxfam or the Red Cross, which rely on public donations and other fundraising activities to provide global relief and development services. Other examples could include local charities near to where you live or work.

Third sector organisations can also include social clubs, special interest societies, religious societies and political parties. Activities will depend on what they have been set up to do. Funding will either come from membership fees, donations, fundraising or government grants.

Feedback on self-assessment question 5.1

Third sector organisations can be funded in any or all of the following ways:

- donations from the public
- grants from charitable foundations and/or funding councils
- government grants and subsidies
- investment from private sources

- fundraising and sponsorship activities
- sales activities.

Feedback on learning activity 5.2

An organisational body is a charity if it is set up as such by the law and has been exclusively established for charitable purposes. Many people have wrongly assumed 'charitable purposes' refers to voluntary work; however, this is not the case.

There are four main types of charitable work:

1   The relief of financial hardship.
2   The advancement of education.
3   The advancement of religion.
4   Other purposes for the benefit of the community.

In summary, a charity has to be based on one of the above activities exclusively: its *raison d'être* is for public benefit.

Feedback on self-assessment question 5.2

The principal roles of the Charity Commission in England and Wales are as follows:

- securing compliance with charity law, and dealing with abuse and poor practice
- enabling charities to work better within an effective legal, accounting and governance framework, keeping pace with developments in society, the economy and the law; and
- promoting sound governance and accountability.

Feedback on learning activity 5.3

The Royal Charter defines the objectives of CIPS as:

- To promote and develop for the public benefit the art and science of purchasing and supply and to encourage the promotion and development of improved methods of purchasing and supply in all organisations.
- To promote and maintain for the benefit of the public high standards of professional skill, ability and integrity among all those engaged in purchasing and supply.
- To educate persons engaged in the practice of purchasing and supply and by means of examination and other methods of assessment to test the skill and knowledge of persons desiring to enter the Institute.

Feedback on self-assessment question 5.3

Purchasing within a charity is impacted by its regulation and legislation, the specific strategic objectives and the interests of its multiple stakeholders.

The strategic objectives of a charity will impact purchasing activities in the following ways:

- Cost effective and efficient use of the organisation's resources and spending budgets.
- Accountability to the members, trustees and, in turn, to the regulators.
- Need for probity in all financial transactions.
- Pursuit of ethical, environmental and corporate social responsibility policies in line with the organisation's objectives.
- Transparent accounting and transactions.
- Compliance to legislation and regulations.
- Acting in alignment with the values and culture of the organisation.

Feedback on learning activity 5.4

You are encouraged to find out what the strategic objectives of the charity are and then see how they align with the principles of CSR. You should be able to note a distinct correlation and alignment between the charity's CSR activities and its objectives.

Feedback on self-assessment question 5.4

Charities are established to serve a public benefit. They rely significantly on the donations and subscriptions of the public and they have a high degree of trust invested in them to fulfil their stated objectives.

Organisations are increasingly recognising the need to measure, track and report on their social and ethical performance. A charity that is unable to do this risks loss of public confidence and trust; furthermore, it risks investigation and potential intervention from its regulator.

Ethical trading policies are important for all charities to adhere to, not least of all, because of their publicly stated and marketed strategic objectives.

Funding perspectives for purchasing

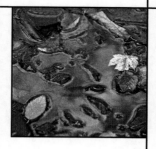

Introduction

Having studied different types of organisation, business sector and the impact these contexts have on purchasing, in this study session we turn our attention to the basic aspects of funding. This has an important bearing on purchasing in terms of determining the cost of goods and services and how they will be paid for. We will consider a simple budgeting cycle for revenue expenditure within organisations, as well as how capital expenditure is funded. You will study the basics of funding public sector infrastructure projects and consider the impact of economic factors such as price inflation.

6

Session learning objectives

After completing this session you should be able to:

6.1 Describe a simple budgeting process for regular goods and services.
6.2 Describe how investment expenditure is requested and appraised in organisations.
6.3 Compare and contrast public and private funding initiatives.
6.4 Analyse the impact of economic factors such as inflation, interest and monetary exchange rates.

Unit content coverage

This study session covers the following topics from the official CIPS unit content document:

Statements of practice

- Recognise the transferability of the fundamental principles of purchase and supply management.
- Appraise the need for different approaches to purchasing in differing organisations and contexts.

Learning objective

2.5 Analyse and explain purchasing and financing capital expenditure items.
- Financing considerations, including benefit/cost analysis (BCA), investment, return of investment (ROI), break-even, post-project appraisal (PPA) and whole-life costing
- Public and private funding initiatives including private finance initiative (PFI), public private partnership (PPP), build-own-operate-transfer (BOOT)
- A simple budgeting cycle

- Economic factors of financing including inflation and interest rates

Prior knowledge

Study sessions 1 – 5 should be covered before this session, because they provide a good foundation to the organisational context and cover several basic areas about how different sectors are funded.

Resources

Internet access is preferable, but not essential. You may also wish to access a library for further reading and additional studies, but this is neither compulsory nor essential.

Timing

You should set aside about 4½ hours to read and complete this session, including learning activities, self-assessment questions, the suggested further reading (if any) and the revision question.

6.1 The budgeting process

This section considers a typical organisation's budgeting cycle and the impact this has on purchasing activities.

Learning activity 6.1

Describe the budget cycle in your own workplace.

Feedback on page 81

It is important for organisations to budget for their expenditure for several reasons. Budgets help organisations plan what resources they need and also how they will pay for them. Often budgets are seen as restrictive, but these controls provide essential governance for organisations to manage their limited resources appropriately. They help set limits on expenditure and instil a sense of discipline and control on spending.

Budgets are usually set on an annual basis and are aligned with the organisation's financial year. A typical annual budgeting process will contain the following steps:

- budgetary requests
- organisational review
- budget allocation
- expenditure, management and monitoring
- interim review and adjustments
- end-of-year reconciliation and start of next year's budget.

In practice the budget cycle is usually a lot more complex, but for our purposes the above steps comprise the key features for setting and reviewing a budget.

Budgetary requests are typically made anywhere between three and six months before the start of the financial year. The budget request needs to contain a reasonable expectation and forecast of all foreseeable expenditure in the year ahead, be it internal (on staff costs and internal charges) or external (on third parties such as rates, fees and supplies). Usually managers are also asked to provide a brief justification as to why they require the expenditure.

An organisational review of all the budget submissions follows. This is led by the finance department (Finance) and considers how much the organisation can afford. When cutbacks are required, there is often a process of exchange where initial requests are rejected and asked to be trimmed down.

Once the budgets are agreed and set by Finance, the manager is informed of the allocation. When the financial year begins, the manager is authorised to spend within his/her budget and is free to use that allocation however they see fit, while working within the guidelines of the organisation. The budget is monitored on a regular basis (weekly or monthly, depending on the needs) to ensure that there is sufficient available for expenditure throughout the remainder of the financial year.

Many organisations undertake an interim financial review of expenditure within budgets. The purpose is to check the current financial position, the forecasts of expenditure for the remainder of the year and to make any necessary adjustments. When an organisation is facing specific cost pressures, the budgets are adjusted part-way through the year. Invariably the adjustments result in budget reductions and so any cost reduction initiatives within the organisation are a welcome reprieve.

Self-assessment question 6.1

How can purchasing contribute to setting the internal budget allocations for third-party expenditure of an organisation?

Feedback on page 82

6.2 Investment expenditure

Investment expenditure is often referred to as 'capital expenditure' because it is expenditure that adds to the capital assets of the organisation. It can include:

- new premises
- plant and machinery
- IT equipment
- infrastructure
- commercial vehicles.

We will look more closely at capital expenditure in study session 17. Budgeting for this type of expenditure is different to the annual budgeting round: it is not financed by the day-to-day cash flow of revenue into the organisation. Instead, it requires investment capital, which might not yield a payback for several years.

To request investment expenditure, an organisation requires a **business case** (sometimes called a 'case for investment') to demonstrate that there is sufficient **return on investment** (ROI).

Learning activity 6.2

List the key components of a business case for financial investment. If you have difficulties thinking of what needs to be included, find out what is included in business cases in your own organisation.

Feedback on page 82

Before a business is developed, many projects require a feasibility study. The purpose of the feasibility study is to check that the project has sufficient financial viability: in other words that the benefits of the project outweigh the costs.

For example, in the UK the Environment Agency undertakes feasibility studies before investing public funding to build new flood defences. The feasibility study considers the lifetime of a potential flood defence project (say, 25 years) and analyses how much the flood defence would cost as well as what the potential cost of flood damage to the local community would be. The potential cost of the flood damage would be saved if the flood defence is built: it constitutes a **tangible benefit** to the community.

The Environment Agency is therefore able to compare the costs: if the cost of building the defences is less than the tangible benefits of avoiding flood damage, then there is a case for investment. This is called a **benefit–cost analysis (BCA)** and leads to a calculation called the benefit/cost ratio: refer to the table below for further information.

Of course, there are other benefits to the community than avoiding the financial losses resulting from flood damage. These **intangible benefits** might include increased public confidence, reduced fear of flooding, as well as an increased attractiveness of the local area. These benefits are intangible because, although they exist, they cannot be measured, quantified or costed into the benefit–cost analysis.

Table 6.1

Benefit/cost ratio	What it means
Less than 1	The cost of investment outweighs the tangible benefits from the project. There is no immediate financial justification for the investment. Most projects are unlikely to proceed.

(continued on next page)

Table 6.1 (continued)

Benefit/cost ratio	What it means
Exactly 1	The cost of investment is the same as the tangible benefits from the project. There is no real financial justification for the investment, although there may be additional contributory factors from intangible benefits. Some, but certainly not all, projects may proceed.
More than 1	The benefits of the project outweigh the costs of investment and there is financial justification for undertaking the project. Most projects will proceed, providing the investment offers sufficient ROI. Some private sector enterprises require the benefit/cost ratio to exceed 3 before the investment is justified.

A benefit–cost analysis is just part of a feasibility study. Other factors may include initial consultations (for public schemes), investigative testing, a check for buildability and planning consent (for construction schemes), and/or possibly even a check that the market can supply the new products or services.

Once the feasibility study has been concluded and agreement has been made to go ahead with the project, a formal business case is developed. The business case is a request and a financial justification for the capital investment.

Typically business cases will include:

- An outline of the project, its rationale and the need it will fulfil.
- A detailed breakdown of the costs of the project in terms of design, construction, operation, maintenance and ultimate disposal.
- A detailed review of the tangible benefits of the project and its return on investment.
- Details of any other intangible benefits.
- An investment schedule detailing when the capital investment is required and over what time period.
- A calculation to show how and when the money will be paid back, including an outline of when the project will break even (or in other words have paid for itself).
- Details of all financing calculations, particularly where future money has needed to be discounted to present values.
- A description of any assumptions that have had to be made in forming the business case.
- An overview of any risks, dependencies and issues, including contingency plans where the risks are significant or potentially disruptive.
- A high-level summary of the next steps and required actions to initiate the project.

Business cases can take weeks or months to prepare because of the detailed analysis and calculations that are required. This is particularly important if large sums of investment capital are being requested.

The business case is reviewed by senior management and finance managers within the organisation. Where funding is external, the business case is sent to the funding body and representations are made on behalf of the beneficiaries to present their case in the best possible light.

6

6

6.3 Private and public funding initiatives

We have already looked at sources of finance for the public and private sectors in the study session 1. This section takes a closer look at the public–private partnership that exists in the UK as an important source of funding for major initiatives.

The government can work in partnership with private sector enterprises to provide services or build facilities for the public. This is done using public–private partnerships, commonly known as PPPs. Since 1997 several PPP schemes have been used as part of the government's modernisation programme. These include building new hospitals, schools, prisons and defence contracts. In the year 2000, the Treasury set up the government agency Partnerships UK to enable the public sector to use PPPs to achieve their objectives. To ensure that the PPP will provide value-for-money service, their costs are compared using a public sector comparator (PSC), which estimates what the cost of the service would be, if it were run by the public sector.

Definition of PPP

PPPs are commercial arrangements between the public sector and the private sector to provide public infrastructure, community facilities or related services with a share of both risk and rewards.

There are several advantages of public–private partnerships. The expertise of the private partner can be used to develop the most advanced facility or service possible, and to achieve best value. This could be done by using innovative design techniques and/or using the latest technology.

By incorporating design and build into the same contract, both costs and development time can be reduced. There may also be an opportunity to reduce the operation and maintenance costs. The private sector has greater experience of effectively managing large projects and completing them within budget.

The use of integrated supply chains can also lead to substantial savings in cost. The introduction of new technology could also improve the level and quality of service. Revenues may also increase as the fees charged to the public may reflect the true cost of the service, rather than a subsidised one. The risks are also not borne totally by the public sector as they can be shared with the private partner.

There are, however, risks associated with PPP schemes. There is often a fear that the government could lose a degree of control over the project or service and that there will be less accountability to the public or even that the quality of the service may suffer. This is particularly so about the issue of safety. These issues, of course, should be addressed in the contract specification, particularly if there is a risk of cutting corners to save money. There may also be the possibility of increased costs to the public if the market price is charged for the service.

There are several different PPP schemes:

- **Operation & maintenance**: the private partner is contracted to operate and maintain the service to the public. Examples include wastewater treatment works, car parks, and recreational parks. The contract is awarded for a term period (say three, five or seven years) and the required service and maintenance standards are specified.
- **Design–build joint ventures**: the contract is formed with one or more lead contractors to design and build new works. The lead contractor co-opts other specialists to undertake key aspects of the work. An example might be a large public infrastructure project (such as a dam, a highway or a sports arena) which needs a design consultant, a constructor, a mechanical/electrical contractor and specialist engineers. The responsibility for the full design, development and completion of the works is contracted out. The contractors form a joint venture to deliver the scheme.
- **Turnkey operation**: similar to the above, where a private partner is contracted to design, construct, operate and maintain the infrastructure. Examples include major transportation links and/or power generation schemes. The contract requires the development of the facility by a certain timescale followed by a period of operation (say, five years) on behalf of the public service, which retains ownership and ultimate responsibility for the service. The advantage is the contractor irons out any snagging items with the works in the first few years of operation and is able to hand over a fully functional operation in a controlled manner.
- **Build–own–operate–transfer (BOOT)**: similar to turnkey projects but where the contractor is required to retain ownership and full accountability for the asset during its period of operation. The advantage for the contractor is that they are able to keep the asset on

their accounting balance sheets and therefore take specific financing advantages during the life of the contract.

The final major financing tool for public sector investment projects is the **private finance initiative (PFI)**. It is a government initiative to provide modern facilities on a basis similar to the BOOT schemes described above. However, in this instance, the private contractor is required to design, build, finance and operate the new facility, commonly referred to as a DBFO contract. In this instance the contractor owns the asset and has financed for it themselves. The public sector is charged for the service on a pay-as-you-go charging facility, which includes several complex financing equations to calculate the price.

The PFI has been widely used in the UK's National Health Service (NHS) for the provision of new medical facilities and hospitals. The NHS provides the medical staff and pays for the service on a patient-bed basis. The main advantage for the public sector of this type of arrangement is that it has greater certainty that the project will be available on time and within budget, as well as knowing in advance exactly how much the service will cost. For the contractor, they know they have a regular revenue stream from a client that can afford to pay.

Self-assessment question 6.3

Describe three different ways in which a new hospital construction project might be funded.

Feedback on page 82

6.4 Economic factors

Over time, prices and costs vary because of numerous economic factors in the market. Although there is not sufficient remit to review the cause and effect of these variations, there is a significant impact on the purchase of goods and services.

Learning activity 6.4

Using internet or local library resources, identify what the Retail Prices Index (RPI) measures and what it assesses to produce its index. You will find the Office for National Statistics is a useful resource http://www.statistics.gov.uk.

Feedback on page 83

Here is a list of factors that will cause prices of goods and services to fluctuate.

Table 6.2

Reasons for price increases	Reasons for price decreases
• Demand exceeds supply • Scarcity of raw materials • Trade restrictions from the supplier • Monopolistic supply • Cartel in the supply market • Last minute demands from the buyer • Number of suppliers reduces • Inflationary pressure in the supply chain	• Market is saturated with supply • New supply markets opened up • Supplier loses major customer contract • Import trading barriers lifted • Goods become surplus to requirement • Goods about to be superseded by new or alternative product • Alternative source of supply are found • Sales representative is falling short of their personal sales quota

6

Self-assessment question 6.4

Identify the risks for a buyer agreeing to fix prices in line with national pricing levels over time.

Feedback on page 83

Revision question

Now try the revision question for this session on page 281.

Summary

This study session has reviewed various funding aspects that have an impact on purchasing activities, including budgets, cases for investment, public schemes and inflationary factors. They are important considerations for anyone involved in purchasing management: fully understanding the flow of money from the buyer into the supply chain is a key aspect of the job.

In the next study session we will begin to focus more closely on the purchasing function by considering key organisational issues that face the function. This is a critical element of your CIPS studies, which will help not just for the examinations, but also throughout your professional purchasing career.

Suggested further reading

You could read the relevant sections of Bailey et al (2005).

Feedback on learning activities and self-assessment questions

Feedback on learning activity 6.1

It will help to record the key events in the budgeting cycle, who gets involved and the timings of these events in a typical calendar year. Note how this links to the financial year of your organisation. You should also note how the budget is split into several different cost items. These will include internal operational expenses (such as staff and cross-charging) and external expenditure from third parties. The external spend is split between regular 'revenue' items which have a regular budgetary allowance, and 'capital' items which may require investment and will add value to the organisation's asset base.

Feedback on self-assessment question 6.1

Purchasing can make a significant contribution by helping departments set budget allocations initially (particularly where purchasing has information about specific market costs). As the year progresses any cost savings from purchasing activities can help reduce the budget spend and therefore support mid-year budget revisions.

Similarly, budgetary information can be very useful for purchasing in that it sets out a plan of the organisation's forecast third-party expenditure. A purchasing function can use this information to manage spending effectively and negotiate the best deals.

Feedback on learning activity 6.2

Put simply, a business case needs to state what the investment is required for, how much money it will cost and what the benefits of the investment are going to be. It is a demonstration to the investor that the project is viable and 'compelling' in terms of financial justification.

Feedback on self-assessment question 6.2

A benefit refers to a gain (or avoided loss) from a project or investment. It can be financial or non-financial, but it usually represents the purpose for the investment. Tangible benefits can be measured and quantified in financial terms: they have a monetary value attached to them which can be calculated. Examples of tangible benefits include increased sales revenue, mitigated costs and/or additional savings. Intangible benefits, however, are difficult to measure and cannot be quantified in financial terms. Although they will have a monetary value attached to them, it is often impossible to calculate. Examples of intangible benefits include increased consumer confidence, increased customer loyalty, greater public awareness and brand promotion.

Feedback on learning activity 6.3

The website has some useful information and background to public–private partnerships which could help with your further studies. The projects database helps locate all the current PPP initiatives in England and Wales.

Feedback on self-assessment question 6.3

Constructing a new hospital facility is a major project that requires the input of many complex and specialist services. The hospital owners have the following methods open to them:

- private finance initiative
- public private partnership
- traditional capital expenditure.

Feedback on learning activity 6.4

The RPI is one of the UK's measures of inflation (or 'cost of living'). It measures the price increase over time of consumer products by comparing a 'basket of items' month on month. At any one time 650 of the top consumer items are compared and their prices indexed back to the price in the UK during January 1987.

The January 1987 prices were indexed as a measure of 100. Where the RPI for a product is now, say, 240 it means that price is now a multiplier of 2.4 times the price in January 1987.

Feedback on self-assessment question 6.4

Some suppliers will try to sell in this pricing strategy in an attempt to index their price discounts to national indices. Their argument is that although markets change and prices fluctuate in response to the economy, the buyer at least can maintain a discount off these price levels.

In reality prices do not all change in harmony with the national averages, there is constant variation. Leaving a deal open to price fluctuations will invariably open up a risk to price increases beyond the control of the buyer. This may place pressure on budgets and/or profitability of certain items.

There are many ways of measuring price fluctuations in a market and, unless the method of measurement has been pre-agreed, this could cause an area of significant tension between the supplier and buyer in the future.

Price certainty allows the organisation to budget for its goods and services and therefore allows a greater degree of control and security for the buying organisation.

6

6

Study session 7

The purchasing organisation

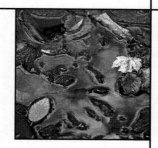

Introduction

This study session focuses on the organisation of the purchasing function. In it you will study the different forms of organisational structure, as well as the various generic roles and responsibilities that exist in a typical purchasing function. We will also consider the role of purchasing as an internal service provider and ask whether this service can be outsourced.

7

Session learning objectives

After completing this session you should be able to:

7.1 Compare and contrast a range of functional models for purchasing.
7.2 Describe the typical roles and responsibilities within a purchasing function.
7.3 Appraise the relative merits of the 'part-time' purchaser.
7.4 Evaluate the merits of centralised vs. decentralised purchasing structures.
7.5 Identify the purchasing function's key customers and describe the role of purchasing as an internal service provider.
7.6 Discuss the arguments for and against outsourcing purchasing activities.

Unit content coverage

This study session covers the following topics from the official CIPS unit content document:

Statements of practice

- Recognise the transferability of the fundamental principles of purchase and supply management.
- Appraise the need for different approaches to purchasing in differing organisations and contexts.
- Compare the diverse legal and regulatory environments in which the procurement activity takes place.

Learning objective

1.5 Evaluate the context of the purchasing function and different purchasing situations.
- Purchasing as a discrete organisational function within the supply chain
- Relationship between the purchaser and a supply market
- The various functional models for purchasing: including centralised, decentralised, centre-led action network (CLAN), lead buyer/business partnering and matrix structure

- Typical division of roles and responsibilities within purchasing
- The part-time purchaser
- Customers of the purchasing function
- Merits of internal versus external outsourcing of supply
- Role of a strategic sourcing unit (SSU) and how it can be measured for effectiveness
- Merits of consortium buying with other independent organisations

Prior knowledge

Study sessions 1 – 6 should be covered before this session, because they provide a solid foundation to the organisational context for purchasing.

Resources

Internet access is preferable, but not essential. You may also wish to access a library for further reading and additional studies, but this is neither compulsory nor essential. In this study session you may find it especially helpful to refer to the purchasing structure and organisation chapter of our recommended text.

Timing

You should set aside about 6 hours to read and complete this session, including learning activities, self-assessment questions, the suggested further reading (if any) and the revision question.

7.1   Organisational models for the purchasing function

There are many different types of organisational design for the purchasing function. As the quote at the start of this study session stated, there is not any singular ideal structure for the profession. In this section we will therefore consider the key features and merits of the following organisational approaches. These apply equally to the purchasing function or any other function within the organisation:

- functional
- divisional
- matrix
- lead buyer
- business partners.

Learning activity 7.1

Draw an organisational structure for purchasing in your own organisation. Make sure you include both formal and informal roles and the reporting

(continued on next page)

Learning activity 7.1 *(continued)*

lines between them. Compare the structure of your own organisation with the descriptions that follow to help you identify what type of approach to purchasing your organisation adopts.

Feedback on page 98

Functional Structures

The functional structure is organised around key tasks and functional activities performed by the organisation. It tends to be a centralised structure with each department reporting into the board of directors. Although this gives a very clear chain of command and encourages specialism in functional expertise, it can tend to fragment the organisation to concentrate only their own tasks and not necessarily work together for the best interests of the company. The diagram below summarises the functional structure:

Figure 7.1

A functional structure is typically found in organisations with limited numbers of products or services, trading in a limited number of countries.

Divisional structures

Divisional organisations are organised around different product sets and/or territories. Each division has functional representation, thus creating a decentralised structure spread across different business units and geographical areas. This helps empower individual business units/divisions with their own responsibilities and accountabilities, and it helps bring the functions closer to the customer. However, divisional structures can lead to independent operating principles and variations in the service offered. The following diagram summarises the divisional structure:

Figure 7.2

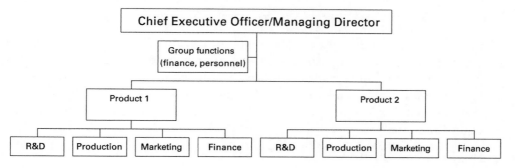

Divisional structures are typically found in organisations offering a multiple number of products/services or trading in several geographical regions.

Matrix structures

The matrix structure tried to gain the best of both worlds by organising itself functionally and divisionally. The divisions tend to be organised around products and/or customer segments, whereas the functional reporting gives a clear accountability into the board of directors. Although it allows large functional structures to get closer to the customer and the product delivery, it can create a conflicting set of reporting lines for staff. What the matrix structure gains in flexibility and proximity to other functions, it can often trade for complexity and increased reporting responsibilities. The following diagram illustrates an example of the matrix structure:

Figure 7.3:

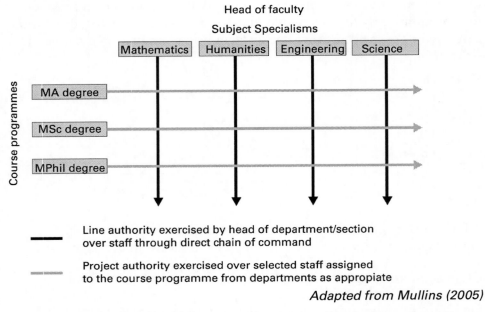

Adapted from Mullins (2005)

Matrix structures will be typically found in large and complex organisations that are trading multiple products/services in geographical areas or regions.

Lead buyers

The 'lead buyer' concept refers to the placement of additional purchasing responsibilities on colleagues within another function. Typically it applies where purchasing activities need to be undertaken within a manufacturing or production department by a non-purchasing member of staff. We will discuss the merits of 'part-time' purchasing later in this study session.

The lead buyer concept has advantages in taking the purchasing activities directly into the fulfilment environment but obvious disadvantages in asking a non-purchasing professional to undertake the responsibilities. The purchasing function extends their team 'membership' to the lead buyer to help the individual adjust to the dual responsibilities. The concept has been very successful in helping purchasing breakdown departmental barriers with other functions.

Business partnering

Business partnering is a more contemporary theme than the lead buyer, – but based on similar objectives – that being to work closely with other

7

functional areas. The business partners are members of the purchasing function placed into the teams of other functions to advise on purchasing matters. This typically happens where other functions have a particularly large or complex third-party spend (for example in other business units or divisions). The business partner acts as a representative of purchasing. They support the other function by reviewing key commercial matters and advising when the purchasing function needs to be brought in to help.

Self-assessment question 7.1

Identify the potential advantages and disadvantages of a purchasing function operating in a matrix structure.

Feedback on page 98

7.2 Purchasing roles and responsibilities

In this section you will turn your attention to the purchasing function itself and study several different roles that exist within it. There are many different types of role and responsibility covered by a typical purchasing department, so we are going to consider only the following generic roles here:

- head of purchasing
- purchasing manager
- senior purchasing manager
- role of a purchasing leadership team
- supplier manager
- contracts manager
- purchasing analyst
- expediter.

Of course, if we were considering small organisations, there might only be a few of the above purchasing roles in existence, or even just one role. In effect the responsibilities are shared across the function.

Learning activity 7.2

Make a list of the purchasing roles and responsibilities within your own workplace and record your observations in the following template:

Table 7.1

Purchasing roles	Responsibilities undertaken by the role

Feedback on page 99

89

Head of purchasing

The head of purchasing (HoP) role has overall responsibility and accountability for all activities in the purchasing function. Arguably this should include all purchasing activities anywhere in the organisation, whether within or outside of the purchasing function. It is also a contentious point as to whether the HoP has responsibility for the management of all third-party expenditure, but this will depend on how the organisation is set up, as few organisations are able to give this full responsibility.

The HoP is there to provide the overall direction, policies and strategy for the procurement function. A lot of the role is about representing the function's interests to other senior managers and promoting the role and benefits of purchasing across the organisation. Stakeholder management, functional leadership and communication are critical skills on top of a thorough understanding of purchasing management.

Depending on an organisation's preference for job titles, the HoP role can be fulfilled by the procurement director, chief purchasing officer and/or the vice president for purchasing.

Purchasing manager

The role of the purchasing manager is to undertake the day-to-day operational purchasing activities. This may be confined to one particular category of expenditure (such as IT software or human resources (HR)) depending on the size and complexity of the organisation, or it may be that the purchasing manager has to take on responsibility for all categories. It has been argued that a good purchasing manager should be able to turn their hand to any category of expenditure because of the transferability of skills. Although this is the case on most occasions, there are some instances where a particular technical skill, behavioural quality or market knowledge are required.

The purchasing manager is responsible for reviewing third-party spend and the market, selecting and appraising suppliers, running competitive enquiries and negotiating with potential suppliers. In general the purchasing manager's responsibility goes as far as the preparing and awarding the contract, at which point the day-to-day responsibilities for managing the contractual relationship are passed on to others.

Depending on an organisation's preference for job titles, the purchasing manager may also be called a sourcing manager, category manager or commodity manager.

Senior purchasing manager

The senior purchasing manager's role is broadly similar to that of the purchasing manager, with the distinction of size and scope of responsibilities. This may also be reflected in the senior purchasing manager assuming team leadership for several purchasing managers. The senior purchasing manager may be responsible for a group of expenditure categories (such as in IT, where there might be individual purchasing managers for software, hardware and telecommunications, or professional services where individual purchasing managers are responsible for HR, legal services and consulting).

Purchasing leadership team

Larger purchasing functions will operate a purchasing leadership team (PLT) which meets on a regular basis to discuss the performance and direction of the purchasing function. The PLT usually comprises the senior management of the purchasing function and is chaired by the HoP. The HoP can use the PLT as an effective means of communicating and consulting on strategic issues affecting the function.

Supplier manager

Supplier managers differ from purchasing managers in that the focus of their role is generally post-contractual award. The role of supplier manager is to ensure that the supplier is managed effectively across the business and that the supplier meets all the requirements that have been stipulated of them. In many cases a supplier will have more than one contract with an organisation – often for a range of products or services. The supplier manager takes on responsibility for the holistic management of the relationship with that supplier using balanced scorecards to take a broader perspective of the supplier's performance than individual contractual measures. This is particularly relevant and effective where supplier development activities or new product innovation is required.

Sometimes supplier managers are called Supplier Relationship Managers to emphasise the focus of the role.

Contracts manager

A contracts manager has a very similar role to the supplier manager but focuses on the contract per se as opposed to the relationship with the supplier. These roles are designed for particularly large or complex supply contracts, where there is a specific need to manage the contract. The contracts manager is responsible for monitoring performance to contract, administering payment as per the contract schedules and issuing specific contractual notices and/or contract change notices. The contracts manager is less concerned about the broader relationship issues with the supplier: rather they focus on ensuring that everything is done to the letter of the contract.

Purchasing analyst

Purchasing analysts support the work of the purchasing function by providing an essential data gathering, research, information processing and data analysis role. This could include market research, financial analysis, cost analysis and/or compliance reporting. These are essential responsibilities of any purchasing function to fulfil. When working alongside a purchasing manager, the purchasing analyst can provide essential information and data that allows the purchasing manager to fulfil his/her responsibilities.

7

Expediter

The role of an expediter is one of the hardest roles to fulfil successfully. In effect the role is there to chase up orders and ensure on-time delivery. This can be particularly important where just-in-time deliveries are required or where supplies are required to meet an important production deadline. If the orders cannot be delivered on time, the subsequent knock-on effects are significant. The expediter is required to chase orders, track deliveries and monitor performance of key suppliers.

Self-assessment question 7.2

Outline the key differences between a purchasing manager and a supplier relationship manager and highlight any potential conflicts in their responsibilities.

Feedback on page 99

7.3 Part-time purchasing responsibilities

The 'part-time' purchaser is a common feature of many organisations. It is rare to find an organisation that gives total responsibility for managing third-party expenditure to the purchasing function. It follows that spend management occurring beyond the remit of the purchasing function is therefore likely to be undertaken by members of staff who are doing so in addition to their own responsibilities. Accordingly, there are both advantages and disadvantages of these types of arrangement.

Learning activity 7.3

Make a list of the functional areas in your own workplace where 'part-time' purchasing activities take place. Do you think this is an appropriate way of managing the third-party spend?

Feedback on page 99

Part-time purchasing is inevitable in most, if not all, organisations. It is therefore imperative that the full advantages and disadvantages of such a set-up are understood and appropriate actions put in place to mitigate any associated risks.

Ideally there would not be any such thing as 'part-time' purchasing. The purchasing function would be fully equipped to work alongside all other functional areas and therefore bring its commercial expertise to bear with their technical skill and market knowledge.

In practice, part-time purchasing occurs for one of three reasons:

- historical reasons before the establishment of a fully professional purchasing function
- technical reasons because the other function(s) believe they are the only ones qualified or knowledgeable to manage the spend
- deliberate avoidance of the purchasing function because they do not want purchasing to be involved or to lose control of the spend.

The term 'maverick spend' is the commonly used term to describe situations in this last category: that is to say where the spend is being deliberately kept out of the management reach of purchasing.

The disadvantages associated with 'part-time' purchasing obviously regard the potential lack of professional spend management. There are concerns about inconsistency with policy, lack of full effectiveness and potential exposure to commercial risks. Furthermore where the organisation has specific policies about purchasing ethics, contact with suppliers and/or tendering rules and procedures, there is a risk that these may not be adhered to.

Given the nature of the 'part-time' term, there is also a risk that the full amount of time cannot be given to the purchasing role, especially where members of staff have other full-time responsibilities to fulfil.

That is, however, not to disregard part-time purchasing or to say it is inappropriate. Part-time purchasing can demonstrate an effective means of spreading purchasing responsibilities throughout the organisation. It can also use the technical skills and knowledge base of other functions where purchasing does not have that capability.

The risks of part-time purchasing are best mitigated by ensuring that the part-time purchasing staff are included wherever practically possible in the purchasing function communications, training and development. It is also useful to ensure these individuals are given support, training and guidance on policy and procedure. Many of these skills and capabilities are available from CIPS if the organisation is unable to offer them itself.

Self-assessment question 7.3

Evaluate the risks associated with 'part-time' purchasing.

Feedback on page 99

7.4 To centralise or decentralise?

The terms 'centralisation' and 'decentralisation' refer to the degree to which responsibility and authority is delegated and the function is correspondingly structured within an organisation.

Where responsibility, authority and accountability for decision making remains tightly controlled and situated in one focal point of the organisation, the function is said to be centralised. Conversely where the decision-making responsibilities, accountability and authority are diversely spread across different parts of the organisation, the function is said to be decentralised.

In practice, many functional structures are centralised and many divisional structures are decentralised, although there are several counter-examples to this generalisation.

Learning activity 7.4

Use the organisational chart you developed for purchasing in your own workplace from Learning Activity 7.1 and identify the degree to which purchasing is centralised or decentralised. Can you identify the reasons for this and the benefits of being organised this way?

Feedback on page 100

The following table outlines the arguments in favour of centralisation and decentralisation.

Table 7.2

Arguments in favour of centralisation	Arguments in favour of decentralisation
• Decisions are easier to communicate and coordinate because they are made in one place	• Responsibility is devolved to localised areas therefore increasing buy-in, motivation, job satisfaction and an entrepreneurial spirit
• Consistency is easy to develop because of the single location	• Decisions can be made with better knowledge of the local environment, culture and customer-needs
• Control on resource allocation is easier	• Customer service and response is easier to manage
• Economies of scale exist (because of one location) and therefore lower administrative overheads and duplication	• Skills development and cross-fertilisation is more likely as staff need to be adaptive to their environment and take on a range of roles
• More opportunity to use specialist skills	• Local decisions can be made quicker without reference to central office
• Quality and speed of decision making is improved	• Greater customer and product knowledge because of day-to-day involvement in operational surroundings
• Policies and procedures are easy to standardise, implement and be adhered to	• Purchasing is more 'visible' and more likely to be involved in local matters

The arguments for and against are equally compelling and therefore can only be truly evaluated in the context of the specific organisational environment.

Further reading on this subject is available in the chapter on purchasing structure and design in Bailey et al (2005).

Self-assessment question 7.4

Which is better for an organisation: centralised purchasing or decentralised purchasing? Give reasons to support your response.

Feedback on page 100

7.5 Customers of purchasing

To conduct spend management programmes and supplier negotiations effectively, the purchasing function is required to assume the role of the client within the supply chain. Purchasing represents the customer to suppliers and quickly assumes the role and behavioural qualities as such.

However, it is worth recognising that purchasing is rarely the end-point consumer in the supply chain: it is usually undertaking the procurement on behalf of another party within the organisation.

This factor has a significant bearing on the purchasing function and the way in which it conducts its day-to-day operational activities.

Learning activity 7.5

List the customers of the purchasing function within your own workplace and identify their specific requirements or demands.

Feedback on page 100

If purchasing acts as an internal service provider for all other functions in terms of managing third-party expenditure, then there are several key facts we need to establish:

- What is the service offered by purchasing?
- How is it measured and monitored?
- Who is best placed to manage the service?

Purchasing service

Clearly the exact scope of service offered by purchasing will vary from one organisation to another. This will depend on the accountability and authority given to the purchasing function. However, in general terms the service will comprise:

- cost and risk management
- provision of goods and services
- provision of data and information about suppliers, markets and products/services
- guidance and implementation of sourcing strategies

- negotiation and formation of contracts
- implementation of an effective purchase-to-pay process.

Measuring the purchasing service

In general the responsibility for measuring the effectiveness and performance of the purchasing service falls on the purchasing leadership. To achieve this, a scorecard (or 'dashboard') is often used, which measures various aspects of the purchasing service in a balanced format.

Other relevant measurement tools could include:

- benefits tracking tool
- contracts database
- purchase-to-pay compliance
- time utilisation sheets
- project-related progress reports
- internal customer feedback.

Sometimes it is difficult to achieve a perfectly balanced measurement approach because of the intangibility of the service provided. There is a natural preference to manage only what can be measured. Purchasing can easily fall into this trap by focusing predominantly on cost savings as their only effective measurable output. Although this is not true, striking a balance with other less quantifiable services can be a challenge to get right.

Managing the purchasing service

The question of who manages the purchasing service is of particular interest. Purchasing may be an internal service provider, but this does not necessarily mean it needs to be managed like a supplier by other functions. The organisation has given accountability and authority to the HoP to perform purchasing activities.

However, it does therefore follow that the HoP has a duty to keep purchasing's customers informed of progress and performance. This is an effective means of keeping them consulted on purchasing matters, as well as giving them confidence that purchasing is providing a good service.

Self-assessment question 7.5

To achieve a balanced measurement of purchasing performance, outline some of key performance metrics that could be measured other than cost savings.

Feedback on page 100

7.6 Outsourcing purchasing responsibilities

Purchasing has been at the forefront of outsourcing and make/buy reviews since the mid-1990s. As an advocate for outsourcing, it should not be surprised to experience a recent trend to reverse the tables and consider whether purchasing itself should be outsourced.

Logically and conceptually this should not present a significant problem for the profession. Purchasing provides a service and the organisation needs that service, whether it is conducted within or outside the organisational boundaries.

However, from an emotive standpoint, we may have an alternative view of this proposition.

Learning activity 7.6

Imagine the impact on your own workplace if the purchasing function was outsourced to a third-party specialist provider. Try to think objectively and identify three advantages and three disadvantages this would offer your organisation.

Feedback on page 101

Refer to the table below for a list of the arguments for and against outsourcing purchasing activities:

Table 7.3

Arguments in favour outsourcing purchasing activities	Arguments against outsourcing purchasing activities
• There are economies of scale by aggregating goods and services with other buying organisations	• The organisation loses a critical commercial skill and knowledge base
• Specialist services and expertise can be bought-in, therefore creating a better service	• Risks of confidentiality and intellectual property protection could be exacerbated
• Risk-reward structures can ensure that the service provider is incentivised to provide the best service	• Aggregation of good and services may lose the distinctive requirements of the organisation
• Administrative efficiency can be created by giving the management to a third party	• The supply of good and services is removed one step further away from the customer and consumer
• A third party can absorb the fluctuation in demands for purchasing activities and flex their resource accordingly	• An additional management layer is needed to manage the third-party service provider

Clearly an evaluation of the arguments for and against outsourcing purchasing activities needs to be done, and this is unlikely to be from within the function itself.

In practice smaller organisations (with smaller third-party spend) have more to gain by using outsourced purchasing service providers, as they are able to take advantage of the economies of scale when buying in bulk. Large organisations are less likely to find these benefits because they already have these advantages of scale: in fact it is possible that they could be giving away some competitive advantage if they allow their spend to be aggregated with that of smaller providers.

Self-assessment question 7.6

Identify three key driving forces behind the reasons why some organisations are considering outsourcing purchasing activities

Feedback on page 101

This study session has focused on several different aspects associated with managing the purchasing function, including the organisational structure, generic roles and responsibilities, the issue of centralisation and the definition and delivery of the purchasing service.

The purpose of this study session has been to equip you with a good understanding of the key organisational contexts facing the purchasing function. This helps you to appraise the need for different approaches to purchasing in differing organisations and contexts.

In the next study session we will consider the nature and structure of supply markets and supply chains as a further area in the purchasing context.

Suggested further reading

In Bailey et al (2005) there is a specific chapter on the design of the purchasing structure.

You could also read the chapter on the design of the purchasing structure in Lysons and Farrington (2006).

Finally you could look at the chapter on organisational structure and design in Mullins (2005).

Feedback on learning activities and self-assessment questions

Feedback on learning activity 7.1

Your structure should resemble an organisation chart for the purchasing function, but should also include other colleagues in the business who carry out purchasing responsibilities. Use your output as a basis for comparison in the remainder of the text.

Feedback on self-assessment question 7.1

Organising purchasing in a matrix structure brings the advantages of both functional and divisional structures. The function retains a clear chain of command and its central coordination, while being able to flex itself into project-based teams and product-based portfolios in local divisions or business units. Purchasing works cross-functionally and can rapidly respond to local issues. It remains close to the customer and is able to transfer its expertise relatively easily.

However, the organisational structure is complex, with staff often having dual reporting lines (one to the project team and the other into purchasing). This can lead to conflicting loyalties for the staff over prioritising their time, resources and effort.

Feedback on learning activity 7.2

You will notice several different roles and responsibilities acting within the same function. The following text outlines several generic roles that might typically exist. Compare your own list with the roles described.

Feedback on self-assessment question 7.2

The purchasing manager is responsible for managing third-party expenditure effectively and sourcing the appropriate supplies on the best commercial terms. The supplier relationship manager is responsible for managing the health of the relationship with a key supplier and working with them collaboratively to improve all-round service for the organisation. Conflict may arise when an existing contract needs to be reviewed or renewed. The supplier relationship manager has an interest in maintaining the goodwill in the relationship which they have invested in over time. The purchasing manager may not be able to assess this intangible factor and will be happy to apply competitive commercial pressures into the relationship.

Feedback on learning activity 7.3

Typical areas might include HR, marketing, engineering and IT where specific market expertise is required to function effectively in the market and with the stakeholders. Often these areas are reluctant to relinquish full responsibility to a 'non-technical' area such as purchasing. The issue concerning appropriateness is particularly difficult to answer. Functions wish to retain control on critical areas of spend because they have an intimate technical knowledge in that area and it is therefore beneficial for them to remain in control of the expenditure. However, if this means the spend management is placed into the hands of a part-time purchaser who has little or no commercial awareness or purchasing capabilities, then there are corresponding risks with this approach.

Feedback on self-assessment question 7.3

The risks associated with 'part-time' purchasing obviously regard the potential lack of professional spend management. There are concerns about inconsistency with policy, lack of full effectiveness and potential exposure to commercial risks, such as poor contract practice or unfavourable commercial terms. Where the organisation has specific policies about purchasing ethics, contact with suppliers and/or tendering rules and procedures, there is a risk that these may not be adhered to. This would have considerable ramifications in some organisations, particularly the public sector.

Given the nature of the 'part-time' term, there is also a risk that the full amount of time cannot be given to the purchasing role, especially where members of staff have other full-time responsibilities to fulfil. This could lead to cutting corners.

Feedback on learning activity 7.4

With an accurate organisation chart and an understanding of your own organisation you should be able to identify whether your purchasing function is centralised into one focal point of responsibilities or decentralised into a diversely spread function. Study the following text to identify some of the reasons and benefits for your function being organised this way.

Feedback on self-assessment question 7.4

There is no better organisational model. As the text above states: the arguments for and against are equally compelling and therefore can only be truly evaluated in the context of the specific organisational environment.

That said, from your own experience you may wish to argue in favour of one model. This is perfectly legitimate and, if that is the case, you can use the above table as a checklist to ensure you have covered all considerations.

Feedback on learning activity 7.5

The customers should many and various, probably as many as there are other functions in your workplace. Here are a couple of examples you might select:

HR is a customer of purchasing. It requires training, recruitment and staff services to be procured on its behalf. These need to provide the right level of service and meet the required budget levels. Given the specific sensitivity of staff-related matters, the suppliers will need to demonstrate appropriate experience and safeguards in dealing with people matters.

Legal is a customer of purchasing. It requires legal advisers and cost draughtsmen to be procured on its behalf. These services need to have the right levels of experience and technical skill, combined with the right level of service and cost effectiveness.

Feedback on self-assessment question 7.5

The list could include:

- cost mitigation and avoidance
- percentage of spend under contract
- number of suppliers in vendor base
- number of preferred suppliers utilised
- internal customer feedback
- number of projects delivered on time

- compliance with policy and procedures
- compliance with approved purchase order and payment routes.

The list is not exhaustive but the point is well made: purchasing's remit is far more than saving costs!

Feedback on learning activity 7.6

Compare your answers with those provided in the following text. Purchasing is in effect a service and, just like any other internal service, it needs to be critically reviewed to establish where the best location for it is.

Feedback on self-assessment question 7.6

Drivers behind the move to outsource purchasing activities include:

- need for cost effectiveness in all areas of the organisation
- current trend to market-test all services
- a supply market for procurement service providers now exists
- risk and accountability can be passed on to third parties
- it reduces headcount in the organisation
- it reduces the complexity of management.

7

7

Supply markets and supply chains

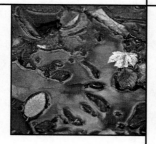

Introduction

So far you have studied the context of different business sectors and specifically looked at the purchasing organisation. This chapter strikes at the heart of understanding effective purchasing management by examining the structural dynamics of supply markets and supply chains. This is critically important for the purchasing professional to appraise and constitutes one of the most influential study sessions of this unit.

Session learning objectives

After completing this session you should be able to:

8.1 Analyse the competition and relative bargaining power of a supply market.
8.2 Describe a range of supply chain classifications.
8.3 With examples, evaluate the relative merits of 'tiered' supply chains.
8.4 Describe and evaluate the role of an agent.

Unit content coverage

This study session covers the following topics from the official CIPS unit content document:

Statements of practice

*   Identify the procurement cycle as it applies to a variety of different organisations and contexts.
*   Recognise the transferability of the fundamental principles of purchase and supply management.
*   Appraise the need for different approaches to purchasing in differing organisations and contexts.

Learning objective

1.5 Evaluate the context of the purchasing function and different purchasing situations.
    *   Purchasing as a discrete organisational function within the supply chain
    *   Relationship between the purchaser and a supply market

'Business success is always about the ability of the individual (or the company) to link a new supply offering with effective demand, in such a way that control over the supply chain value is retained. The most successful will always...leverage it effectively against customers'
Andrew Cox (1997)

8

8

Prior knowledge

Study sessions 1 – 7 should be covered before this session, because they provide a solid foundation to the supply market context for purchasing.

Resources

Internet access is preferable, but not essential. You may also wish to access a library for further reading and additional studies, but this is neither compulsory nor essential.

Timing

You should set aside about 4 hours to read and complete this session, including learning activities, self-assessment questions, the suggested further reading (if any) and the revision question.

8.1   Supply markets

Any review of supply markets, the relative levels of competition within them and/or the strength of the buyer's power has to start with a study of supply and demand from first principles.

We need to start with a basic understanding of the relative market strengths.

Buyer dominance occurs when supply exceeds demand. Suppliers are numerous, levels of competition are high, there are plenty of alternative sources of supply and switching costs are nominal; meanwhile buyers are relatively few and have consolidated or low/restricted demand. In these circumstances the buyer is said to have relative power and leverage over the supply market. This typically has a strong influence on the bargaining position of the parties such that the price is low.

Conversely **supplier dominance** occurs when demand exceeds supply. Suppliers are relatively few, there is little or no competition and either few alternative sources of supply or relatively high switching costs; meanwhile buyers are plentiful and demand for the supply is high or unrestricted. In these circumstances the suppliers have relative power and leverage over the buying market. This typically has a strong influence on the bargaining position of the parties such that the price is high.

This is summarised in table 8.1.

Table 8.1 Characteristics of supply markets

Characteristics of supply market	Characteristics of buying market	Relative power, leverage and bargaining positions	Influence on price
• Numerous suppliers • Plenty of alternatives • Low switching costs • High competition	• Few buyers • Consolidated demand • Low/restricted demand	• Buyer dominance • Leverage and bargaining position favours the buyer	• Prices kept low
• Few suppliers • Few alternative sources • High switching costs • Low competition	• Many buyers • High demand	• Supplier dominance • Leverage and bargaining position favours the supplier	• Prices kept high

Table 8.1 is of course a huge simplification on reality, but it does provide a useful guide to the relative bargaining power between buyer and supplier. Figure 8.1 illustrates how this relationship balances when comparing the buying market with the supply market.

Figure 8.1:

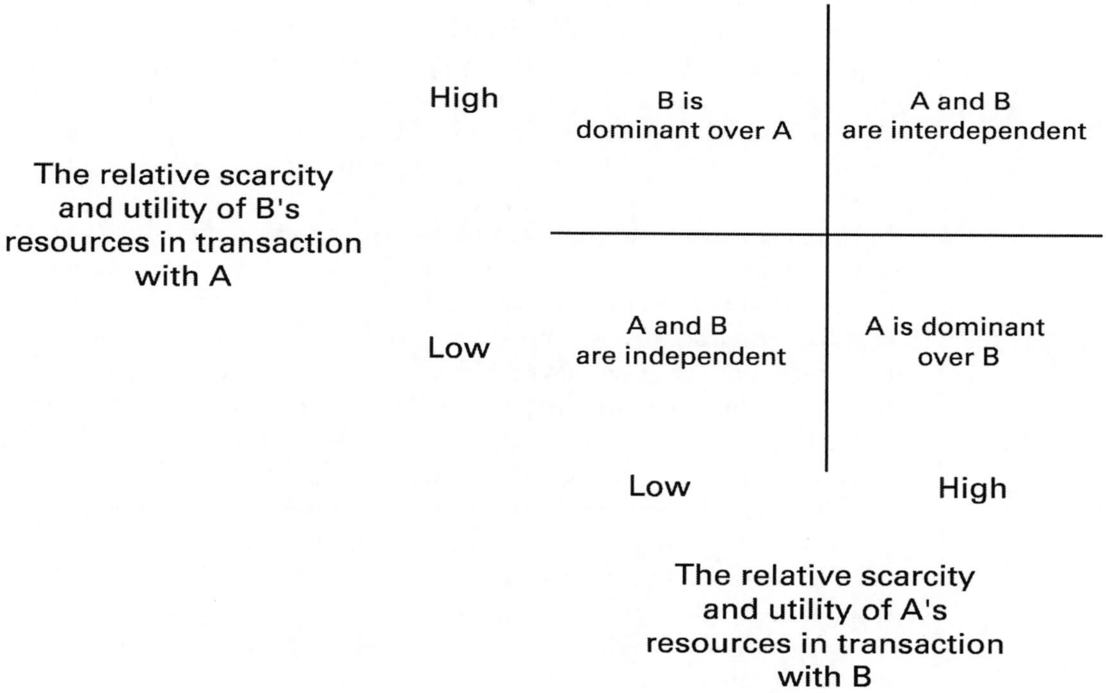

The relative scarcity and utility of B's resources in transaction with A

	Low	High
High	B is dominant over A	A and B are interdependent
Low	A and B are independent	A is dominant over B

The relative scarcity and utility of A's resources in transaction with B

Source: adapted from Cox et al 2002

105

Learning activity 8.1

Using the above diagram as a guide, identify three supply markets your own organisation buys from and evaluate the relative bargaining positions of parties.

Feedback on page 113

Classical economics supports the above but tends to focus on the quantum of supply and demand in terms of the number of participants in the market. Important terms such **monopoly**, **oligopoly**, **monopsony** and **cartel** have become influential economic and commercial themes. Here are their definitions:

- **Monopoly** refers to a highly restricted supply market that is typically represented a single participant. An example of a monopoly is the local wastewater and sewerage service provider: there is only one supplier in the locality and there is no realistic alternative. In this situation the supplier has very high relative power over buyers, but fortunately this is a regulated market for the purposes of consumer protection and welfare.
- **Oligopoly** refers to a restricted supply market that is typically represented by very few participants (say between two and six). Because the level of competition is relatively limited, the market maintains relative bargaining power over its potential buyers. An example of an oligopoly in the UK is the sugar production market where there are two principal producers and several very small independents. This supply market is aptly described in Cox et al (2002). Other similar situations include the provision of national telecommunications services and the operation of retail supermarkets.
- **Monopsony** refers to a highly restricted buying market in which one buyer dominates: it is the opposite of a monopoly. The buyer can use this position of power to bargaining the best terms possible from the suppliers. An example of a monopsony is a tobacco grower that has no choice other than sell his/her tobacco to one cigarette company that is the only buyer for his product. The cigarette company therefore virtually controls the price at which it buys the product.
- **Cartel** refers to a restricted marketplace in which the participants agree to collude and therefore control prices. The most famous contemporary cartel is the Organisation of Petroleum Exporting Countries (OPEC) which, particularly in the 1970s, restricted oil production and sales, while fixing high prices. By restricting supply to a market of high demand, they were able to sustain their high prices and therefore return lucrative profit.

The number of participants in the market is not the sole measure of competitiveness, nor is it the only indicator of relative bargaining power. Cox (1997) explores the concept of **critical assets** and their importance

within a supply market for making money. He defines a critical asset as: '...
that supply chain resource (or combination of resources), which is of such
importance to the process of value appropriation and accumulation, that the
possession of it gives its owner or controller the power to define and allocate
value'.

In his work, Cox provides several well-established examples of critical assets
(such as Microsoft's operating system and Intel's processing capabilities) but
he fails to provide a full list or catalogue of critical assets, although in Cox et
al (2002) the theories are expanded and several supply markets are explored
in detail.

Self-assessment question 8.1

Define the terms 'monopoly' and 'monopsony' in relation to buying from a
supply market and the effect these conditions might have on price.

Feedback on page 113

8

8.2 Supply chains

Supply chains are defined as the interlinking sets of two or more markets
comprising a process of provision of goods and services to a customer.

In study session 3 we described a simple supply chain for automotive
production that linked the raw materials to parts-production; the parts
production to components production; the components production to
sub-assembly; the sub-assembly to main assembler; the main assembler to
retailer; and finally the retailer to the consumer. We noted that, although
this was relatively easy to conceptualise and describe, in reality the supply
chain is far more complex than this.

Learning activity 8.2

Taking the supply of a major product or service to your own workplace,
describe the supply chain(s) that sit behind it. Using an appropriate
diagram, illustrate how the markets are linked to form the end-product/
service.

Feedback on page 113

Professor Christine Harland describes four different levels of supply chain,
shown in figure 8.2.

Figure 8.2: Four different levels of supply chain

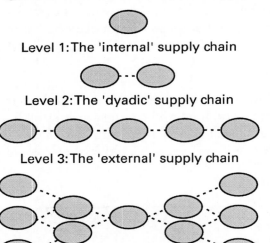

Level 1: The 'internal' supply chain

Level 2: The 'dyadic' supply chain

Level 3: The 'external' supply chain

Level 4: The 'network'

Source: Harland (1996)

The descriptions in Harland's taxonomy comprise four simple definitions of supply. They define the supply chain based on the numbers of players and the organisational boundaries of their operations. Although this helps us to conceptualise and simplify an otherwise complex model, in practice supply chains are very different. This is particularly so in today's dynamic environment where acquisition, mergers, integration and outsourcing are common activities. Many organisations span two or more markets whereas some of their competitors will only focus on one market; the models are therefore, at best, a gross simplification. Cox and Thompson (1998) have argued that supply chains need to be described by the process of *activities* that transform a set of raw materials to finished goods and services for use by an end-consumer. Although this concept applies irrespective of organisational boundaries, it is helpful for the practical purposes of purchasing and supply chain management, to overlay the existing organisational boundaries, thus helping to understand who does what.

Cox (1997) has argued that the concept of the supply chain is insufficient and that it can only be fully understood when it is mapped with a parallel **value chain**. This (not to be confused with Porter's value chain) refers to the process by which money is exchanged through the supply chain in response to the supply offerings. In effect the value chain flows in the opposite direction to the supply chain. The value chain is not however a mirror image because each market player in the chain charges varying amounts and applies a different margin of profit. Cox proceeds to argue that firms will set up in a chosen market within the supply chain so that they can take the best margin they are able, given the resources and assets at their disposal.

In terms of Harland's descriptions, we will consider the third level ('external' supply chain) in the remainder of this section, as the others are considered elsewhere in this study guide. In effect this type of supply chain model is a *linear* model.

From a purchasing perspective, a key aspect of to defining and making the most of the supply chain is the process of **supply chain management**

(SCM). SCM has developed from the observation of Japanese operations management practices in several highly successful manufacturing industries, such as automotive and electrical goods. The key features and benefits of a SCM approach are as follows:

1   **Elimination of waste**: through better resource planning, improved supply chain communications, quality management and improved demand management. This is achieved by considering the supply chain as a whole unit rather than a series of independently competing companies.

2   **Greater efficiency**: through higher utilisation of assets and resources, automation of process, better use of technology, elimination of waste (as above), stockless purchasing and just-in-time deliveries.

3   **Shared resources and capabilities**: through parties in the supply chain working together and collaboratively supporting the process of supply. It removes the unnecessary elements of competition and duplication, whilst encouraging open communication and innovation.

4   **Synergy**: buyers and suppliers share resources, capabilities, problems and ideas by working together jointly. The process promotes open communication and learning, therefore helping the individual companies improve their own operational effectiveness.

5   **Cost-base reduction**: through supplier rationalisation, automated processes and supply base 'tiering' making the whole transaction process less costly, quicker, simpler and more efficient.

6   **Customer focus**: maintaining a focus on the end-consumer at all times throughout the supply chain helps ensure quality and fitness-for-purpose.

7   **Greater competitiveness in the market**: the net effect of SCM achieved through the elimination of waste and unnecessary cost.

8   **Innovation**: through communication and joint working, using the ideas and shared resources of other supply chain partners. The innovations are usually implemented into the operational supply chain and the benefits distributed to all parties. For example, an improvement in the production process at one part of the supply chain means operating costs are lower, this benefit can be passed on to customers as an overall cost reduction on the price.

Further study on the supply chains and the SCM concept is available in Bailey et al (2005) in their chapter about management aspects.

Self-assessment question 8.2

Evaluate the benefits of conceptual supply chain models and outline how their practical application.

Feedback on page 113

8.3   Tiered supply chains and networks

We noted in the previous section that the linear supply chain model is a gross simplification of reality. In practice most supply chains look more like Harland's level 4 supply chain: the 'network'. Every organisation has multiple suppliers, who in turn have their own multiple suppliers. Most suppliers supply to more than one buyer organisation, but few if any supply to exactly the same buyers. The result is a complex web of interlinked supply relationships, best described by the network model.

Supply chains and networks that work together with the SCM approach are called **supply networks** and organisations that take the lead to establish these networks are said to take a **network sourcing** approach. Some of the best and most well-known examples are found in the Japanese automotive manufacturing industry.

Learning activity 8.3

Review the supply base for your own workplace and identify two or three examples of supply networks in action. Try to take examples from different industries so as to broaden your experience and understanding of the concepts.

Feedback on page 114

The key characteristics of a supply network include:

- Suppliers bring their own set of distinct competencies to the project / team and are sourced and utilised on this basis.
- Suppliers and supply relationships are formed and adapted according to the needs of the job(s).
- Relationships and structures are fluid rather than hierarchical.
- Supplier relations are generally close working and collaborative.
- Shared resources, joint-development, synergy and innovation are key features.
- Suppliers might collaborate on one project, while competing on another (the term **co-opetition** is used to describe this).
- Suppliers may supply to each other and/or work for each other on projects.
- At least one party in the network takes responsibility for coordinating the network for the needs of the client or customer.

When the network regularly works together for the continuous production of goods and services for an end-customer, the supply network takes on the **network sourcing** model. Professor Peter Hines (1994) describes network sourcing as the follows:

1 A tiered supply structure with heavy reliance on small firms.
2 A small number of direct suppliers with individual part numbers sourced from one supplier but within a competitive dual sourcing environment.
3 High degrees of asset specificity among suppliers and risk sharing between customer and supplier alike.
4 A maximum buy strategy by each company within the semi-permanent supply network, but a maximum make strategy within these networks.

5 A high degree of bilateral design employing the skills and knowledge of both customer and supplier alike.

6 A high degree of supplier innovation in both new products and processes.

7 Close, long-term relations between network members involving a high level of trust, openness and profit-sharing.

8 The use of rigorous supplier grading systems increasingly giving way to supplier self-certification.

9 A high level of supplier coordination by the customer company at each level of the tiered supply chain.

10 A significant effort made by customers at each of these levels to develop their suppliers.

One regular theme within the networked supply school of thought is that of the tiered supply chain. Put simply it refers to different levels (tiers) within the supply chain taking on responsibility for the coordination and management of different aspects of the supply chain activities. A good example of this is the automotive industry where suppliers to the final assembler will assume responsibility for the sub-assembly of their component parts. There are also many examples of this supply chain arrangement in non-production environments through the use of managed service suppliers (see study session 16 for further details).

There are relative merits of tiered supply chains. Although they remove the day-to-day management and coordination of multiple suppliers from the customer, they do add an additional management layer and the additional costs associated with managing the tiers.

Self-assessment question 8.3

Evaluate the relative merits of a fluid supply network.

Feedback on page 114

8.4 Role of an agent

Agents are used at key points in the supply chain for linkage purposes. The role of an agent will vary according the specifics of the situation, but could include:

- to bring parties and alliances together
- to provide key introductions
- to assist with selling
- to provide market information from diverse sources
- to manage upstream / downstream relationships
- to represent a client or supplier (for negotiation or public relations purposes, etc).

In practice, agents add very little to the *transformation* process within the supply chain. They do not produce or manufacture anything; they add very little *tangible* value. However, in many situations their input and role is critical and they do significant intangible value: indeed in today's increasingly service-based economy, the role of the agent is burgeoning.

Learning activity 8.4

List three different types of agent (with examples) and describe the service they provide

Feedback on page 115

The key features of agents are as follows:

- provider of a service: no physical product
- position of 'trusted adviser' to the client
- does not enter into the supply chain contract directly (as in the examples of the sports agency or the engineer) but helps set up and negotiate the deal
- usually comprises a market 'expert'
- uses information and knowledge as their key differentiator
- leverages **information asymmetry** to be of value to the client (in other words, they know the market, you do not, therefore you pay them to help you).

The insurance industry is a classic example of a supply chain that has historically used agents extensively. However, technology and, in particular, the advent of the internet as had the impact of reducing the agent's bargaining position. Until the mid 1980s the consumer used an insurance broker to search the market and find the best insurance deal. The customer paid the broker a fee and the broker usually took a commission from the chosen insurer. Direct Line was the first insurance company to challenge this model by advertising directly to the consumer and charging lower premiums. They did not have to pay the broker any introduction fee or commission and therefore could undercut the competition. Direct Line has been tremendously successful and virtually all other insurers have copied them, particularly now the internet is widely accessible. The result has been a process of **disintermediation** in the insurance industry for the benefit of the consumer and the detriment of the insurance broker.

Self-assessment question 8.4

Evaluate the potential advantages and disadvantages of buying from an agent

Feedback on page 115

Revision question

Now try the revision question for this session on page 281.

Summary

This study session has provided a rapid overview of the key features, benefits and issues in supply markets and supply chains. We have considered the relative bargaining power of buyers and suppliers to a market and then proceeded to evaluate the supply chain models, the concept of supply chain management and supply networks. A lot of the information provided here only touches upon this subject: additional reading has been provided for you should you wish to study further.

The next study session focuses in on specific purchasing activities and, in particular, the key activities in the purchasing life cycle.

Suggested further reading

You could read the relevant sections of Bailey et al (2005), Cox (1997), Cox et al (2002), Hines (1994) and Womack et al (1990).

Feedback on learning activities and self-assessment questions

Feedback on learning activity 8.1

It is unlikely that you will have identified any practical examples that exactly match these theoretical guides, but you should be able to have identified a likeness towards one or other of the positions.

Feedback on self-assessment question 8.1

A monopoly refers to a supply market that has just a single supplier. As a result, the supplier has relative bargaining power over buyers as there is no alternative and prices are therefore likely to be high. A monopsony is in effect the opposite where there is a single buyer in the market who has relative bargaining power over buyers and prices are therefore likely to be low.

Feedback on learning activity 8.2

Supply chains are rarely linear and you probably have noted how quickly a product within a market quickly branches out to be supplied by several other supply chains. The exercise demonstrates two things: (1) that supply chains are complex, despite the relatively simple concept; and (2) that it is important for purchasers to understand how individual products and component parts are made up. The complexity of supply chains is discussed further in the remaining text.

Feedback on self-assessment question 8.2

Harland described a simple taxonomy of four levels of supply chain. They define the supply chain based on the numbers of players and the organisational boundaries of their operations. Although this helps us to conceptualise and simplify an otherwise complex model, in practice

8

8

supply chains are very different. This is particularly so in today's dynamic environment where acquisition, mergers, integration and outsourcing are common activities. Many organisations span two or more markets whereas some of their competitors will only focus on one market; the models are therefore, at best, a major simplification helping us to understand the nature of transactions in conceptual form only. Harland's model is has conceptual value but only limited practical application.

Cox and Thompson argued that supply chains need to be described by the process of *activities* that transform a set of raw materials to finished goods and services for use by an end-consumer. Although this concept applies irrespective of organisational boundaries, it is helpful for the practical purposes of purchasing and supply chain management, to overlay the existing organisational boundaries, thus helping to understand who does what in practical terms.

Cox argued that the concept of the supply chain is insufficient and that it can only be fully understood when it is mapped with a parallel value chain. This refers to the process by which money is exchanged through the supply chain in response to the supply offerings. In effect the value chain flows in the opposite direction to the supply chain. The value chain is not, however, a mirror image because each market player in the chain charges varying amounts and applies a different margin of profit. Although this, too, is a simplification and conceptualisation of reality, it does provide an additional dimension to the supply-chain exchange process. In practical terms it helps to identify which entities in the supply chain receive the largest proportion of money for their involvement.

Feedback on learning activity 8.3

There are examples in many industries, although they may not be as well defined as the Japanese automotive manufacturing industry. Some examples include:

- IT solutions and applications development: where suppliers become co-dependent and many competitors both supply to each other and buy from each other.
- 'Managed Service' industries, such as HR, training and professional services where a lead provider offers a 'one-stop shop' and coordinates the network of suppliers to meet the client demand on a case by case basis.
- Construction and engineering industries: where main contractors will form specific supply networks of subcontractors and specialist suppliers for the benefit of fulfilling specific client projects
- Most assembly and production industries now operate tightly managed supply networks in order to control cost, quality and delivery time.

Feedback on self-assessment question 8.3

Suppliers bring their own set of distinct competencies to the project or team and are sourced and used on this basis. This therefore means that suppliers are solely used on the basis of their expertise and specialisms.

Relationships and structures are fluid rather than hierarchical and supplier relations are generally close working and collaborative. This often involves shared resources, joint development, synergy and innovation leading to continuous improvement, cost reduction and greater efficiency in the supply chain.

At least one party in the network is required to take responsibility for coordinating the network for the needs of the client or customer. This can be a burdensome management task unless the network is used to working together on a regular basis.

Careful management and ethical sourcing standards are required where the network is particularly fluid, especially to avoid issues of reciprocal trading and offset.

The model is predicated on the basis of supply chain collaboration and there is a risk that the competitive edge could be lost if relationships become too comfortable.

Feedback on learning activity 8.4

There are many different types of agent. Here are just a few examples:

- Public relations agency: manages the image, press relations and external communications for a company, a brand or an individual.
- Sports agency: manages the negotiations and contract management for a professional sports player.
- Broker: advises client on market products (for example financial services products) and forms a deal for the client with the chosen market provider.
- Consulting engineer: represents the client in a construction or engineering project and manages the contract on their behalf.

Feedback on self-assessment question 8.4

Agents rely on 'information asymmetry' in the supply chain. They do not contribute directly to the transformation process, but they add value by bringing information and knowledge to one of the parties in the supply chain in return for a fee/commission. The merits of an agency depend very much on the value of the information to the client. In many ways the client is paying unnecessarily for an information service which it does not need (it could do the job itself), but expediency and efficiency usually mean that the agent is worth commissioning. The additional tier in the supply chain adds cost, but if the value the agent brings outweighs the cost of their fees, then this is acceptable.

8

8

The purchasing life cycle

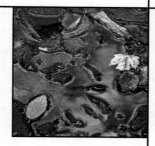

Introduction

So far this study guide has focused on elements associated with the organisation and its position in the supply chain. This study session focuses on specific aspects of purchasing as an activity and provides a pivotal chapter for the remaining text in this guide. You will study the discrete stages in a typical purchasing life cycle, learn how to identify key members of a cross-functional team, and understand how to determine the business requirements for a purchase. Finally you will learn why it is insufficient to purchase on price alone.

'The idea of the purchasing cycle is often employed to indicate the main activities in which purchasing might be involved.'
Bailey et al (2005)

Session learning objectives

After completing this session you should be able to:

9.1 Describe the key stages in the purchasing life cycle.
9.2 Identify the constituent members of a cross-functional purchasing team and describe their respective roles.
9.3 Explain the need for clearly defined business requirements and how they should be prioritised.
9.4 Explain why purchasing on price alone is insufficient.

Unit content coverage

This study session covers the following topics from the official CIPS unit content document:

Statements of practice

- Identify the procurement cycle as it applies to a variety of different organisations and contexts.
- Recognise the transferability of the fundamental principles of purchase and supply management.
- Appraise the need for different approaches to purchasing in differing organisations and contexts.

Learning objective

2.2 Identify and explain different methods of purchasing
  - Classification of supply chains, tiered supply, managed services and the role of an agent
  - The purchasing cycle, its key stages and its relative transferability
  - Importance of cross-functional teams, varying cross-functional requirements and the impact of this on purchases

- Methods of purchase:
  - Spot-buying and one-off purchases
  - Long-term supply relationships
  - Framework agreements and call-off arrangements
  - Projects: how scoped, purchased and paid for
  - Low value orders including use of purchasing-cards
  - Typical purchase-to-pay (P2P) methods
- Merits of competitive tendering: the key stages, appraisal and evaluation of tenders, and merits of e-tendering
- Good practice and its application to purchasing including benchmarking
- Consumables
- Call-off orders

Prior knowledge

Study sessions 1 – 8 should be covered before this session, because they provide a solid foundation to the organisational context for purchasing.

Resources

Internet access is preferable, but not essential. You may also wish to access a library for further reading and additional studies, but this is neither compulsory nor essential.

Timing

You should set aside about 4½ hours to complete this session, including all reading, learning activities, self-assessment questions and sample assessments or examination questions.

9.1 Purchasing life cycle

Learning activity 9.1

Imagine you are about to purchase some new equipment for your organisation. Using the steps outlined below, identify the correct sequence in the purchasing process:

1 Negotiate the price with the preferred supplier.
2 Manage the maintenance and warranty contract.
3 Select the preferred supplier.
4 Appraise the supply market.
5 Award the contract.
6 Define the business requirements.

(continued on next page)

In this opening learning activity you have identified most of the main stages that compose the purchasing life cycle and placed them into their correct sequence. The purchasing life cycle is typified by figure 9.1 in which ten stages in the life of the purchasing activity have been identified. There is some dispute as to the title of the cycle – some refer to it as the purchasing cycle or the purchase process – but these are inadequate descriptions. The correct title is the **purchasing life cycle** because it describes the end-to-end stages in the life of both the purchasing activity and the purchase itself. The process is cyclical because once a product has been consumed and/or disposed of, a replacement is often required thus repeating the activities.

Figure 9.1: The purchasing life cycle

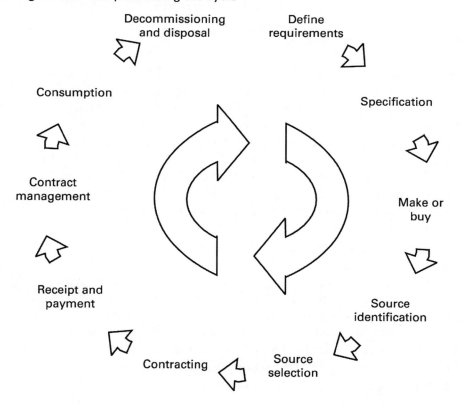

Stage 1: define requirements

The life cycle starts with the initial identification and definition of need. The business has a requirement and a purchase is required to fulfil it. This represents the initial demand for goods or services and purchasing has a significant role to play in helping the business define and prioritise the requirements. You will study this critical stage in the cycle later in this study session.

Stage 2: specification

The specification represents the documented statement of requirements. It is the formalisation of the initial need into a technical document, which may contain any of the following: a design, a set of technical/quality standards, a bill of quantities and/or an inventory of components and materials. The specification is used by suppliers to price the need and to check that their supplies meet the correct technical requirements. Purchasing plays an important role in helping develop the specification by giving critical supply market information and advising on the cost implications of certain specified requirements.

Stage 3: make or buy

The 'make or buy' decision is a critical choice requiring a good understanding of the requirements as well as that of the relative competencies of the market and the organisation. The 'make' decision involves the organisation proceeding to fulfil the need internally, whilst the 'buy' decision requires the organisation to purchase from a third party. The relative merits of internal supply are reviewed later in study session 19.

Stage 4: source identification

This stage involves searching and analysing the supply market: it is about identifying suitable and appropriate sources of supply that will fulfil the acceptance criteria of the requirements. This may involve advertising for suitable expressions of interest (such as the *Official Journal of the European Union* for public sector procurement) or other forms of pre-qualification exercise. The purpose is to establish a body of suitably qualified and compliant suppliers with which to create competitive bidding. As expressions of interest are received, so it is the role of purchasing to help the business appraise each potential supplier for their suitability.

Stage 5: source selection

Selecting the source involves identifying the preferred supplier to supply the goods or services required. This may involve seeking inviting the pre-qualified group of suppliers to tender or alternatively requesting proposals from a few carefully selected suppliers. A predetermined set of 'order winning criteria' needs to be established to assess the suppliers' propositions. This will involve a range of criteria – not just cost – including service, quality, innovation, delivery and performance.

Stage 6: contracting

Once the preferred supplier has been selected a series of negotiations and exchanges will take place to agree the final commercial and contractual details. This can be a complex process in itself and details of these activities have been outlined in other CIPS study guides. Once the contract has been agreed and signed, the parties are committed to ensuring the purchase and supply go ahead.

Stage 7: receipt and payment

Payment for goods and services usually occurs after receipt, although this is not always the case. The purchase-to-pay process (P2P process) can be complex and it is important to ensure this is undertaken efficiently and effectively to prevent sourcing errors. P2P is considered in detail in study session 10.

Stage 8: contract management

Having signed the agreement, the supplier and their performance need to be managed. This stage is referred to as 'contract management' but can equally relate to supply management and/or supplier relationship management. The role of purchasing is to ensure that the supplier delivers to the contractual commitments: on time and to the right specification. In simple purchases, this stage can precede the receipt and payment stage; whereas in longer-term, more complex purchases contract management is ongoing beyond individual deliveries.

Stage 9: consumption

Consumption is a critical stage in the purchasing life cycle, as it considers the needs of the business in terms of use and maintenance of the purchased goods. Many goods have separate maintenance agreements, which need to be managed during the lifetime of the product. Purchasing's role is to support the ongoing monitoring and evaluation of the goods, so that additional and/or remedial purchases can be made if necessary.

Stage 10: decommissioning and disposal

The end of the life cycle involves disposal of the product. This is becoming increasingly important as awareness and care for the environment grows. Many products and works now need to consider how they will be decommissioned, recycled and disposed of before their initial purchase. If considered too lightly, this could be a very expensive and risky stage in the process for organisations.

Self-assessment question 9.1

Using the ten-step purchasing life cycle, compare and contrast the purchase of goods and services. Identify which stages of the life cycle are relevant for either purchase.

Feedback on page 127

9

9.2 Cross-functional purchasing teams

Learning activity 9.2

From your own workplace identify a purchasing project that used cross-functional teamwork and describe the roles and responsibilities of each member.

Feedback on page 127

Cross-functional teams play a critical role in achieving buy-in and compliance to purchasing projects. Purchasing rarely operates as the single conduit to the supply base and it is very unlikely to be the sole 'customer' of the services and products supplied. Establishing and maintaining effective cross-functional support is a vital skill for purchasing managers.

Figure 9.2 shows a basic 'three tier' governance structure for a cross-functional project-based team.

Figure 9.2: Governance structure for a cross-functional project-based team

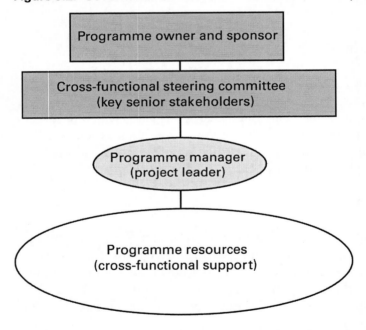

The tiers are required for effective division of responsibilities, direction-setting and escalation. They also allow different levels of seniority in the organisation to become involved in the project.

Programme owner/sponsor

The Head of Purchasing or Chief Procurement Officer (CPO) needs to take responsibility and ownership for the delivery of a cross-functional purchasing project. This is a functional role for which the CPO has functional accountability. The CPO acts in 'sponsorship' capacity to give the programme a senior lead, mandate and delegated authority.

Steering committee

The role of the steering committee is to ensure senior buy-in and support for the purchasing project. It needs to be reported to on a regular basis and be chaired by the CPO. The steering committee acts in an advisory capacity to the CPO to enable the strategy to be developed 'legitimately'. Members of the steering committee comprise senior managers from stakeholder groups within the organisation.

Programme manager

The programme manager takes responsibility for the day-to-day activities of the purchasing project, ensuring that progress keeps to plan and regular reports are made. They act as a focal point to the project and help coordinate resources and budgets under the direction of the CPO. For a purchasing project, it is likely that this individual comes from the purchasing function but this may not be the case if the project is not purchasing-led.

Programme resources

The team comprises a range of colleagues both within and outside purchasing. Cross-functional representation is required both for consultation purposes and for the use of specialist skills such as human resources (HR), legal, risk and finance. Team members may not necessarily be full-time, but they will meet together regularly and have an equal say in the project. Where the project is led by another function, purchasing will be required to provide a specialist role in this team as part of the cross-functional representation.

9

Self-assessment question 9.2

List the potential cross-functional teams members involved in sourcing a new recruitment agency for the finance specialists.

Feedback on page 127

9.3 Business requirements

Learning activity 9.3

Imagine you work for a regional building firm and are in the process of establishing a preferred supplier agreement with a ready-mix concrete provider for delivery to your construction sites.

Identify and rank your top five business priorities for the supply of concrete.

Feedback on page 128

This learning activity has highlighted three key learning points:

- There is more than one key business criterion when purchasing goods and services.
- Not all criteria are of equal importance.
- The business criteria form a 'hierarchy of needs'.

Figure 9.3 illustrates the concept of a hierarchy of needs.

Figure 9.3: Hierarchy of needs

The pyramid diagram represents a hierarchy of the business requirements for any purchased product or service in the organisation, much like Maslow's hierarchy of needs for the individual.

The relative priority of the hierarchy needs to be determined for each purchase made: it cannot be assumed that service is more important than cost but less important than quality and so on. Before proceeding to identify and appraise potential suppliers, purchasing needs to understand and define each business requirement in quantifiable terms. This will then help determine the sourcing criteria and the performance metrics of the purchased goods.

Self-assessment question 9.3

For each of the five generic business requirements listed below, provide specific examples of the business requirements and an indication of how they might be measured or assessed.

(continued on next page)

Self-assessment question 9.3 *(continued)*

Business requirement	Specific examples	Sample measures
Cost		
Service		
Quality		
Delivery		
Security of supply		

Feedback on page 128

9.4 Purchasing on price alone.

In the previous section you learned about the range of business requirements that purchasing needs to take into consideration when specifying and purchasing a product or service. This section focuses on the key aspect of price.

Price is often the focus for purchasing and there are obvious risks associated with focusing purely on price alone.

Learning activity 9.4

Imagine you have been asked to negotiate the cost of purchasing an important machine tool for a production plant. What factors are you likely to consider?

Feedback on page 128

The key learning point from the activity is that the cost to the organisation is always more than just the price of the product itself. Figure 9.4, an 'iceberg' diagram, illustrates this point:

Figure 9.4: Costs associated with the acquisition of a product or service

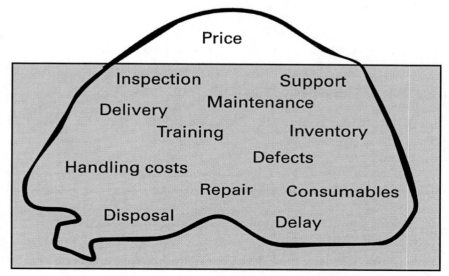

Source: adapted from Bailey et al (2005)

9

Price is the most visible cost, and often the biggest individual component in the total cost of the acquisition. However, the figure 9.4 helps us to remember that there are usually many other costs associated with the acquisition of a product or service than just the price alone. These additional costs are hidden from the initial price, and suppliers rarely bring attention to them, for obvious reasons.

Bailey et al (2005) state:

'The total acquisition cost is more than simply price, and has a bearing on developing the wider role of purchasing into total cost management. It is the total you actually pay for goods and services, including such things as tooling, duty, inventory-carrying costs, inspection, remedy or rectification and so on.

'It is an obvious fact, yet a commonly ignored one, that a low price may lead to a high total acquisition cost.'

The total acquisition cost referred to comprises the price, plus all other associated costs of owning, operating and eventually disposing of a product. This is defined as the total costs of ownership (TCO), also known as 'whole life costing' (or total life cycle costing) because it represents the full cost of the product to the organisation.

TCO is a relatively easy concept to understand for products, components and works – that is, tangible goods – but it equally applies to services. The costs of a service include the price (or fee) of the service itself, plus all the related costs of receiving the service into the organisation.

There are many risks associated with buying on price alone, because price is an insufficient indicator. Focusing on only the price means that other 'hidden' costs are not considered or managed effectively. It can also mean that other business requirements such as service, quality or delivery are overlooked.

Self-assessment question 9.4

Bailey et al (2005) state that '…a low price may lead to a high total acquisition cost.' Explain what is meant by this comment.

Feedback on page 129

Revision question

Now try the revision question for this session on page 281.

Summary

In this study session you have considered the full purchasing life cycle as a series of process steps in the end-to-end lifespan of a product or service as it is purchased and consumed. You have also studied in detail specific elements associated with the purchasing activity, including cross-functional teamwork, the need to establish broad business requirements and the dangers of buying on price alone. The next study session looks at specific methods of purchase.

Suggested further reading

You could read the relevant sections of Bailey et al (2005) and Lysons and Farrington (2006).

Feedback on learning activities and self-assessment questions

Feedback on learning activity 9.1

The correct sequence should be: 6, 10, 4, 11, 3, 1, 5, 8, 7, 2, 9.

In this exercise you have identified many – but not all – of the key stages in the purchasing life cycle and placed them into the correct sequence. The rest of this section of the study session looks at this in further detail.

Feedback on self-assessment question 9.1

The process is equally valid for purchasing products or services, although some of the terminology is more geared towards that of products. Given that one of the key features of a service is that it is consumed at the point of delivery, the decommissioning and disposal stage is not relevant for services.

One of the key learning outcomes of this is to recognise the transferability of some of the key purchasing principles, of which, the purchasing life cycle is one. This means that, in effect, the life cycle is equally applicable to any purchased item, albeit with a degree of customisation.

Feedback on learning activity 9.2

You should be able to identify the individual contributions of each team member and observe that, as well as representing different functional interests, they also perform different roles and responsibilities.

Use the remainder of this section to identify formal roles within the team.

Feedback on self-assessment question 9.2

This is a relatively simple purchasing project and unlikely to require a full-blown steering committee. If the sourcing requirement is part of a larger initiative (such as a purchasing programme or an HR recruitment drive) then the owners of these broader initiatives are likely to want to sponsor this specific initiative.

Although sourcing is a specific purchasing activity, in this case it is recommended that HR is involved (from a recruitment policy and

9

procedures standpoint) and finance (as the end user/customer). During the purchasing life cycle, legal may also need to be involved to form the contract.

Feedback on learning activity 9.3

Your list of priorities should look something like this:

1   security of supply
2   safety, regulatory and legislative compliance
3   on-time delivery
4   quality
5   cost.

You may have a different priority: the issues are open for debate. However, the purpose of the exercise is to recognise that there are a range of business criteria that need to be considered when sourcing any purchase.

In this particular instance, security of supply is of utmost importance because without the concrete the building work cannot be undertaken. Regulatory and legislative compliance is of equal priority because of the obvious ramifications. On-time delivery has to be one of the most important considerations, especially given the nature of the product being sourced. Finally, quality and cost need to be considered to ensure the building works are technically and commercially viable.

Feedback on self-assessment question 9.3

There are many examples you could have selected; here is a sample to compare your responses with.

Business requirement	Specific examples	Sample measures
Cost	Disposal costs	Estimated sum (£)
	Maintenance costs	Annual sum (£)
	Unit cost	Unit price (£)
Service	Response times	Elapsed time (days, hours)
	Reliability	Percentage downtime
Quality	Compliance to standards	Percentage compliance
	Compliance to specification	Percentage compliance
	Limited defects	Parts per million
Delivery	Lead time	X days
	Tolerance on delivery	Accuracy ± 1 hour
Security of supply	Feasibility of supply	Yes/No
	Alternatives	Yes/No

Feedback on learning activity 9.4

You do not need to be an expert in purchasing capital machine tool items to answer this question. There are several elements involved in the total cost, including: the initial price, installation and testing costs, cost of maintenance and servicing, cost of spares, operational costs (such as energy consumption and any consequential impact of down-time), life-expectancy, lease cost (if relevant), costs of decommissioning and disposal.

9

Feedback on self-assessment question 9.4

The total costs of ownership include much more than just the price: they include the costs of owning, operating, maintaining and disposing of the goods throughout their life. If a buyer focuses purely on lowering the price, then it is likely that the other costs will increase. The price of products and services is only lowest when quality, service, delivery and all other business requirements are compromised. In this event, the product or service is likely to be more expensive to maintain (or alternatively have a shorter life span, thus requiring re-acquisition more often).

9

9

Study session 10
Methods of purchase

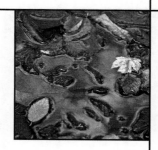

Introduction

This study session covers a broad range of subjects associated with different methods of purchase. It studies simple transactional purchasing such as spot-buying and low-value orders. It also reviews more complex purchasing methods such as long-term relationships, framework agreements and project procurement.

Central to the purchasing process is the purchase-to-payment process (P2P). P2P provides the bedrock for professional buying and, ultimately, strategic procurement. In this study session you will learn more about P2P and its central role in purchasing.

> 'Purchasing and supply managers long have been interested in reducing the time and administrative cost involved in ordering... In progressive firms, the purchasing and supply unit focuses on adding value, not time-consuming paperwork.'
> **Dobler and Burt (1996)**

Session learning objectives

After completing this session you should be able to:

10.1 Evaluate the merits of spot-buying.
10.2 Assess the merits of long-term supply relationships.
10.3 With appropriate examples, describe how framework and call-off agreements operate.
10.4 Outline how a major project is scoped, purchased and paid for.
10.5 Identify solutions for purchasing 'low-value' orders.
10.6 Describe the key elements in a typical 'purchase-to-pay' process.

10

Unit content coverage

This study session covers the following topics from the official CIPS unit content document:

Statements of practice

- Identify the procurement cycle as it applies to a variety of different organisations and contexts.
- Recognise the transferability of the fundamental principles of purchase and supply management.
- Appraise the need for different approaches to purchasing in differing organisations and contexts.
- Recognise best practice procurement processes and consider how they can be adapted and transferred to other contexts.

Learning objective

2.2 Identify and explain different methods of purchasing

- Classification of supply chains, tiered supply, managed services and the role of an agent
- The purchasing cycle, its key stages and its relative transferability
- Importance of cross-functional teams, varying cross-functional requirements and the impact of this on purchases
- Methods of purchase:
  - Spot-buying and one-off purchases
  - Long-term supply relationships
  - Framework agreements and call-off arrangements
  - Projects: how scoped, purchased and paid for
  - Low value orders including use of purchasing-cards
  - Typical purchase-to-pay (P2P) methods
- Merits of competitive tendering: the key stages, appraisal and evaluation of tenders, and merits of e-tendering
- Good practice and its application to purchasing including benchmarking
- Consumables
- Call-off orders

Prior knowledge

Study sessions 1 – 8 should be covered, and specifically study session 9.

Resources

Internet access is preferable, but not essential. You may also wish to access a library for further reading and additional studies, but this is neither compulsory nor essential.

Timing

You should set aside about 6 hours to read and complete this session, including learning activities, self-assessment questions, the suggested further reading (if any) and the revision question.

10.1 Spot-buying

Spot-buying relates to purchases that are ordered and paid for immediately. It can include over-the-counter trade, telephone orders, electronic/internet purchases and commodity market trading.

In a commodity market the price fluctuates constantly and therefore spot-buying fixes the price at the instant the order is made and confirmed. Similarly, for electronic or over-the-counter trade, the purchase is made subject to an agreed, current price list and the current terms and conditions of trade.

Feedback on page 143

Learning activity 10.1

Using the template below, prepare a list of purchase items that are appropriate for spot-buying and a list of those that are not:

Appropriate for spot-buying	Inappropriate for spot-buying

10

Spot-buying is a very efficient and easy method of purchase. Because of its simplicity and the immediacy of the transaction, there is little administration and so the costs of transaction are kept to a minimum. In effect, the main focus of spot-buying is price: once that is agreed, the purchase can proceed without delay.

Spot-buying should be used when:

1 The goods are easily specified and designed (that is, of limited or no variation).
2 The price fluctuates with market dynamics and therefore needs to be fixed at any given time.
3 The purchase/use/consumption is required immediately.
4 Payment can be made instantly.
5 The order can be fulfilled at once.
6 The terms and conditions of trade are acceptable to both parties.

If the purchase fulfils these criteria then it is likely to be a candidate for spot-buying.

The advantages of spot-buying lie in the simplicity of the transaction. The focus is on the price, with all other elements being standardised (or 'commoditised'). This means the relative lead time to acquire the goods is short and the costs of transaction are relatively inexpensive. A good spot-buyer learns to index and track spot-prices over time so that the price trends can be observed and forecast for the future. This then allows the buyer to forward-project the best time to purchase and the most suitable quantity/volume.

However, if the buyer gets it wrong the effects can be considerable. Spot-buying at the wrong time can mean excessive prices, or poor quality in the case of perishable goods. In effect, the spot-purchase is making a speculative bid for goods.

Further study on purchasing commodities and perishable stock is available in study session 15. The recommended text also contains an excellent introductory chapter on the subject of buying commodities and some of the inherent risks that the buyer needs to manage (Bailey et al 2005).

Self-assessment question 10.1

Identify some of the main risks associated with spot-buying.

Feedback on page 143

10.2 Long-term supply relationships

Purchasing transactions that occur regularly over time are often described as a 'relationship' between the buyer and supplier. Many purchasers find that there are advantages in aggregating demand over a longer period and structuring the contract accordingly. This section looks at the relative merits of long-term supply relations.

Learning activity 10.2

Identify one or more long-term supply contracts from your own organisation and describe their key features (including the type of contract, the terms of purchase, the behaviour of the supplier, the nature of the relationship, the type of communication that exists and so on). In what ways do these relationships differ from short-term and spot-purchase relationships?

Feedback on page 143

Longer-term supply relationships are often characterised by 'closer' working relations. This subject is covered in detail in the CIPS Level 4 Managing Purchasing and Supply Relationships unit and will only be covered at a summary level here.

In essence, contract requirements are aggregated over time for the following reasons:

1   They reduce the costs of re-tendering and re-contracting.
2   They promote efficiency and productivity.
3   They allow greater economies of scale to be realised.
4   Preferential terms of service/supply can be achieved.
5   There is a greater focus on delivery and quality, rather than winning the next order.
6   They reduce the costs of exit and/or switching supply.
7   They allow supplier and buyer learning to be enhanced.
8   Collaboration and continuous improvement can be enhanced.
9   Effective communication and shared understanding is established and maintained.
10 Effective buyer leverage can be maintained.

One description of long-term close-working relationships is that of 'partnership sourcing' also called 'partnering'.

The CBI and DTI define partnership sourcing as follows:

'Partnership sourcing is a commitment by customers/suppliers, regardless of size, to a long-term relationship based on clear mutually agreed objectives to strive for world class capability and competitiveness.'

Partnership sourcing has received a lot of academic attention in the purchasing profession during the past 20 years and has become the backbone of the lean supply school of thought. Further reading on this subject includes Lamming (1993) and Hines (1994) both of whom are fully referenced at the end of this course book.

Some of the critics of partnership sourcing have argued that the concept has been falsely promoted as a 'panacea' for solving all supply chain issues. One of the most vocal critics has been Cox (1997) who describes the partnership concept as 'myopic'.

Here are some of the reasons why long-term close-working relationships sometimes fail:

1   Relations can become too close, resulting in complacency and lost competitiveness.
2   Innovation can become stifled.
3   Switching costs can increase, leaving the buyer 'tied' to the supplier.
4   Long-term relationships require additional management resource and time to set up and maintain, which might be unnecessary for some purchases.
5   Requirements change over time and some long-term relationships may not be able to cater for the new requirements.
6   Contract change during the mid-term of a relationship can be costly and disruptive.
7   Buyers can lose touch with market knowledge.
8   Over-reliance on the supplier can build up, thus creating dependency for more services.
9   Effective buyer leverage can be lost.
10 Relations can become stale and unproductive.

In summary, it is not possible to say whether long-term relationships are advantageous or not: the answer will depend on the specific circumstances of supply. However, it is evident that long-term relationships are often considered to be favourable, as long as there is sufficient in-built flexibility to allow for changing circumstances.

Self-assessment question 10.2

Compare and contrast the relative advantages and disadvantages of long-term supply relationships.

Feedback on page 143

10

10.3 Framework and call-off agreements

Where long-term contracts are made up of many smaller repeat transactions, a special contracting mechanism is required to cover the needs of the relationship and the individual transactions. This is called a **framework agreement**: the contract operates as a framework or 'umbrella' for each of the individual transactions for a certain period of time.

An example of a framework agreement is a maintenance contract, where individual jobs and services are 'called off' during the lifetime of the agreement. The full agreement is covered by the terms of the framework agreement, while the individual transactions have specific conditions of their own. This is explained in more detail later in the text.

Learning activity 10.3

Identify a framework agreement from your own workplace and describe its main characteristics. Include a description of the purchases it covers and the differences between the individual transactions and the full contract.

Feedback on page 144

There are many different names for framework agreements and the contracting method they represent. Here are some examples:

- serial contracting
- framework agreements
- call-off contracts
- term contracts.

Essentially, they represent the same method of contracting with a third party with only subtle differences.

Serial contracting is based on the rationale that the consolidation of expenditure increases a buyer's leverage in the market place and provides a far more attractive workload proposition for the supplier. Quite simply it works by stringing together a series of smaller contracts so that the same supplier is retained for a longer period, without the need for re-tendering. For the supplier this means the potential of a steady workload that they do not have to compete for or risk losing to a competitor. In essence it moves small projects and transactions away from the arms-length basis of spot-purchase and introduces a longer-term basis for the relationship. Serial contracting is not difficult to manage and it does not contravene public procurement directives – it is an eminently sensible approach to managing procurement workload.

Framework agreements are similar to serial contracts, except that they operate for a given period of time rather than a specific number of transactions. They are also called term contracts and/or call-off contracts. The idea is very similar to serial contracting and it produces similar cost and productivity advantages. The mechanism operates at two distinct levels: the framework agreement operates for the term of the appointment

10

and stipulates the general conditions of engagement. However, it rarely contains any orders or guarantees of work; it is purely a governing set of terms and conditions. Within these terms of appointment, the client will call-off individual jobs or transactions (sometimes called 'episodes') using a purchase order or a similar type of ordering document. Each work episode is conducted as a separate contract, albeit on the preferential terms of service agreed in the governing framework agreement. In effect mobilisation and lead times are quickened because the up-front contract administration has been reduced to simple call-off order.

Typical contents of a framework agreement:

- governing terms and conditions
- duration of agreement
- no workload guarantees
- annual review and escalation mechanisms
- agreed price lists and discount structures
- service-level agreement
- general specification.

Typical contents of a call-off order:

- order details (volume/quantity, cost, delivery date)
- specific details (such as specification or schedule variations)
- name of requisitioner
- allocated budget number
- authorised signature.

Self-assessment question 10.3

Identify four examples of goods or services that would be appropriate to purchase using call-off contracts, clearly stating the rationale for your choice.

Feedback on page 144

10.4 Buying projects

In many ways buying a project is not very different from buying any other product or service. However, given the additional complexities involved in managing a project, there are some additional considerations required to procure projects successfully.

Learning activity 10.4

Identify several projects procured in your own organisation and compare the purchasing process with that of other goods and services. Describe the key differences.

Feedback on page 145

Scoping and specifying projects

When buying any product or service, one of the most critical factors is getting the specification correct. Buying projects is no different: the project needs to have its boundaries defined so that everybody knows what is in-scope and out-of-scope. As well as scope, projects also need to be specified in terms of their objectives, the deliverables, the proposed methodology and the available resources. Where time is an important factor, a deadline needs to be established together with a break down of individual stages that make up the full delivery.

Pricing projects

Projects are usually priced in one of two ways: either as a sum of their component prices or as a lump sum in totality. Both figures appear as a total sum, but they are made up in very different ways. The component price approach comprises a sum of all the input prices (typically for plant, labour, materials and subcontractors). The price is broken down to this granular level so that if the need for resources alters it is easy to cost the effect of changes to the project. Where a lump sum is quoted, there is no granularity as to how the price has been established and so variations can become a costly source of dispute.

Project variation

Most projects provide a mechanism for change control, either through variation orders or contract change notices. This gives the client the opportunity to vary the details to the contract and to have those variations costed in an open and consistent manner. Projects need to change for a variety of reasons:

1 unexpected events occur
2 business requirements change
3 change of key personnel can create new priorities
4 new facts are discovered
5 markets change and products evolve
6 something goes wrong or one party fails to deliver.

There are many other reasons why projects change – many of which are perfectly reasonable. If the price has been built up by individual components it is far easier to calculate the cost of change. However, where the price is a fixed lump sum there is not that luxury of flexibility. Suppliers are then asked to quote for the change and a negotiation ensues.

In some industries, project variations can be extremely costly and a source of considerable tension and conflict. Based on empirical research, Cox and Thompson (1998) calculated that at any given time there is approximately £4 billion in dispute in the UK construction industry alone.

Paying for projects

Given the complex nature of many major projects and the fact that they can take a long time to complete, payment is often staged in line with completion. Some projects require monthly invoices and reconciliation, whereas others require the completion of key 'milestones'. A milestone refers to a key stage in the project that is easy to identify and define. In the example of a house-building project, typical milestones might include the completion of each of the following: design, groundworks, main structure, interior plumbing/fittings and decoration.

Self-assessment question 10.4

Define the terms 'change control' and 'milestone payments'.

Feedback on page 145

10.5 Low-value orders

Low value orders refer to purchasing transactions of little monetary worth. Where it is not possible to aggregate these items, they need to be purchased individually thus creating administrative efficiency.

Learning activity 10.5

Prepare a list of typical low-value order items

Feedback on page 145

Bailey et al (2005) claim that the average purchasing transaction costs an organisation £125 to administer, thus making a £1,000 order actually cost 12.5% more at £1,125. If this is the case, then the administration cost on lower value items will be considerably more than 12.5%.

To increase the administrative efficiency of buying low-value items, the following methods of purchase are available, amongst others:

* purchasing cards
* travel and expenses cards
* catalogue sourcing
* e-procurement
* petty cash.

Purchasing cards

The purchasing card is a common approach used by many organisations. It operates like a credit card, allowing the named user to purchase goods and services within a specified authorisation limit. The card can be restricted to specified expenditure items only, thus restricting the likelihood of fraudulent use.

At the end of each month, the organisation is sent a consolidated bill of all the month's expenditure for reconciliation purposes. Organisations can use this information to track expenditure trends and ensure that spend is being managed appropriately.

Travel and expenses cards

Travel and expenses (T&E) cards operate in exactly the same way as purchasing cards but are limited to travel expenditure only (such as rail fares, hotel accommodation, air travel, car parking and so on). These cards tend to have wider use than purchasing cards throughout the organisation, hence the need to operate two different card schemes. T&E cards are issued in line with a travel policy, which staff are required to comply with.

Catalogue sourcing

Many low-value order items are consolidated into catalogues for easy identifying and ordering purposes. The supplier provides a large quantity of stock items to select from and operates a monthly accounting system for their clients, leaving the buyer to place orders by phone, fax or e-mail. Typical items in catalogues include: stationery, office supplies, corporate workwear, tools, spares, IT consumables and IT peripherals.

E-procurement

The introduction of internet technology and electronic commerce has led to a number of efficient purchasing innovations. These include: e-procurement, e-sourcing and online catalogues. In effect, the supplier is offering buyers the opportunity of ordering goods over the internet, thus saving time and administrative cost.

Petty cash

Petty cash is a very traditional method of managing low-value order items, which is still in place in many smaller organisations today. In effect, the company provides a 'float' from which staff pay for goods and return a receipt. The system is fraught with risks of potential losses and fraud and, for these reasons, petty cash is actively discouraged by professional practices.

Self-assessment question 10.5

Explain why low-value order items need specific methods of purchase.

Feedback on page 145

10.6 Purchase-to-pay (P2P)

Purchase-to-pay (P2P) represents the full end-to-end process between requisitioning an order, having it fulfilled and paying for the order; it is the 'cradle to grave' process for an order.

Feedback on page 146

Learning activity 10.6

Arrange the following P2P process steps in sequence:

1 Goods receipt.
2 Inbound inspection.
3 Requisition.
4 Payment.
5 Three-way match.
6 Delivery and invoice.
7 Order placement.
8 Goods dispatch.

Requisitioning and order placement

An order is an instruction to do something, such as supply goods or carry out work. This is often conducted using a purchase order, for which there are accompanying standard terms and conditions. The order needs to state clearly what is required, when and for how much. If the supplier accepts the order a legal contract has been formed.

Goods dispatch

On receipt of an acceptable and unambiguous order, the supplier carries out the order requirements by dispatching the goods to the buyer's stated location. The supplier arranges transportation and usually carries the risk of loss or damage to the goods while they are in transit.

Delivery and invoicing

Goods are usually accompanied with documentation requiring the buyer to sign for their receipt. Sometimes an invoice accompanies this paperwork, but often the invoice follows later. In signing for the goods, the supplier is requesting proof of receipt. Sometimes suppliers request that the buyer takes responsibility for the goods as soon as they are received, even if they have not been inspected or paid for.

Inbound inspection

The buyer is required to inspect the goods and make sure that they fulfil the requirements of the original order. This includes quantity, quality and technical integrity. Once the buyer is satisfied that the goods meet the specified requirements, the payment process can commence. If the goods are unsatisfactory, they need to be returned and replaced.

Goods receipt

Satisfied that the goods meet the specified requirements, the buyer issues a goods receipt note (GRN) to confirm receipt of the goods and to initiate the payment process formally. If the supplier has only made a part-delivery, the buyer is required to issue a partial GRN. Some organisations require their staff to operate a different system for services (because services are consumed at the point of delivery). In these cases, the buyer issues a service receipt note (SRN).

Three-way match

The GRNs and/or SRNs are sent with the supplier's invoice to the accounts payable office. If the P2P process has not been automated, then this creates a considerable amount of paperwork which can incur the risk of losses/errors unless very well managed.

Accounts payable check to make sure that the invoice matches the order requirements (in terms of cost, quality, quantity and description). They also check to ensure the order has been received properly (by the GRN/SRN). This process is called the 'three-way match'. When all three documents match, authorisation is given for the payment to be made.

Payment

Payment is the last step in the P2P process and concludes the contractual requirements of the order. Once the three-way match has been made, payment is authorised for release.

For further information about the P2P process, the recommended text (Bailey et al 2005) has a detailed description in its chapter on purchasing systems.

10

Self-assessment question 10.6

Explain why it is important to have a consistent P2P process.

Feedback on page 146

Revision question

Now try the revision question for this session on page 282.

Summary

This study session has covered a broad range of subjects associated with different methods of purchase. It has covered simple transactional purchasing such as spot-buying and low-value orders. It has also covered more complex purchasing methods such as long-term relationships, framework agreements and project procurement.

Central to the purchasing process is P2P. P2P provides the bedrock for professional buying and, ultimately, strategic procurement.

In the following study session, you will continue the theme of purchasing methods by studying the tendering process in detail.

Suggested further reading

You could read the relevant sections of Bailey et al (2005), Dobler and Burt (1996), Hines (1994), Lamming (1993) and Lysons and Farrington (2006).

Feedback on learning activities and self-assessment questions

Feedback on learning activity 10.1

Here is a list of examples, of which there are many other possible answers:

Appropriate for spot-buying:	Inappropriate for spot-buying
Commodities	Services
Goods for resale (retail items)	Capital works
Energy	Transportation
Financial products	Outsourcing
Foreign exchange	Maintenance repair and operations

Feedback on self-assessment question 10.1

Spot-buying is an instantaneous method of purchase which suits a number of specific goods, particularly when the price fluctuates. Because the price fluctuates over time, it is difficult to predict. This therefore comprises the biggest commercial risk: if the goods are bought at the time of a peak price, they may lose value very quickly.

Other main risks associated with spot-buying include quality (for perishable items) and transit (where transportation and delivery is required). Where the transaction occurs over international boundaries, foreign currency fluctuations could create risks. Similarly, where there is internet and/or telephone trading, appropriate risks of security need to be assured against.

Feedback on learning activity 10.2

Long-term supply contracts cover a series of transactions and therefore need to consider the contractual performance in the round. Aggregation over time means more certainty of custom for the supplier and this in turn should be reciprocated with preferential terms of supply and economies of scale. When managing the performance of the contract, a long-term view should be taken by both parties. For the supplier this should be reflected in treating the customer as a long-term customer.

Feedback on self-assessment question 10.2

The potential advantages of long-term supply relations are:

- They reduce the costs of re-tendering and re-contracting.
- They promote efficiency and productivity.

- They allow greater economies of scale to be realised.
- Preferential terms of service/supply can be achieved.
- There is a greater focus on delivery and quality, rather than winning the next order.
- They reduce the costs of exit and/or switching supply.
- They allow supplier and buyer learning to be enhanced.
- Collaboration and continuous improvement can be enhanced.
- Effective communication and shared understanding is established and maintained.
- Effective buyer leverage can be maintained.
  The potential disadvantages of long-term relations are:
- Relations can become too close, resulting in complacency and lost competitiveness.
- Innovation can become stifled.
- Switching costs can increase, leaving the buyer 'tied' to the supplier.
- Long-term relationships require additional management resource and time to set up and maintain, which might be unnecessary for some purchases.
- Requirements change over time and some long-term relationships may not be able to cater for the new requirements.
- Contract change during the mid-term of a relationship can be costly and disruptive.
- Buyers can lose touch with market knowledge.
- Over-reliance on the supplier can build up, thus creating dependency for more services.
- Effective buyer leverage can be lost.
- Relations can become stale and unproductive.

Feedback on learning activity 10.3

The full nature of framework agreements is outlined in the remaining text of this section. In your example you should have observed that the framework agreement covers the broader aspects of the buyer-supplier relationship (including over-arching terms and conditions such as payment, service-levels, indemnity, liability, confidentiality and intellectual property). The individual transactions have an ordering process of their own within the framework of the broader agreement where specific terms are agreed (such as quantity, delivery, cost, specification and so on).

Keep a record of your example for revision purposes.

Feedback on self-assessment question 10.3

The rationale for using a call-off contract depends on the regularity and standardisation of the goods and services to be purchased, particularly if the exact volume is not known in advance. The following examples are appropriate:

- recruitment
- couriers
- travel
- stationery

- IT maintenance
- spares
- financial consulting services.

Feedback on learning activity 10.4

In essence the purchasing process and sequence of activities remains exactly the same. However, there are some additional considerations required when procuring projects. These include:

1 scoping and specifying the nature of the project
2 pricing the project
3 allowing for variations
4 paying for projects.

Project management could also be added to this list, but this is a major discipline in its own right and subject to the scope of another unit in the CIPS Graduate Diploma itself.

Feedback on self-assessment question 10.4

Many projects change because of unforeseen events or changes in the life of long-term project. Change control refers to the process of managing variations and amendments in a contract for a project.

Milestone payments refer to periodic payments that are made during the life of a project. Each milestone represents the completion of a key stage within the build-up of the project, for which a proportionate sum of money is allocated.

Feedback on learning activity 10.5

Typical low-value order items include:

- spares
- stationery
- travel
- books
- subscriptions
- office supplies
- computer peripherals
- couriers
- shrinkwrap software
- flowers.

Feedback on self-assessment question 10.5

All purchasing transactions cost the organisation money to administer. For low-value orders, this cost represents a significantly large proportion of the total cost of the item. Lower value items tend to have less risk because of the smaller monetary sums involved; they tend to be simpler, more standardised and easier to acquire.

10

For all these reasons, low-value items need administratively efficient methods of purchase. The acquisition of low-value goods should be simple, easy-to-use and inexpensive; it simply is not cost-effective to manage them in any other way.

Feedback on learning activity 10.6

The correct order should be: 3; 7; 8; 6; 2; 1; 5; 4

The remaining text in this section of the study session explains each of these process steps in detail.

Feedback on self-assessment question 10.6

The P2P process determines the way in which an organisation orders and pays for goods and services from third-party suppliers. Many organisations spend over 40% of their turnover on external purchases. This represents considerable sums of money and the risks of error or fraud in the payment systems would be significant if they were not managed appropriately.

Consistent P2P processes are required to ensure easy and efficient management of orders and payments. Without a controlled and consistent process, the organisation is vulnerable to financial errors and/or fraud.

The tender process

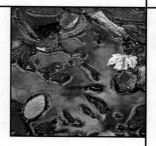

'Competition is at the core of the success or failure of firms.'
Michael Porter (1980)

Introduction

This study session follows on directly from the previous by considering a specific method of purchase: the tender.

Tendering is a robust structured process of creating effective competition for business in a supply market. This study session reviews the merits of both paper-based and electronic tendering. It will also look in detail at the tender process and identified the key components of an invitation to tender.

Session learning objectives

After completing this session you should be able to:

11.1 Evaluate the importance of competition to support purchasing activities.
11.2 Appraise the relative merits of tendering.
11.3 Describe the key stages in a tender process.
11.4 List the requirements of an invitation to tender (ITT).
11.5 Appraise the relative merits of e-tenders.

11

Unit content coverage

This study session covers the following topics from the official CIPS unit content document:

Statements of practice

*   Identify the procurement cycle as it applies to a variety of different organisations and contexts.
*   Recognise the transferability of the fundamental principles of purchase and supply management.
*   Appraise the need for different approaches to purchasing in differing organisations and contexts.
*   Recognise best practice procurement processes and consider how they can be adapted and transferred to other contexts.

Learning objective

2.2 Identify and explain different methods of purchasing
*   Classification of supply chains, tiered supply, managed services and the role of an agent
*   The purchasing cycle, its key stages and its relative transferability
*   Importance of cross-functional teams, varying cross-functional requirements and the impact of this on purchases
*   Methods of purchase:

- • Spot-buying and one-off purchases
- • Long-term supply relationships
- • Framework agreements and call-off arrangements
- • Projects: how scoped, purchased and paid for
- • Low value orders including use of purchasing-cards
- • Typical purchase-to-pay (P2P) methods
- Merits of competitive tendering: the key stages, appraisal and evaluation of tenders, and merits of e-tendering
- Good practice and its application to purchasing including benchmarking
- Consumables
- Call-off orders

Prior knowledge

Study sessions 1 – 8 should be covered, and specifically study sessions 9 and 10.

Resources

Internet access is preferable, but not essential. You may also wish to access a library for further reading and additional studies, but this is neither compulsory nor essential.

Timing

You should set aside about 4½ hours to read and complete this session, including learning activities, self-assessment questions, the suggested further reading (if any) and the revision question.

11.1 Competition

Learning activity 11.1

From your own workplace (or an organisation you are familiar with), identify a supply market where there is no competition. Describe how effective it is to purchase from this market.

Feedback on page 157

As noted in Michael Porter's opening statement to this study session, competition lies at the heart of business success or failure. Without competition in a supply market, buyers are likely to experience:

- • excessive pricing
- • supplier collusion
- • stifled innovation

- poor service levels (in terms of delivery or response times)
- poor quality.

According to Porter (1980), the following conditions lend themselves to giving power to suppliers:

- concentration of suppliers
- lack of dependence on the customer's business
- switching costs facing the customer
- uniquely differentiated product (unavailable elsewhere)
- the threat of forward integration.

Where the suppliers are powerful and there is little or no effective competition, the buyer has very little effective leverage on the supply market. There is a risk that the buyer will experience all the issues that were listed above.

Michael Porter goes on to say that the buyer's goal is to find mechanisms to offset or surmount the sources of supplier power. Further reading on this subject is available in the chapter on strategy towards buyers and suppliers in Porter (1980).

The advantages of creating competition in a supply market are as follows:

- prices and costs are minimised
- quality and service is maximised
- continuous improvement occurs regularly
- innovation and new products emerge.

In the remainder of this study session, we will study the tender process as a controlled means of creating effective competition in a supply market.

11

Self-assessment question 11.1

Explain the potential consequences of a supplier failing to respond to competition that has been introduced by a purchaser.

Feedback on page 157

11.2 Tendering

Learning activity 11.2

From your own workplace identify the reasons why tendering is or is not used to purchase goods and services.

Feedback on page 157

The CIPS Purchasing Policies and Procedures define the following terms:

Invitation to tender (ITT)	'A document, or more usually a set of documents (including specifications, drawings etc) sent to all firms selected to bid for a contract, or all firms replying to an open invitation. The ITT package should contain all the technical, commercial and procedural information required for a potential supplier to make an offer. Each potential supplier must receive the same information.'
Tender	'Strictly, the response from a potential supplier to an Invitation to Tender. The Tender process consists in attracting competing bids from suppliers against a set of specifications and other requirements, within a pre-determined timescale, and evaluating them objectively. A tender process may be openly advertised, with any potential supplier free to bid, or confined to a number of pre-qualified suppliers who are known to be likely to be able to satisfy the requirement.'

Tenders differ from quotations and estimates in that they constitute a firm offer to undertake the supply of goods or services for a price. They include the specification and delivery requirements, together with terms and conditions. Quotations, however, only provide a statement of the price and not necessarily the full terms and conditions of supply; further discussion and negotiation is required before agreement. Estimates are indicative, non-binding prices that are liable to change.

Dobler and Burt (1996) have identified the following five conditions for the appropriate use of competitive tendering:

1   The value of the goods or services to be purchased must be large enough to justify the expense (for both buyer and supplier).
2   The specification of the goods and services needs to be clearly defined for both the buyer and the supplier alike. From this, the supplier needs to be able to cost the supply of the goods or services accurately.
3   The market must comprise an adequate number of suppliers.
4   The suppliers must be technically qualified and competent to fulfil the requirements. Similarly they must actually *want* the business.
5   There must be sufficient time available to allow the tender process to be fulfilled.

Conversely, Dobler and Burt also identified four conditions when competitive bidding should *not* be used:

1   The cost of supplying the goods and services is impossible to estimate with certainty.
2   Cost is not the only criteria, others are equally important (such as quality, service and/or technical competence).
3   Situations where the specification and/or scope are likely to change.
4   Situations in which special tooling and/or other set up costs are major factors (where these issues and costs are better resolved through direct supplier negotiation).

Dobler and Burt argue that if these nine conditions are all satisfied, then competitive tendering usually results in the lowest price. Arguments therefore in favour of tendering are that it provides a professional, structured and consistent method of sharing information with suppliers, eliciting their competitive bids and sourcing competitive supply. The process is robust, auditable and effective.

Criticisms against tendering have included the administrative effort required to manage the tender process and the time it takes. Some critics argue that tendering removes the opportunity for supplier innovation and creativity, therefore reducing the bidding process to a price war. Although there is some merit in these criticisms, it usually depends on how the tender process has been structured and used by the buyer.

Self-assessment question 11.2

Identify two specific goods or services where it is inappropriate to use a tender process as an effective method of purchasing.

Feedback on page 158

11.3 The tender process

Learning activity 11.3

Arrange the following stages of a typical tender process in the correct sequence:

1   Confirmation of intention to tender
2   Evaluation of tenders
3   ITT
4   Tenders received
5   Contract award
6   Preparation of tender documentation
7   Post-tender negotiation
8   Further information / questions from tenderers
9   Pre-qualification of tenderers
10 Short-listing of tenders

Feedback on page 158

11

Preparation of tender documentation:

Before any of the tender process commences, the documentation needs to be drawn up. Investing time up front and doing this thoroughly will help clarify the requirements and lead for a far easier procedure for all concerned. The golden rule here is that the suppliers' tender submissions can only ever be as good as the tender request.

Typically tender documents should contain:

- the specification of materials, services or equipment required (including quantities, quality and technical design standards)
- a description of the relationship expected with the supplier
- the proposed terms and conditions of the future contract
- a general description of the tender evaluation criteria
- details of the instructions, the deadlines, the contact points and any associated procedures that the tenderers must follow
- a request to confirm the tenderers' intention to tender.

Pre-qualification of tenderers

Pre-qualification is an essential part of creating the correct level of competition among the tenderers. The short list of pre-qualified tenderers needs to be long enough to create effective competitive pressures but short enough to manage efficiently. Typically a short list of between four and eight tenderers is sufficient.

Pre-qualification can occur through several mechanisms. Often opportunities are advertised (such as in the *Official Journal of the European Union* for large public tenders inside the European Union) and potential bidders are invited to submit an 'expression of interest'. The buyer uses the information collected in the expressions of interest to select the best pre-qualified short list of tenderers. This list will receive the ITT.

Invitation to tender

The ITT contains the specific instructions for tenderers about the procedures that need to be followed and the scope/specification of the goods and services required. This is covered in further detail in the next section of this study session.

Questions and further information

During the tender period, it is sometimes necessary to issue further information to the tenderers to help them prepare their bids. This may be as a result of a question raised by one of the tenderers, or as a result of new information that has come to light.

The new information should be sent to each tenderer in writing so that there is no misunderstanding or misinterpretation of communication. The same information needs to go to each tenderer and be sent at the same time, so as to give equal consideration to all parties.

Evaluation of tender submissions

Once the tenders have been received and confirmation of receipt sent back to the tenderers, the buyer needs to evaluate the tender submissions and rank the bids. This is rarely done in isolation; the buyer usually works with their business stakeholders so that a common objective view can be formed. The evaluation is made on several pre-determined criteria which may include aspects of cost, service, quality, delivery and innovation. In effect, these criteria should relate directly back to the original business requirements (discussed in study session 9).

Post-tender negotiation

Having ranked the tenders, the buyer invites the top tenderers to discuss their bids and seek further clarification on any outstanding matters. Usually the buyer selects at least the top two tenderers so that the competitive edge can be maintained. During these discussions further negotiation can take place to change aspects of the supplier's bid. This is called **post-tender negotiation** (PTN) and forms an effective leverage tool to lower prices before the contract award.

Contract award

The final stage of the tender process is the contract award itself. In essence, the tender constitutes a formal offer by the supplier. If accepted on face value, then the terms and conditions outlined in the supplier's tender become the agreed contract. The buyer needs to be aware of this fact and ensure that the appropriate discussions have taken place as part of the PTN and that the correct documentation is being used to form the contract.

Self-assessment question 11.3

Describe some of the areas of discussion during a post-tender negotiation

Feedback on page 158

11

11.4 Invitation to tender (ITT)

Learning activity 11.4

Identify an ITT from your own workplace and list its contents.

Feedback on page 158

Instruction to tenderers

The instructions need to be written very accurately so that there is no confusion, ambiguity or misunderstanding between the tenderers. Typical content of the instructions will be:

- deadline for tender submissions
- acceptable format of tender submissions (for example paper or electronic copies)
- point of contact for queries
- need for compliance with the ITT documentation
- whether alternative proposals are allowed
- confidentiality requirements

- non-collusion instructions
- request to confirm a tenderer's intention to bid
- any other procedures (such as extensions of time or variations).

Overview of the award process

The tenderers need to know what award process is going to be and the timescales required. This allows them to tailor their submission to the exact requirements of the client and therefore give the buyer a better proposal. In particular, tenderers want to know what will happen after they submitted their tender and when the contract is likely to be awarded.

Scope and objectives

The ITT needs to state what the scope of the tender includes and excludes. These requirements need to be precise so that the tenderer can price them accurately and there are no 'nasty surprises' later in the process.

By stating the objectives of the tender, the buyer is allowing the tenderers a greater opportunity to deliver a bid that will fully meet their needs.

Specification

The specification is in effect a detailed 'statement of requirements'. It could state technical standards, quality standards, design parameters, methodologies and process, and so on. Getting the right specification and giving the tenderer detailed information ensures that a more realistic and accurate tender will be submitted, thus making for a better contract.

Bill of quantities

Not all tenders need to have a bill of quantities, but they are regularly used in tenders for major projects such as construction. The bill of quantities is a full listing of all the resources and materials that a contract is likely to need to use to fulfil the requirements. In a construction tender, this might include the volume of concrete, the number of bricks and the amount of soil that needs to be moved, among other items.

The tenderer is able to price the individual items so that, if there is a variation in the contract, the change in the overall cost can be calculated.

Pricing requirements

Finally, and perhaps most importantly, the ITT needs to give clear instructions as to how the tenderers should be pricing their submissions. This needs to include:

- the type of price (fixed, lump sum, firm, variable and so on)
- the units of measurement (time, size, quality and so on)
- the format of any breakdown
- the currency
- payment terms
- how long the price needs to remain valid
- any other details required.

The overriding purpose is to ensure that when the tenders are received back in, the buyer is able to make a like-for-like comparison on the issue of cost.

Self-assessment question 11.4

Explain the importance of consistency while tendering.

Feedback on page 158

11.5 E-tendering

E-tenders refer to the process of competitive bidding over the internet, sometimes referred to as e-auctions or, more correctly, on-line reverse auctions.

Learning activity 11.5

As a learning activity to increase your knowledge of e-tenders and e-auctions, read the CIPS Introduction to e-auctions paper, which can be found on the CIPS website.

To access the paper you need to go to the overview page of the e-business section in the professional resources webpage (accessible from the CIPS Homepage).

An e-tender operates as a live 'bidding' event on the internet where tenderers have the opportunity to place as many bids as they wish during the tender period. The principles are exactly the same as a standard paper-based tender, but the operation is different.

With e-tenders, the process is as follows:

1   Once suppliers have been pre-qualified and short-listed for the tender, they are sent a brief ITT which notifies them of the forthcoming tender, its scope and its deadlines.
2   Tenderers are then briefed on the nature of the goods and services to be tendered and, in particular, how the e-tender will be run. They are given the time and log-in details of the e-tender event and allowed some 'preparation time' once the tender document has been released (usually two weeks) before the event itself.
3   The e-tender event may only take a few hours. The tenderers are given their personal log-in details (the URL address and password) and they bid simultaneously during the event.
4   The internet technology allows tenderers to see the price submitted by all other bidders but de-personalises the submissions so that each tenderer remains anonymous.
5   The e-tender is called a reverse auction because rather than tenderers bids increasing, the bids decrease over time. The tenderers can view the other bids and therefore know whether their bid is lowest or not.

11

6   Once the tender event is closed, the passwords and e-tender site are de-activated and the bids are scrutinised to ensure compliance.
7   As with paper-based tenders, there is a period of PTN to clarify outstanding matters and agree the contract award.

In general, the competitive nature of e-tenders and in particular the transparency of other bids lead to lower prices than paper-based tenders. The whole process is quicker and a lot more efficient on the administration. For example, all the bids are electronically submitted and automatically displayed in a like-for-like comparison. Because all the submissions and correspondence has been done electronically, there is also a robust audit trail for accountability purposes.

One of the notable differences of e-tenders is the amount of upfront preparation time required to brief tenderers. This is longer than paper-based tenders, but is required to elicit high quality bids. Overall the elapsed process time is shorter.

E-tenders can be more expensive than paper-based tenders because of the technology involved, but this cost is usually more then recouped by the price savings from the tender itself.

The four tests required to ensure an e-tender will be successful are:

1   The goods and services must be able to be specified accurately.
2   The value of the goods or services to be tendered must be high enough to warrant the cost of the e-tender (this threshold is usually £200,000).
3   There needs to be at least four competing suppliers in the market.
4   There needs to be an *appetite* for the business.

If the above four criteria are satisfied, then the e-tender is likely to be a success.

Self-assessment question 11.5

Identify four potential advantages of an e-tender.

Feedback on page 159

Revision question

Now try the revision question for this session on page 282.

Summary

Tendering is a robust structured process of creating effective competition for business in a supply market. This study session has reviewed the merits of both paper-based and electronic tendering. It has looked in detail at the tender process and identified the key components of an ITT.

The following study session concludes your study of methods of purchase by considering 'best practice' purchasing methods.

Suggested further reading

You could read the relevant sections of Bailey et al (2005), CIPS (1998), Dobler and Burt (1996), Lysons and Farrington (2006) and Porter (1980).

Feedback on learning activities and self-assessment questions

Feedback on learning activity 11.1

Competitive markets can be identified by the number of suppliers in the market and the degree of rivalry between them. In effect, competition is a factor of supply and demand. Markets without competition could be monopoly markets (where there is just one supplier) or oligopoly markets (where there just a few suppliers acting in collusion).

Purchasing is not as effective in markets where there is no competition, because of the lack of effective demand. Suppliers have sufficient demand and can select the clients they wish to work for. They are also at liberty to command the price they wish to charge.

Many monopoly or oligopoly markets are regulated to protect consumers and minimise opportunistic behaviour.

Examples of supply markets where there is very little competition include: water and sewerage supply, medical services, rates, rail transport and professional subscriptions.

Feedback on self-assessment question 11.1

If competition has been effectively introduced by a purchaser, then existing suppliers are facing the threat of losing business, while new suppliers are facing the opportunity of winning new business. If a supplier fails to respond to competition, then other suppliers are likely to gain the business. This could be due any of the following reasons: lower prices, better quality, better service, more innovation and so on.

Feedback on learning activity 11.2

If you do not know the answers to this question, then your purchasing policy and/or procedures may be able to help. In general tendering is employed to create a structured and controlled competitive enquiry process in a supply market. Tenders provide a consistent method of sharing commercial information with a selected group of suppliers; they also provide a consistent and structured approach to receiving competitive bids from the supply market.

Some organisations do not use tendering as it is seen to be unnecessarily administrative and inefficient, but this view is not supported by everyone.

11

Feedback on self-assessment question 11.2

There are many instances where purchases will not warrant a tender process because they do not fulfil the nine conditions (as identified by Dobler and Burt in the text). An example would be where the value of the goods or service does not warrant the tender, for example a small training programme valued at £10,000. Other examples of inappropriate tendering could include the supply of specialist design services, where there is only one or two specialist designers in the market.

However, assuming the goods and services do fulfil the tendering criteria, then they can be purchased effectively through a tender process.

Feedback on learning activity 11.3

The correct sequence should be: 6; 9; 3; 1; 8; 4; 2; 10; 7; 5.

The process is discussed in detail in the remaining text of this section.

Feedback on self-assessment question 11.3

Typical areas of discussion with short-listed tenderers during a post-tender negotiation may include:

- the prices within the tender
- the terms and conditions of the proposed contract
- deadlines and delivery dates
- methodology and/or process to be adopted
- quality standards
- scope
- resources.

Feedback on learning activity 11.4

Typically an ITT may comprise the following documentation:

- instructions to the tenderers
- overview of the award process
- scope and objectives
- timescales
- specification
- bill of quantities
- pricing requirements.

Feedback on self-assessment question 11.4

Consistency is an essential tenet of tendering for the following reasons:

1   It provides fair competition – the same rules apply to all.
2   It gives the tenderers confidence that they have an equal opportunity of winning the contract.
3   The competition is enhanced, because everyone knows there are no special favours.

4   It allows the buyer to evaluate the tender submissions on a like-for-like basis.

Feedback on self-assessment question 11.5

Here are some of the advantages of e-tenders:

1   Competitive: usually produces better results than paper-based tenders.
2   Transparency: therefore less opportunity for fraud.
3   Quick process: total elapsed time is shorter than paper-based tenders.
4   Efficient: less administration with an e-tender.
5   Audit trail: all records kept electronically for scrutiny and accountability.

11

11

Best practice purchasing

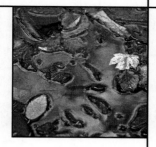

Introduction

Best practice is a controversial term among some business academics but in reality simply refers to an organisation's drive to improve its operational practices. This study session will consider what best practice means for purchasing. It will also consider the process of benchmarking and the benefits that can be attained by comparing practices and learning from others. One of the biggest recent advances in best practice has been that of automating the purchasing processes. Internet technology has revolutionised many procurement procedures and brought significant benefits as a result and the final section of this study session will look at those in more detail.

Session learning objectives

After completing this session you should be able to:

12.1 Explain why it is necessary to strive for best practice.
12.2 Describe the process of benchmarking.
12.3 With examples, identify ways in which technology can assist best practice.

Unit specification coverage

This study session covers the following topics from the official CIPS unit specification:

Statements of practice

- Identify the procurement cycle as it applies to a variety of different organisations and contexts.
- Recognise the transferability of the fundamental principles of purchase and supply management.
- Appraise the need for different approaches to purchasing in differing organisations and contexts.
- Recognise best practice procurement processes and consider how they can be adapted and transferred to other contexts.

Learning objectives

2.2 Identify and explain different methods of purchasing
  - Classification of supply chains, tiered supply, managed services and the role of an agent
  - The purchasing cycle, its key stages and its relative transferability

- Importance of cross-functional teams, varying cross-functional requirements and the impact of this on purchases
- Methods of purchase:
  - Spot-buying and one-off purchases
  - Long-term supply relationships
  - Framework agreements and call-off arrangements
  - Projects: how scoped, purchased and paid for
  - Low value orders including use of purchasing-cards
  - Typical purchase-to-pay (P2P) methods
- Merits of competitive tendering: the key stages, appraisal and evaluation of tenders, and merits of e-tendering
- Good practice and its application to purchasing including benchmarking
- Consumables
- Call-off orders

Prior knowledge

Study sessions 1 – 8 should be covered, and specifically study session 9.

Resources

Internet access is preferable, but not essential. You may also wish to access a library for further reading and additional studies, but this is neither compulsory nor essential.

Timing

You should set aside about 3 hours to read and complete this session, including learning activities, self-assessment questions, the suggested further reading (if any) and the revision question.

12.1 Best practice

Learning activity 12.1

In the opening quotation to this study session, Professor Andrew Cox states that generalisable rules cannot be developed for the most appropriate actions for companies to take to become more competitive. This statement tends to contradict many views that organisations should be striving for best practice. Consider these two opposing views and decide which you support. Give reasons for your choice.

Feedback on page 169

Given the controversy facing the concept, why is it that so many organisations strive to achieve best practice in their respective industries?

To answer this challenge, we need to understand the nature of competitive markets and their impact on organisations operating in them. The nature of competition is such that it is impossible to become complacent in the search for continuous improvement or competitive advantage. Nobody wants to be second best, but perhaps more importantly, few companies can afford to be known for providing inferior goods or services. Competition therefore drives organisations to be as good as they can be.

Few markets are dynamic, they are constantly changing and developing. What was true for the market last year is very unlikely to be the case for the market this year or next. Here are a few examples of the changes experienced in markets:

- new competitors enter the market
- some existing companies merge
- some existing companies exit the market
- continuous improvement brings out new versions of existing products
- innovation develops new products
- legislation and regulations change the rules
- politics and socioeconomic change
- consumer behaviour, trends and fashion change.

If a company does not change and develop with market dynamics, then there is a risk that it might lose touch with its customers' needs and start to incur losses (in terms of profit and/or market share). Development, change and continuous improvement are therefore a critical component of survival in a competitive market. It is therefore essential that every company strives to find the best practice it needs to compete successfully.

Best practice for purchasing will clearly mean different things to different organisations. Here are some examples of so-called best practices:

- supplier rationalisation
- just-in-time deliveries
- business process re-engineering
- network sourcing
- enterprise resources planning (ERP) systems (such as SAP)
- product portfolio analysis
- supply chain management
- e-procurement
- supplier relationship management
- customer and/or supplier portals.

The list could go on. What is important to note is that each of these concepts has at one time been heralded to be the latest 'best practice' for purchasing. But it is obvious that this cannot be the case: there is no evidence to support that any one of these is better or worse than any of the others.

However, it is true that any of these concepts could constitute the best practice for a particular organisation in its specific circumstances. For

12

example it makes sense for a manufacturing company with reliable demand forecasts to reduce its stockholding and therefore save money. Stockless purchasing and just-in-time deliveries will constitute best practice in these circumstances, providing there is no adverse risk placed on the company's production schedule.

In the above example, stockless purchasing and just-in-time constitute best practice – not just for that organisation – but probably for most organisations in that specific industry. It would not necessarily be best practice for all organisations though. For example, stock is still needed in many industrial sectors where contingency is required for sudden peaks and troughs in demand. In these circumstances stockless purchasing and just-in-time is not best practice and could seriously jeopardise production.

Self-assessment question 12.1

Define the terms 'industry practice' and 'best practice'

Feedback on page 169

12.2 Benchmarking.

Benchmarking is a continuous process of measuring and improving products, services and processes against those of other leading practitioners. In stems from the Japanese word *dantotsu* meaning 'striving for the best of the best'. The process involves studying other (usually better performing) practices and comparing what they do with your own practices. Benchmarking brings about improvements in operational performance by extracting and learning about better practices from elsewhere and then adopting them in your own organisation to enhance performance.

Learning activity 12.2

Using library and/or internet resources, find out more about benchmarking and list some of the potential benefits of benchmarking other operations.

One site of help is the Benchmarking Centre: http://www.benchmarking.co.uk. Note: you will need to register to gain access, but registration and access are free.

Feedback on page 169

Although not fully developed as a management technique until 1979 by the Xerox Corporation, one of the most famous examples of benchmarking involved Toyota in 1958. At the time, Toyota was a small family-run business that had been struggling in post-war Japan and the political tension between the Japanese government and the unions of the time.

As the nephew of its owner, Eiji Toyoda and his production engineer Taiichi Ohno were sent to Detroit in the USA to study Ford's system of mass production so that they might learn the latest techniques. They concluded that they were unable to copy the same practices because of geographical and topographical reasons (there simply was not the space for mass production). However, during their study visit they had become fascinated with the shelf-filling techniques at the local supermarket.

Toyoda and Ohno copied and adapted the idea of regular small-scale stock replenishment from their vendors and over time developed the now world-famous and leading edge 'Toyota production system'.

This is an example of generic benchmarking, where Toyota was able to compare and learn from another industry and then adapt the learning successfully to their organisational context.

There are four main types of benchmarking:

1   **Internal**: where internal functions, product lines, business units and/ or teams make comparisons between themselves and adopt the learning from each other.
2   **Competitive**: where competing organisations make comparisons (either collaboratively or covertly) and adopt the learning and better practices from each other. Reverse engineering is a form of competitive benchmarking where a competitor's product is acquired and dismantled to learn how it has been manufactured.
3   **Functional**: where functional disciplines make generic comparisons, either within the same industry or across a range of industries. The Procurement Strategy Council run by the Corporate Executive Board is an example of functional benchmarking for purchasing functions.
4   **Generic**: where comparisons are made between organisations and their business processes, regardless of whichever industry they come from, as seen in the Toyota example above.

Table 12.1 outlines the general 15-step process that a benchmarking exercise will go through (adapted from Oakland 1993).

Table 12.1

Plan	1. Select department(s) or process group(s) for benchmarking
	2. Identify the best competitor
	3. Identify the benchmarks
	4. Bring the appropriate team
	5. Decide information and data collection methodology
	6. Use data collection methodology
	7. Prepare for visits and interact with target organisations
Analyse	8. Compare the organisation and its competitors using the benchmark data
	9. Catalogue the information and create a specialist 'competence centre'

(continued on next page)

12

Table 12.1 *(continued)*

10. Understand the 'enabling' process as well as performance measures

Develop   11. Set new performance standards

12. Develop action plans to achieve goals

Improve   13. Implement specific actions and ensure these are integrated into the business process

Review   14. Monitor the improvements made and the results

15. Review the benchmarks

Source: Adapted from Oakland (1993)

Professor Andrew Cox (1997) has argued: '…no amount of effort directed towards describing what individual companies are doing, or have done in the past, can provide a basis for understanding what any other company ought to do now or in the future. …even if companies are in the same industries, they start from where they are now and not from where their competitors are.'

Although these statements may be true for companies seeking to find the ideal 'best practice', they do tend to fly in the face of all the practical benefits that organisations have reaped from benchmarking exercises over recent years. Every individual recognises that it can compare itself with others and learn from what they do that is better. This is one of the natural laws that is true of both society and business. Benchmarking has proved its contribution in helping organisations enhance their performance.

12

Self-assessment question 12.2

Why do organisations benchmark?

Feedback on page 170

12.3 Technology and best practice purchasing

In recent years there have been several significant developments in 'best practice' purchasing through applications of technology in purchasing and supply processes. Many of these rely on internet technology as a means of rapidly sharing and exchanging information. As such, many automated processes have been found to have found significant benefits over previous manual or paper-based systems. The contribution of technology towards best practice has been considerable.

Learning activity 12.3

Consider the impact of internet technology on the purchasing function and supply base at your own workplace, or an organisation with which you are

(continued on next page)

Learning activity 12.3 *(continued)*
familiar. Identify the systems and processes that have been transformed and
outline the benefits this technology has brought.

Feedback on page 170

The need for electronic commerce (e-commerce) stems from the demand
within both industries and government to make better use of the
information technology tools that are now widely available. The tools
can improve the quality of customer reaction, improve productivity and
efficiency of business processes, and improve the speed and quality of
information exchange both within and across organisations. In fact, every
point and process along the value chain can be impacted and improved
through the application of information technology.

Traditionally the definition of e-commerce focused on electronic data
interchange (EDI) as a primary means of organisations conducting business
electronically through a pre-established contractual relationship. The advent
of the internet has revolutionised this approach and opened it up to form
a broadly accessible portal for all. Increasingly today organisations are
using internet technology to automate and streamline purchase requisition,
approval, fulfilment and payment processes.

Here are the benefits:

- significant cost savings
- significant time savings
- greater accuracy
- quicker updates
- greater reliability
- improved business relationships
- auditable processes and data repositories.

The economic forces motivating the shift to electronic commerce are both
internal and external. Competitive forces are driving organisations to find
cost efficient processes with greater effectiveness and reliability.

Some of the generic types of technology that assist purchasing include:

Electronic data interchange (EDI): referred originally to direct secure links
between organisations' computer systems for the convenience of sharing
information and sending/receiving documents (such as purchase orders and
invoices). The key operational feature is that EDI comprises an exchange
between buyer and supplier without paperwork. Typical information that is
transferred includes:

1   Query handling: such as a reservation system for travel tickets.
2   Monetary data system: allowing electronic transfer of funds (for salaries,
    payments and debits).
3   Trade data: including quotations, delivery/dispatch instructions, credit
    notes and receipts.
4   Technical data: such as product specifications. This includes technical
    drawings and design information using computer-aided design systems.

12

Bar coding and electronic point of sale (ePOS): the impact of bar coding and electronic point of sale devices can be seen everywhere. Bar codes comprise several narrow and wide black lines which when scanned represent contain coded data about the product they represent. This information is presented in a unique 13-digit code (called an EAN number) which can be linked to computer systems to access information such as: product codes, product description, classifications, key dates, supplier information and prices.

Bar coding extends itself from retail through to stock management and replenishment. It allows inbound and outbound logistics to be automated. When linked to retail and electronic point of sale, the bar coding system allows suppliers to automatically know when an item of stock has been sold. Not only does this provide very accurate retail trend data, it also allows suppliers to replenish stock on an automatic basis, if required.

E-procurement and e-sourcing: this was discussed briefly in the previous study section, but can be broadened considerably to encompass many different aspects of the purchasing life cycle. Internet technology has allowed both sourcing and tendering activities to become automated, as well as the more transactional activities of ordering, invoicing and payment.

With the right systems integration every aspect of the purchasing life cycle can now be fully automated – and be linked through to finance systems such as the general ledger – thus generating massive cost and time savings for both the buyer and supplier.

12

Self-assessment question 12.3

Outline the risks associated with e-commerce.

Feedback on page 170

Revision question

There is no revision question for this session.

Summary

Best practice is a controversial term among some business academics but in reality simply refers to an organisation's drive to improve its operational practices. This study session has also considered the process of benchmarking and the benefits that can be attained by comparing practices and learning from others. One of the biggest recent advances in best practice has been that of automating the purchasing processes. Internet technology has revolutionised many procurement procedures and brought significant benefits as a result.

The next study session starts to look at the customer perspective and understand their impacts on purchasing.

Suggested further reading

You could read the relevant sections in Bailey et al (2005), Cox (1997) and Oakland (1993).

Feedback on learning activities and self-assessment questions

Feedback on learning activity 12.1

This is a challenging task as it forces you to think about what 'best practice' really means and whether every organisation can adopt the same rules. Cox is arguing that best practice differs from one organisation to another, because what works for one will not necessarily work for another organisation. Cox's arguments are based on his view that 'contingent circumstances' determine what the organisation needs to do – and that therefore each organisation's circumstances differ – or, in other words, what is best practice for one organisation, may not be best for another.

Although this view is fundamentally correct, there are many generally accepted guidelines on good practice. The opponents of Cox's view argue that there are several established operational practices that are considered better than others and that because they are better than the others, they are therefore termed 'best practice'. They have many practical examples to support this view.

Both arguments have merits and good students should be able to see beyond the semantics at the centre of the debate.

Feedback on self-assessment question 12.1

Best practice refers to the operational systems, processes and procedures that are best for an organisation, given its specific circumstances and context. Best practice is contentious when it is promoted as a generic 'best-for-all' solution.

Industry practice refers to operational systems, processes and procedures that are generally recognised as standard across a particular industry: there may often be best practice for that specific industrial sector.

Feedback on learning activity 12.2

The potential advantages of benchmarking include:

- significantly reduces waste, rework and duplication
- increases awareness of what you do and how well you are doing it
- process understanding leads to more effective management
- helps set credible targets
- identifies what to change and why
- removes blinkers and 'not invented here' attitudes
- provides external focus
- enables organisation to learn from outside.

12

Feedback on self-assessment question 12.2

Organisations compare themselves with each other for several reasons. These could be to:

- become more competitive
- maintain market position and share
- keep up with innovation
- develop true measures of productivity
- establish effective goals and objectives
- develop industry best practices
- define customer requirements
- remove insular attitudes and behaviour within the organisation
- develop objective evaluation processes
- develop systematic approaches to improvement.

Feedback on learning activity 12.3

Internet technology has helped with information sharing, using the internet as a medium for exchanging information and promoting organisations. It also has helped with communications, through e-mail and other messaging services.

You may have identified several specific applications for your workplace and its suppliers, such as e-procurement, hosted web services, e-invoicing and electronic fund transfer, electronic data interchange and so on. Your list will provide a useful revision aid for the CIPS exams.

In each of these examples, the technology has brought automation to administrative tasks and processes. This has had the effect of speeding up the processes and reducing the administrative cost. By removing manual processing, there is less human error and a greater degree of reliability. The use of technology platforms provides a robust audit trail as well as accountable back-up systems.

Although these benefits were available among the better-managed processes, automating them through internet technologies has had the effect of significantly improving their performance. For purchasing, this helped revolutionise the transactional elements of the profession.

Feedback on self-assessment question 12.3

The risks associated with e-commerce include:

- data systems security and fraud risks (such as allowing third parties access to personal information, commercially sensitive data and/or payment information)
- keying and data entry risks (such as incorrect payment amounts or recipient details)
- systems failure and down-time (preventing the systems and processes to be used and therefore causing business disruption)
- systems errors and computer viruses (potentially causing valuable data to be lost irrevocably or confidential data to be exposed through spyware or worming tools).

There is also the issue of set up cost and maintenance, both of which can be considerable if the payback has not been accurately forecast.

Understanding customer needs

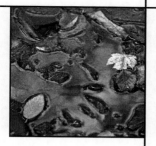

Introduction

This study session introduces the needs of the customer and looks at their impact on purchasing. It observes that there are often multiple customer groups, each requiring their own attention and requirements. This study session will also review the different sources and types of customer feedback, as well as how purchasing contributes directly to serving the customer.

'No customers, no business – no business, no job!'
David Ford (1998)

Session learning objectives

After completing this session you should be able to:

13.1 With examples, identify a range of customer groups both internal and external to the organisation.
13.2 Describe how customer feedback is formulated.
13.3 Outline the ways in which purchasing activity can contribute to customer satisfaction.

Unit content coverage

This study session covers the following topics from the official CIPS unit content document:

Statements of practice

- Recognise the transferability of the fundamental principles of purchase and supply management.
- Appraise the need for different approaches to purchasing in differing organisations and contexts.

Learning objective

2.1 Analyse and explain different types of product and customer requirements.

Prior knowledge

Must cover study session 1 initially.

Resources

Internet access is preferable, but not essential. You may also wish to access a library for further reading and additional studies, but this is neither compulsory nor essential.

13

Timing

You should set aside about 3½ hours to read and complete this session, including learning activities, self-assessment questions, the suggested further reading (if any) and the revision question.

13.1 Customer groups

Learning activity 13.1

List the potential customer groups for the following: a farmer, a university lecturer, a hospital and a water company.

For example, the customer groups of a schoolteacher might include: the parent of schoolchildren, the local education authority, the governors of the school and the pupils themselves.

Feedback on page 179

The above exercise demonstrates clearly that there is rarely just one customer group for an organisation: there are often several. For each of the organisations listed in the learning activity there is a direct customer and one or more indirect customers. For example, the university lecturer has a direct customer in its university and the fee-paying students who attend. But there are also indirect customers in terms of the examinations board and/ or professional institute, as well as the government who gives the university grants and awards.

Arguably some of these indirect customers could also be defined as stakeholders, but since there is a financial supply relationship between the organisation the role is more than just a stakeholder.

Balancing the needs of these different customers can be difficult and create internal tensions for organisations. For example, the farmer mentioned in the above learning activity, may have to supply three different types of customer (the public, food producers and retail customers). In this scenario, the farmer needs to develop different processes for supplying each of the customers. These processes need to consider different forms of marketing, distribution, packaging, logistics, volumes, payment and quality.

As well as external customers, in larger divisionalised and functional organisations the needs of the internal customer have to be recognised. As with external supply chains, inside the organisation there is a supply chain with different functions providing a service to their counterparts.

Some typical service functions include: finance, human resources (HR), legal, public relations (PR) and information technology (IT). Purchasing should also be considered in this list as discussed in study session 7. Each of these functions provides an internal service to other functions and business units, therefore creating an internal supply chain of services. You will study more about the internal supply chain in study session 19.

One of the important distinctions to be aware of is the differences in perspective between the customer and the supplier. Whereas the supplier is focusing on effectiveness and the efficiency with which it can be delivered, the customer is interested in the effectiveness and quality of the goods/ service delivered. Where the difference of perspectives on efficiency involve cost, this could easily lead to a conflict of interests.

Self-assessment question 13.1

List some of the potential internal customers of an organisation's purchasing function.

Feedback on page 180

13.2 Customer feedback

Learning activity 13.2

List the potential sources of customer feedback in your own workplace.

Feedback on page 180

It has been often said that 'feedback is a gift': even if at the time the nature of the feedback seems unsavoury, the fact that somebody else is sharing their perspective provides a valuable insight.

This is particularly the case with customer feedback: as the quote at the start of this study session states: '…no customers, no business – no business, no job'. Without customer feedback, organisations are operating blindly: they produce their goods and services without the benefit of knowing what their customers really think and run the strong risk of getting it wrong.

It is therefore essential that every organisation actively seeks and gathers feedback on itself and its products or services. As part of its customer relationship management, an organisation needs to develop a systematic method of actively seeking, collating, analysing and understanding feedback from its customers.

Here are some of the generic sources of customer feedback that an organisation might consider.

Market research surveys

These usually comprise customer interviews and/or survey questionnaires that are administered by independent market research agencies on behalf of the customer. The customer may be named, or anonymous, depending

13

on how it is perceived that this may change the results. When surveying members of the public, large numbers are often required to make the data statistically relevant. They need to take account of demographics, geography, wealth and other relevant factors. It should be noted that these types of surveys will be able to assess the perception and consumer awareness of an organisation and its products, because customers and non-customers can be surveyed.

Feedback surveys

Many products and services are delivered with questionnaire surveys for the consumer to complete and return. However, the return rate varies from product to product and only averages 45% across industries. Sometimes organisations employ customer services agencies to solicit feedback through direct tele-marketing in the hope that customers find it easier to talk freely on the phone rather than go to the inconvenience of filling in and posting off a form. The feedback from these sources is restricted to customers who have received the organisation's product or service and therefore is more likely to be specific about the actual purchase.

Focus groups

Focus groups involve members of the public being asked to spend time discussing or giving feedback in groups. They tend to take longer (up to half a day) and be a lot more detailed. Researchers use focus groups to understand customer thoughts and attitudes in depth: they therefore need to select a representative sample of the population. This might be of their current customer base, or their prospective customer base. The attendees of focus groups are usually paid a nominal sum of money to take part.

Trials and market testing

When new products and services are being developed they go through a series of prior tests and assessments to ensure that the launch will be a success. These trials will consider marketing, packaging, pricing and even aspects of functionality, such as colour, taste and appearance. It is essential that organisations really understand what the consumer feels about the product to ensure that it is a success when it is launched on the market.

Sometimes, small samples of the market are tested with the product before a full national launch. For example, Barclays Bank tested the new personal identification number (PIN) systems for its Barclaycard credit cards in the Northampton region of the UK before rolling the process out nationwide. This type of market testing helps to assess what public reaction is going to be and gives organisations an opportunity of adjusting any last minute marketing plans.

Customer relationship management data

In the previous study session the advantages that e-commerce technology has brought to buyer–supplier relationships was illustrated through the development of electronic data interchange (EDI). The same technology is able to gather data about consumer spending for detailed analysis. Electronic point of sale technology allows organisations to know which products are being bought, how much they are being sold for, which part of the country they are being sold and through which retailer. This is very powerful customer data and allows the supply chain to understand the nature of demand far more accurately. Supermarkets have been highly effective in using this information to their advantage over recent years.

Complaints

The final and somewhat obvious source of customer feedback is from complaints. Many organisations develop their own customer complaints systems to capture as much information as possible about the areas where the need to improve. The also hope that, in listening to the customer's complaint, they will be able to respond favourably and win back the customer's loyalty.

Internal customers

Gathering feedback from external customers is clearly of significant benefit to an organisation. Equally, internal functions need to gather feedback from their customers and stakeholders. This is useful for understanding how the function performs, how effective it is and what quality of service it provides. It is always helpful to receive this feedback and to use it to identify areas for improvement.

Some internal service functions produce their own 'service charters' that inform their internal customers how they will respond to situations and what level of service they intend providing. In many ways, these operate like an internal service level agreement, without the contractual underpinning. Service functions use the service charter to monitor and assess their performance on a regular basis.

Self-assessment question 13.2

Identify ways in which a purchasing function could gather feedback from its internal customers.

Feedback on page 180

13

13.3 Purchasing and the customer

Learning activity 13.3

List the services provided by the purchasing function to other functional areas in an organisation.

Feedback on page 180

Although purchasing has a strong external focus, this is almost entirely supply-facing. As the customers of a purchasing function are usually other internal functions, it is easy for purchasing to lose sight of the organisation's customer.

Every activity within an organisation has an impact on the customer; it may not be direct (as in marketing, production or customer services) but most activities are systemic. Or, in other words, the organisation works like a system, whereby its actions and behaviour are all interlinked. Purchasing will therefore definitely have indirect impact on the customer.

Here are some ways in which purchasing may have direct impact on the customer:

- Purchasing buys goods for resale: that is, products that are passed on immediately to the customer without any changes. Examples include retail such as branded goods in supermarkets and (do-it-yourself) DIY stores.
- Purchasing sources goods and services to support a 'value added services' customer offering. This usually takes the form of a 'product wrap': typically a range of additional products and services made available to customers if they buy the principal product. Examples include credit cards and professional subscription memberships.
- Purchasing sources product warranties and/or insurances for the customer from specialist service providers. Examples will include maintenance care cover for electrical goods.
- Purchasing gets invited to be involved in a supply chain audit or development programme, which includes the participation of customers and suppliers within the supply chain.

The indirect ways in which purchasing impacts the customer are more obvious, for example:

- Purchasing has a significant influence on the quality of bought-in goods and components for production.
- Purchasing has significant influence on the delivery lead-times and the service received from suppliers, thus allowing better service through to the customer.
- Purchasing sources suppliers and agencies that work with the organisation to impact the customer (such as marketing, packaging, logistics and IT).
- Purchasing reduces the costs and the risks of third-party expenditure, allowing the organisation to provide better and less expensive products and services for the customer.
- Purchasing is regularly involved in supplier innovation and new product development initiatives that allow the organisation to diversify and add new products to its existing range.

Self-assessment question 13.3

Describe the ways in which purchasing can influence the quality of an organisation's product.

Feedback on page 181

13

Revision question

Now try the revision question for this session on page 282.

Summary

This study session has provided an introduction to the needs of the customer and their impact on purchasing. It has observed that there are often multiple customer groups, each requiring their own attention and requirements. You have studied the different sources and types of customer feedback and also how purchasing contributes directly to serving the customer.

The following study session look specifically at the needs of purchasing directly for the consumer.

Suggested further reading

You could read the relevant sections of Ford et al (1998).

Feedback on learning activities and self-assessment questions

Feedback on learning activity 13.1

Here is a non-exhaustive list potential customer groups for each of the four entities:

Farmer:

- supermarket
- food producer
- general public.

University lecturer:

- students
- university
- professional institute and/or examinations board
- government.

Hospital:

- general public
- government.

Water company:

- the general public
- local shops, schools, businesses, hospitals and industries
- fire service
- government/water regulator.

13

Feedback on self-assessment question 13.1

The customers could be many and various, probably as many as there are other functions in the organisation. Here are a couple of examples you might select:

HR is a customer of purchasing. It requires training, recruitment and staff services to be procured on its behalf. These need to provide the right level of service and meet the required budget levels. Given the specific sensitivity of staff-related matters, the suppliers will need to demonstrate appropriate experience and safeguards in dealing with people matters.

Legal is a customer of purchasing. It requires legal advisers and cost draughtsmen to be procured on its behalf. These services need to have the right levels of experience and technical skill, combined with the right level of service and cost effectiveness.

Feedback on learning activity 13.2

Customer feedback can come from any of the following sources:

- market research surveys
- feedback surveys
- focus groups
- trials and market testing
- customer relationship management data
- complaints
- correspondence (of praise/complaint)
- press and other media
- nominations for recognition (such as awards or prizes).

Feedback on self-assessment question 13.2

Purchasing can gather feedback from its internal customers using the following methods:

- surveys and feedback questionnaires
- 360 degree feedback and appraisal
- purchasing data bases and general ledger
- purchasing 'helpdesk'
- stakeholder relationship management
- regular two-way update meetings
- informal discussions.

Feedback on learning activity 13.3

Purchasing provides the following services to other functional areas in an organisation:

- sourcing of supplies
- establishment of supplier relationships
- supply market/chain information
- supplier information

- commercial advice/guidance
- transactional processing support.

Feedback on self-assessment question 13.3

There are many ways in which purchasing can support the quality of an organisation's product. These include:

- establishing quality assurance procedures with suppliers to increase the quality of bought-in goods, components and services
- pre-qualifying and selecting reliable, quality-conscious suppliers
- reducing lead-times on critical purchases
- sourcing the best quality goods for the allocated budget
- establishing quality control procedures to inspect goods and services, so that defects are minimised
- creating and maintaining effective supplier relations and good communication systems with suppliers to increase the quality of their delivery
- using purchasing's supply market knowledge and working with production to design for quality.

13

13

Purchasing for the consumer

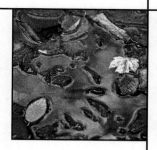

'Any customer can have a car painted any colour that he wants so long as it is black'
Henry Ford, 1909

Introduction

This study session considers the specific needs of the consumer and what it means to purchase 'goods for resale'. Many of the purchasing activities are exactly the same as for any other goods, but with some notable differences about the legislative and regulatory framework.

In this study session you will learn how to differentiate between customers and consumers and identify the key customer requirements in goods for resale. You will also study some of the basic legislative and regulatory frameworks for the protection of consumers as well as the importance of corporate social responsibility (CSR) to consumer confidence.

Session learning objectives

After completing this session you should be able to:

14.1 Explain the difference between customers and consumers.
14.2 Identify the key customer requirements in goods for resale.
14.3 Describe the legislative and regulatory framework for the protection of consumers.
14.4 Explain the importance of CSR to consumer confidence.

Unit content coverage

This study session covers the following topics from the official CIPS unit content document:

Statements of practice

- Recognise the transferability of the fundamental principles of purchase and supply management.
- Appraise the need for different approaches to purchasing in differing organisations and contexts.
- Compare the diverse legal and regulatory environments in which the procurement activity takes place.
- Discuss the ethical implications of purchasing in different contexts.

Learning objective

2.1 Analyse and explain different types of product and customer requirements.

14

Prior knowledge

Should cover study session 1 initially and specifically study session 13 beforehand.

Resources

Internet access is preferable, but not essential. You may also wish to access a library for further reading and additional studies, but this is neither compulsory nor essential.

Timing

You should set aside about 4 hours to read and complete this session, including learning activities, self-assessment questions, the suggested further reading (if any) and the revision question.

14.1 Consumers and customers

Learning activity 14.1

For a supply chain that you are familiar with, identify the respective customers of each tier as well as the ultimate end consumer. What is the difference between the consumer and the other customers?

Feedback on page 192

Consumers refer to members of the public who purchase goods and services for their use and consumption. They represent the end delivery point of most supply chains because they do not sell the goods onwards. There are, of course, exceptions to these rules but in the main this principle holds.

The Dictionary of Finance and Investment Terms defines consumer goods as: '…goods bought for personal or household use, as distinguished from capital goods or producer's goods, which are used to produce other goods. The general economic meaning of consumer goods encompasses consumer services'.

Typically, consumer goods will include: retail items such as clothing, food and branded goods, as well as manufactured items such as cars and electrical goods. Consumer services include utilities, legal services and entertainment, among others.

The differences between consumer goods and producer's goods (sometimes referred to as industrial goods) can be noted in some of the following aspects:

- volumes and order quantities
- marketing and branding
- packaging and presentation of the product

- legislation (see section 14.3)
- payment terms and conditions

Figure 14.1 shows the four different types of buyer–supplier relationship that can exist when supplying consumer goods and producer goods. Most business for professional purchasers is B2B (business-to-business). The examples shown in the diagram illustrate online examples of the type of relationship.

Figure 14.1: Four different types of buyer–supplier relationship

	Business (buyer)	Consumer (buyer)
Business (supplier)	B2B (eg Ford Motors and one of its component suppliers)	B2C (eg amazon.com)
Consumer (supplier)	C2B (eg facebook.com)	C2C (eg e-bay.com)

Self-assessment question 14.1

Explain why it is necessary to distinguish between consumers and customers.

Feedback on page 192

14.2 Goods for resale

Learning activity 14.2

Reflect on your own experiences when buying retail items as a consumer and identify some of your key requirements as a buyer. Try to rank these in priority order.

Feedback on page 192

Purchasing goods for resale has much in common with other types of buying, but there are some major differences too. In the UK, the retail sector accounts for approximately 25% of Britain's gross domestic product. It is therefore essential this sector operates efficiently and maintains low costs. Given that retail does not manufacture anything (as discussed in study session 3), a lot of the cost-base is going to come from the cost of the purchased goods.

Figure 14.2 illustrates the typical retail supply chain, indicating the freedom with which consumers and retailers are able to shop around for the best products to buy. In practice, however, the supply chains are far more complex than this simple schematic. Many retailers have exclusive distribution agreements with key suppliers in an attempt to dominate the market.

Figure 14.2: the typical retail supply chain

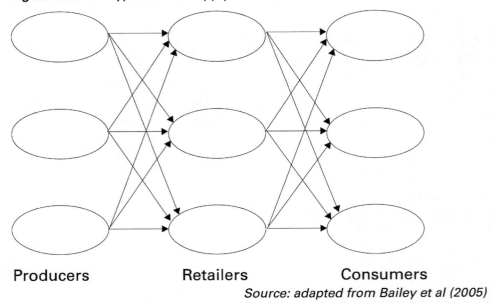

Producers   Retailers   Consumers

Source: adapted from Bailey et al (2005)

All retailers need to plan what they are going to sell: this is referred to as merchandise planning. There are many considerations that retailers have to work through, not least the market, positioning and branding. This is based on the retailing adage: 'what you sell in who you are'. At this level, merchandise management becomes part of the overall corporate planning for a retailer.

Here are some of the considerations involved in merchandise planning:

- range of products (often referred to as the 'product mix'), in terms functionality, quality and price
- understanding the target consumer profile and consumer trends
- changes of tastes and fashion
- mix of branded versus own-label products
- stock and inventory management
- distribution and logistics.

A retailer develops the product mix to maximise the potential sales from each customer. The mix changes over time in line with seasons, tastes and fashions. The merchandiser has to track contemporary themes among the

14

target customer base and ensure that customer feedback is regular and accurate. Typical issues that a merchandiser might consider are:

- Is the product suitable for our store image and brand?
- Is the product appropriate for our target market?
- Where should the product be positioned in the store?
- Can the target market afford the asking price?
- What is the likely demand for this product?
- How readily available is the supply and how scalable is it?
- What are the terms of purchase?

Given the direct link between the products that are bought and the customer's demand, here are some of the specific considerations that a merchandise buyer needs to make:

- Can the supplier meet the delivery requirements for all points of sale?
- How quickly can the supplier vary stock levels?
- How much volume is forecast and how can this be used to lower unit costs?
- When will the supplier need to be paid?
- Is the supplier prepared to lower costs for better shelf positioning?
- Do the products meet the quality and legislative standards required?
- How easy is it to terminate / exit the supply agreement?
- What other products does the supplier have?
- How strong is the supplier's brand when compared with our own?

Own-label products

Many supermarkets and national retail chains now offer their own range of products. In food stores, these are often marketed as 'value' brands: they offer the customer better value for money by giving them the same product for lower cost. These items tend to be volume-related products, where the retailer can buy large quantity orders with regular demand from producers at low cost.

Many producers supply their own branded goods in parallel with non-branded goods (often referred to as 'white-label' goods) to maximise their revenues and maintain efficient factory operations. The white-labelled products may be of a lower specification or lower quality which, while providing a similar functionality, cost considerably less to produce.

In supermarkets, own-labels may include: bread, staple fruit and vegetables, cereals, canned foods and basic frozen foods. Do-it-yourself (DIY) stores are able to provide a wider range of own-label goods because of the non-perishable aspect of the goods, therefore allowing them to source the products from low-cost country manufacturers.

14

Self-assessment question 14.2

Define the term 'white-labelling' and provide an example to illustrate your answer.

Feedback on page 193

14.3 Consumer protection

Learning activity 14.3

Use the internet to identify a consumer welfare association's website for your country and identify the basic rights of consumers, as well as any statutory legislation available to protect consumers.

Feedback on page 193

The legal framework of many countries enshrines the principle of caveat emptor (let the buyer be aware). This places the burden of risk on the customer to establish that the goods are satisfactory before making the purchase: it shifts the power balance in favour of the supplier. However, there have been some significant moves to change this balance of power in recent years.

Since the 1960s, there has been a succession of legislation introduced to protect the consumer and members of the public. These have included the introduction of statutory legislation to increase the responsibilities and accountability of the supplier, as well as the introduction of regulators to specific markets to act in the capacity of a 'watchdog'.

The purpose of this burgeoning legislation has been to protect the consumer from unscrupulous and/or irresponsible practices by the supplier. As competition has increased in retail markets, so has the need for greater control and regulation. In effect the law has attempted strike a balance of responsibility between the consumer and retailer in *proportion* to their ability. The consumer is a member of the public who does not necessarily have full knowledge or technical ability to assess the product at the point of sale, whereas the supplier has had the opportunity to employ professional and technically competent staff to review and assess the goods before placing on the market.

Here are some of the legal requirements of consumer goods.

Safety

It is an offence for a supplier to sell consumers goods – whether new or second-hand – unless they are safe. This does not apply to antiques or to goods that are in need of repair or reconditioning. If new goods are found to be unsafe, then the consumer may have grounds for a legal claim against the manufacturer.

Satisfactory quality

The Sale of Goods Act 1979 (as amended by the Sale & Supply of Goods Act 1994 and the Sale and Supply of goods to Consumers Regulations 2002) requires that goods must meet the standards that any reasonable person would expect, given their description, the price and all other relevant information. In some circumstances, the retailer may be liable for any statement made by the manufacturer about the goods in question.

14

Satisfactory quality includes: the functionality of the goods, their appearance and finish, their safety, the durability and whether they are free from defects and/or minor faults.

Fit-for-purpose

This refers to the intended purpose that goods of this type are generally sold for and the need for them to be produced appropriately. For example, a garden spade is manufactured for digging purposes, so if it bends or breaks while being used to knock a stake into the ground the consumer cannot argue that the spade was not fit-for-purpose.

Goods also need to be fit for any specific or particular purpose made known to the seller at the time of the agreement.

As described

The Sale of Goods Act 1979 (as amended) also requires consumer goods to correspond with any description that is applied to them at the point of sale. If they do not then there may be a case for misrepresentation by the retailer.

No grounds for complaint

The consumer does not have any grounds for complaint if they:

- were told about the defect beforehand
- examined the item when it was bought and was able to see the defect
- bought the item knowing that it was not fit for the purpose they wanted
- did the damage themselves
- made a mistake when buying the item
- simply changed their mind.

Self-assessment question 14.3

Identify the key concerns of a consumer watchdog.

Feedback on page 193

14

14.4 CSR and consumer confidence.

CSR stands for corporate social responsibility. It is a business principle that encompasses ethical trading, social responsibility and environmental sustainability. Although it relates to all aspects of all organisational activities, purchasing and supply has particular emphasis on the practices of external third party suppliers and their contracts with the organisation.

Learning activity 14.4

Using the internet, identify and read the CIPS Principles of CSR document to identify the major benefits of corporate social responsibility.

There is no feedback on this learning activity.

(continued on next page)

Table 14.1 summarises the CIPS Principles of CSR.

Table 14.1

Environmental responsibility:
'We must consider the obligations we have to our surroundings, from local to global.'

Human rights:
'We will honour and observe and not exploit fundamental human entitlements.'

Equality and diversity:
'In our purchasing activities we will commit to improve our organisation's performance in relation to fairness to all.'

Corporate governance:
'Our system of internal and external reporting and responsibility matches our espoused values.'

Sustainability:
'We will proactively promote sustainable practices and products throughout the supply chain without jeopardising future security.'

Impact on society:
'We will add value to the communities and societies upon which our organisation has an influence, either directly or indirectly.'

Ethics and ethical trading:
'All our purchasing activities will be transacted with due regard to the needs and challenges of all involved parties.'

Biodiversity:
'Through our purchasing activities we will proactively avoid reducing the number of interdependent species around us.'

To translate these principles into practical action for purchasers, CIPS has also published the following 'handy hints' for purchasing professionals:

Table 14.2 Handy hints for purchasing professionals

Link to overall CSR policy:	Link with the organisation's overall CSR policy and exert influence on its approach from the supply-side perspective
Align the procurement strategy:	Ensure the CSR sourcing strategy delivers what the organisation as a whole is aiming for and its commitments are entirely practicable within overall existing policies in more general terms, such as value for money or cost reduction
Identify importance:	Identify which aspects of CSR are likely to be important to the organisation overall, and particularly within its supply chain
Get corporate buy-in:	Get high-level corporate buy-in for a CSR policy for the supply side and communicate this to suppliers
Review products for CSR risk:	Review products/services/suppliers for potential benefits or risks from CSR impact, and identify the likelihood and potential impact of risk/reward from each

(continued on next page)

14

Table 14.2 *(continued)*

Prioritise analysis and actions:	Prioritise analysis and action on higher risk/reward areas and the likely impact throughout the supply chain
Balance the impact with strategy:	Balance the CSR impact within the organisation's overall CSR sourcing strategy: for example adjusting risk calculations to account for CSR issues
Involve suppliers:	Involve suppliers in the analysis. If there is a potentially excellent supplier who is poor on a particular aspect of CSR then assess whether it is worth working with them to improve this specific aspect of their business
Rank your risks:	No two organisations will have exactly the same requirements, and therefore a unique risk rank model will need to be developed that encompasses social environmental and economic risks

The benefits of having a robust CSR policy and ensuring that all suppliers are complying with the organisation's standards – especially those who produce goods for resale – are significant for several reasons:

1 The reputation and branding of the organisation are enhanced.
2 Consumers have greater confidence in the values of the organisation and/or product.
3 Consumers have a stronger loyalty and affinity to the brand.
4 There is less likelihood of a lawsuit or public media event causing reputational damage.
5 There are commercial benefits in adopting environmentally sustainable practices such as recycling.
6 The organisation can be viewed as an 'employer of choice'.
7 Suppliers recognise that the organisation will not tolerate unacceptable practices.

Conversely, if CSR is not taken into consideration adequately, the potential risks are considerable.

Self-assessment question 14.4

Identify the risks of a retailer failing to adopt a robust CSR policy.

Feedback on page 193

14

Revision question

Now try the revision question for this session on page 282.

Summary

This study session has looked at the specific needs of the consumer and what it means to purchase 'goods for resale'. Many of the purchasing activities are exactly the same as for any other goods, but with some notable differences regarding the legislative and regulatory framework.

In this study session you have learned how to differentiate between customers and consumers and identify the key customer requirements in goods for resale. You have studied some of the basic legislative and regulatory frameworks for the protection of consumers and also the importance of CSR to consumer confidence.

In the following study sessions several key distinctions are made between types of purchase, with the first of these studying the differences between products and services.

Suggested further reading

You could read the relevant sections of Bailey et al (2005).

Feedback on learning activities and self-assessment questions

Feedback on learning activity 14.1

The customers in the supply chain example you have chosen will be the recipients of the goods or services that they have bought. These goods and services will be used and/or passed on to provide further goods and services to the next set of customers in the supply chain. Where the products are consumed (that is, used up) the customer acts as a consumer. The consumer represents the end delivery point of the supply chain: that is to say, once the goods have been consumed, there is no product to pass on for other customers.

One example of this is from rubber tyre manufacturing. The tyre manufacturers' customers include the automotive assemblers (such as Ford, Toyota and General Motors) and distributors to the after-market. In the after-market, replacement tyres are bought by the public from local garages and repair centres. The public represent the end consumer. Similarly, in automotive production the tyres form an essential component of the finished product which is sold, through dealerships, to the general public as the end consumer.

Feedback on self-assessment question 14.1

Making the distinction between consumers and customers is important for a number of reasons, including:

- the difference in regulatory and legislative frameworks
- the difference in technical understanding, requiring more advice and explanation to be given to consumers
- the difference in payment and credit terms and conditions
- the different buying tends and behaviour, requiring different approaches to marketing and, in particular for consumers, branding.

Feedback on learning activity 14.2

As a consumer, the buyer is interested in ensuring:

- the goods for sale match their stated descriptions
- the goods for sale are fit for purpose (that is they fulfil their need)

- they are safe
- they are of the right quality
- they are the right price.

Although the order may differ depending on what you are buying, the same criteria will still apply.

Feedback on self-assessment question 14.2

White-labelling refers to the practice of manufacturers using their operations to produce non-branded goods for retailers to label with their own-brand.

Examples of white-labelled goods include: bread; ready-meals; basic garden and DIY tools; personal computer (PC) peripherals; stationery items and cosmetics.

Feedback on learning activity 14.3

There are several consumer welfare bodies operating in the UK, including Trading Standards (http://www.tradingstandards.gov.uk), Consumer Direct (http://www.consumerdirect.gove.uk) and the Consumers' Association, more commonly known as Which? (http://www.which.co.uk).

The advice will vary depending on the country. In the United Kingdom, legislation and consumer rights vary slightly between Scotland and the nations of England, Wales and Northern Ireland.

In the UK, consumers are entitled to have goods that are safe, of satisfactory quality, fit-for-purpose and 'as described'.

Relevant statutory instruments in England and Wales include: The Sale of Goods Act (1979, as amended) and the Unfair Contract Terms Act (1977).

Feedback on self-assessment question 14.3

Consumer watchdogs are independent bodies that are established to protect the welfare of the consumer against unscrupulous and/or irresponsible practices by the retailer and/or manufacturer. The consumer is a member of the public who does not necessarily have full knowledge or technical ability to assess the product at the point of sale, whilst the supplier has had the opportunity to employ professional and technically competent staff to review and assess the goods prior to placing on the market.

One of the most well-known consumer watchdogs in the UK is the charity Consumers' Association established in 1957 and publishing regularly under the banner of Which? whose aim is to develop and maintain 'a fair consumer world where everyone makes confident choices'.

Feedback on self-assessment question 14.4

The risks of a retailer failing to adopt a robust CSR policy are as follows:

- the reputation and branding of the organisation is at risk from a potential lawsuit or public media event

14

- consumers may lose confidence in the values of the organisation and/or product
- consumers may lose their loyalty and affinity to the brand
- the commercial benefits of adopting environmentally sustainable practices such as recycling are lost
- the organisation is unlikely to be viewed as an 'employer of choice'
- suppliers do not recognise that the organisation will not tolerate unacceptable practices.

14

Segmentation: direct and indirect purchasing

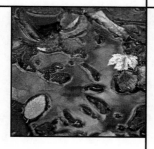

Introduction

The next few study sessions consider different ways of segmenting purchases. These are critically important considerations for a purchasing manager to be aware of, as they help to determine the different contexts in which purchasing is required to act and also the different ways in which specific purchases need to be managed.

This study session segments purchases by the direct or indirect contribution they make to an organisation's primary tasks. You will study the contributions that purchasing can make either directly to the production and operations process, or indirectly to supporting the organisation's overheads and infrastructure. This session also looks at some of the specific requirements of buying commodities and perishable items, as well as the differences of buying for production and buying for stock.

'In practice, ... if a price gets too out of line with world prices it becomes almost impossible to resist the pressure to renegotiate.'
Bailey et al (2005)

Session learning objectives

After completing this session you should be able to:

15.1 Compare and contrast the key characteristics of direct and indirect purchases.
15.2 With examples, describe how raw materials and commodities are purchased.
15.3 Using appropriate examples, explain how the contribution of purchasing impacts the bottom line.
15.4 Describe the key considerations when buying for production vs. buying for stock.
15.5 Describe the key purchasing requirements when buying perishable items.

Unit content coverage

This study session covers the following topics from the official CIPS unit content document:

Statements of practice

- Identify the procurement cycle as it applies to a variety of different organisations and contexts.
- Recognise the transferability of the fundamental principles of purchase and supply management.
- Appraise the need for different approaches to purchasing in differing organisations and contexts.
- Recognise good practice procurement processes and consider how they can be adapted and transferred to other contexts.

15

Learning objectives

2.2 Identify and explain different methods of purchasing.
- Classification of supply chains, tiered supply, managed services and the role of an agent
- The purchasing cycle, its key stages and its relative transferability
- Importance of cross-functional teams, varying cross-functional requirements and the impact of this on purchases
- Methods of purchase:
  - Spot-buying and one-off purchases
  - Long-term supply relationships
  - Framework agreements and call-off arrangements
  - Projects: how scoped, purchased and paid for
  - Low value orders including use of purchasing-cards
  - Typical purchase-to-pay (P2P) methods
- Merits of competitive tendering: the key stages, appraisal and evaluation of tenders, and merits of e-tendering
- Good practice and its application to purchasing including benchmarking
- Consumables
- Call-off orders

2.3 Analyse and explain different ways of purchasing raw materials and commodities.
- Recognise the key differences between direct and indirect purchasing
- Methods of purchasing raw materials and commodity items and key considerations including finance and the futures markets
- Contribution of purchasing to the bottom line
- Purchasing for stock
- Purchasing for production
- Key considerations when purchasing perishable items

Prior knowledge

Study sessions 8 – 12 should be covered before this one.

Resources

Access to the internet is preferable, but not essential. You may also wish to access a library for further reading and additional studies, but this is neither compulsory nor essential.

Timing

You should set aside about 5 hours to read and complete this session, including learning activities, self-assessment questions, the suggested further reading (if any) and the revision question.

15.1 Direct and indirect purchases

The terms 'direct' and 'indirect' refer to the supply chain feeds of goods and services into an organisation. **Direct purchases** are bought from the primary supply chain that flows through the organisation and of which the organisation is a part. For example, a food producer's direct purchases will include ingredients, flavourings and raw foods. **Indirect purchases** are bought from secondary and support supply chains, which help the organisation meet their objectives, but are not part of the operations process themselves. For example, a food producer needs to buy energy, facilities management and maintenance services to support its primary function of producing food.

In retail, the goods for resale represent the direct purchases, whereas the overheads of providing retail premises and all its support functions constitute indirect purchases.

Learning activity 15.1

From your own workplace, draw up a list of direct and indirect purchases to help you distinguish between the two types.

Feedback on page 206

Figure 15.1 outlines the 'value chain' model developed by Michael Porter. It provides a basic analytical framework for organisations to identify where individual business functions add value and costs to their overall operations.

In effect, there are two supply chains. The primary supply chain flows from left to right through the organisation and involves the organisation taking in bought goods and services (inward logistics), transforming them through a value-adding operations process and then selling them onwards (through outbound logistics). These types of purchase refer to direct purchasing (sometimes called supply chain purchasing).

The secondary/support supply chains feed the organisation and are shown beneath the primary supply chain. As well as the internal functions shown (procurement, human resources (HR), technology and infrastructure), they include all the support goods and services required to run the organisation. These types refer to indirect purchasing.

Figure 15.1: The 'value chain' model

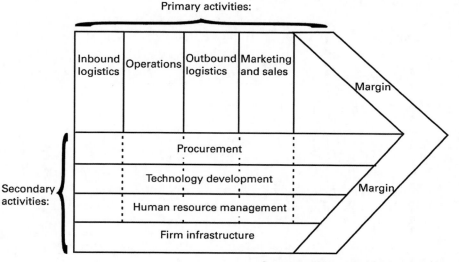

Source: Adapted from: Porter (1985)

The distinction between direct and indirect purchasing is important and has a significant impact on the organisation, hence justifying the need to segment purchases.

In general, direct purchases:

- Have a direct impact on the unit price of the product/goods manufactured by the organisation. If the cost of the direct purchase is lowered, so is the unit price of the out-turning goods.
- Need to have their specification designed and built to fit with other parts, products or components to match the operations process.
- Require specific quality standards that have a direct impact on the quality, number of defects and costs of the out-turning goods.
- Need to be delivered within a specific time schedule and/or lead time to meet the production schedule.
- Sometimes need to be purchased for stock, in order to keep spares available to service fluctuations in levels of demand. Alternatively, they need to ensure that elaborate stockless purchasing and/or just-in-time systems are maintained in order to keep the production process operating.
- Are usually repeated purchases where a relationship is developed with the supplier and the opportunity for two-way collaboration.

By contrast, indirect purchases:

- Impact the general expenses (or 'overheads') of the organisation and therefore only indirectly effect the cost of production if the overhead is attributed to the unit costs.
- Will still need to rely on an accurate specification and quality, but this will have less impact on the production process itself.
- Still need to observe delivery/lead times but, as with quality, there is less impact on the production process itself.
- Do not have such a great demand for stock, because there is less direct impact on maintaining the production process.
- Have a mixture of regular and one-off purchases requiring a range of supplier relations.

Self-assessment question 15.1

With examples, explain what is meant by indirect purchasing.

Feedback on page 206

15.2 Raw materials & commodities

Learning activity 15.2

Using resources from the local library, a quality national newspaper or the internet, identify a list of typical commodities and try to define what a commodity item is.

Feedback on page 206

The main issue when purchasing commodities and raw materials is that of the fluctuating market. Commodities are price sensitive and as a result the price can change rapidly. This gives the purchaser a major challenge, particularly if large quantities are required to support the organisation's production processes.

Here are some of the inherent risks involved in purchasing commodities:

- The price fluctuations mean that there is a risk of buying at too higher a price, when competitors may be buying at considerably lower prices.
- If the commodity is a major component / ingredient of the production process, high prices can have a significant impact on the production costs.
- There is a risk that cost increases of your product cannot be passed on to customers – your market may not be as fluid as the commodity's.
- If the price of the commodity drops significantly, the value of your stock may also drop significantly – potentially giving a balance sheet problem.
- If the price of the commodity increases at a higher rate than your own market price rises, your organisation may have cash flow difficulties (particularly as most commodities required immediate payment).

Table 15.1 outlines some of the major uses of commodities and illustrates the significant impact of price changes.

Table 15.1 Major uses of commodities

Aluminium	Used as a base metal for many manufactured goods, including household items, cars and casing for electrical goods. It is particularly favoured for its relatively light weight compared with other metals.
Cocoa	Used as a base ingredient for chocolate, foods and drinks: one of the most volatile commodities.
Coffee	Used for coffee drinks and other food products: also volatile.
Copper	Used as a base metal, particularly for cabling and wiring.
Cotton	Provides over 50% of the world's clothing materials.
Gas oil	Covers crude oil and oil products and used as the world's primary source of fuel and energy.
Gold	A precious metal that has historically provided one of the indices for currency and foreign exchange: now traded for investment purposes.
Grains	Covers the like of wheat, barley, maize, oats and rye and is used as a staple ingredient of many food products.
Lead	Used for the production of batteries and some limited house building products (such as flashing) because of its malleable qualities.
Nickel	Used to produce stainless steel and other metal alloys.
Rubber	Used primarily for vehicle tyres, but also for clothing, household products and light industrial products.
Silver	Used as an industrial metal but also traded as a precious metal for investment purposes: can be a volatile market.
Soya beans	Because of its high protein content, the soya bean is one of the highest value food commodities. It is used for food products (such as cooking oil) and animal feeds.
Tin	Used as a base metal for manufacturing (such as automotive) and canned products.
Wool	Used as one of the staple materials for clothing and carpets.

The price fluctuations are widely reported: many of the quality national newspapers will report the figures in their financial pages. CIPS publishes

15

commodity price indices in the back of its fortnightly magazine *Supply Management*.

Why the price volatility?

The price fluctuation of commodities is easy to observe in normal everyday domestic life. For example, in supermarkets the prices of fruit and vegetables change with the seasons and, although it is now possible to buy many products out of season, the prices reflect the difficulty that the retailers have had in sourcing them.

Here are some of the main reasons why commodity pricing fluctuates:

- interest rates, such as the minimum lending rate
- currency fluctuations, such as the relative strength of sterling
- inflation, such as the effect of increased material and labour costs
- government policies, such as import controls or stockpiling
- 'glut' or shortage supply factors
- relationships between importing and exporting countries.

One of the main reasons, however, is that of crop harvests, which are heavily affected by weather, seasons and natural events such as plant disease. Good harvests produce over-supply in a market, forcing prices down; whereas poor harvests and crop failures create major shortages and therefore increase prices.

Political and economic stability also play an important role: wars, strikes, riots and revolutions will all destabilise the economy and potentially disrupt harvests.

To combat these fluctuations, the world commodity markets trade prices with each other. A commodities trader will speculate on harvest yields, the market and the prices to make a profit; however, if this speculation is wrong, then a loss ensues. In purchasing, the role of the buyer is to mitigate the risk of fluctuating commodities and to ensure continuity of supply.

For further reading on this complex subject refer to the 'Buying Commodities' chapter in Bailey et al (2005) or to Buckley (1996), both of which are referenced at the end of this study session.

15

Self-assessment question 15.2

Identify four principal factors that influence global commodity prices.

Feedback on page 207

15.3 Purchasing's contribution

Learning activity 15.3

List the ways in which purchasing activities in your own workplace contribute to the overall corporate objectives.

Feedback on page 207

Direct purchases

With direct materials, purchasing is providing an operational service for the production team. The primary supply chain is an extension of the internal production process and purchasing provides the commercial gateway between the two.

This means that there is a very specific and direct impact from purchasing activities. If the supply chain costs are lowered then the overall costs of production are also lowered, therefore giving the organisation additional competitive advantage.

In this case, the contribution of purchasing goes right to the 'bottom line' (that is, the operating profit of the company as calculated in the 'bottom line' of the profit and loss (P&L) accounts). Every pound saved from the costs of materials effectively translates to a pound retained in the business.

Where purchasing initiates a cost reduction programme across all direct materials, there can be a dramatic impact on the overall profitability of the organisation. Many organisations spend between 30% and 70% of their overall production costs on third-party goods and services. A 5% saving on these costs has a significant impact on profits.

For example, a manufacturing company with a £100 million turnover might typically spend £60 million on third-party supplies for production, with £35 million on staff costs and other expenses (such as indirect purchases) and a healthy £5 million profit (5%). If a cost reduction programme on the direct materials can save an average of just 1% (that is £600,000), then the profits have the potential to increase to £5.6 million.

In this above example, a 1% cost saving in direct purchases has increased profitability by 12%. By contrast, if the proportion of costs to turnover remained constant, then to make an equivalent increase in profitability, the company's turnover would need to rise from £100 million to £112 million.

This simple illustration demonstrates the powerful contribution of purchasing to the bottom line of the company. A relatively small saving on costs can create a significant rise in the company's profitability. For some organisations, this could be the difference between making a loss and making a profit: such is the impact of managing third-party expenditure effectively.

Indirect purchases

Indirect purchasing does not have the same direct impact on the costs of production. Nevertheless it does impact the bottom line in similar powerful ways.

Take the fictitious manufacturing company discussed above. It had a turnover of £100 million of which £60 million was spent on direct purchases and a further £35 million on staff and other expenses, leaving a £5 million profit. Supposing the £35 million expenses comprised £15 million staff and internal costs, with the remaining £20 million on third-party indirect spend.

15

This would mean that a 1% cost reduction across all indirect purchases could yield a total saving of £200,000, thus reducing the £35 million expenses to £34.8 million and increasing profit to £5.2 million.

In this example, a 1% cost saving on indirect purchases has increased profitability by 4%.

Types of saving

The contribution of purchasing to direct and indirect expenditure has been illustrated powerfully. In either case, the company in question has reduced its operating costs and therefore increased its profitability.

This example does, however, contain several assumptions that, in practice, may not be quite as straightforward. In particular, it assumes that (1) all savings are automatically cost reductions and (2) the saved money is retained as profit and not spent elsewhere.

Taking this second point first, the issue is one of budget allocation. If purchasing manages a £200,000 cost reduction on indirect expenses, then the company has three choices of what to do with the saving:

1   It can hold on to the saving and keep it as a direct contribution to profits, as the examples have shown. To do this, purchasing needs to work with its colleagues in the finance function to ensure that the saving is removed from the relevant budgets, so that the money is no longer available to spend elsewhere. Many finance departments operate a 'revised annual forecasting' process where budgets are periodically adjusted during the fiscal year.
2   The budget holders can spend the £200,000 on additional goods and services, thereby getting more for their money.
3   The £200,000 saving can be re-attributed to other budgets or to be used as investment finance.

In the last two options, the procurement saving has helped the business with other initiatives. The saving has not directly contributed to the company's profitability.

In effect there are three types of saving:

1   **Cost reduction (P&L)**: the saving reduces the overall cost of a purchase by £x and, as a result, £x is removed from the budget. The saving is seen to directly impact the 'bottom line' of the P&L accounts: profitability has been increased by £x because the saving has not been spent elsewhere.
2   **Cost reduction (non-P&L)**: as above, but where the money is not removed from the budget: it has been kept available for spending elsewhere therefore failing to have an impact on the bottom line. The business still gets a benefit from the saving, but this is seen as getting more for your money rather than a saving itself.
3   **Cost avoidance**: purchasing has made a saving by reducing the impact of an additional cost that would have otherwise been incurred. For example, a supplier raises his/her prices by 3% for the year ahead but, after negotiation with purchasing, agrees to waive the increase this year.

15

In this scenario purchasing has helped the business to avoid the cost of the price rise. It is a saving but has zero impact on the bottom line.

Self-assessment question 15.3

Describe how purchasing can influence and reduce the an organisation's overhead costs.

Feedback on page 207

15.4 Buying for stock

Stock refers to additional materials and goods that are purchased as back up or spare resources. It helps in times of supply shortage or if a supplier has delivery problems, therefore reducing the risk of stopping the production process.

In recent years, holding stock has been seen as a detrimental activity that adds cost to the organisation but little value. As such, the concept of 'stockless purchasing' has become increasingly popular.

Nevertheless, every organisation holds something in stock, even if it just items of stationery.

Learning activity 15.4

Identify the items of stock that are held in your own organisation and the reasons why they are held.

Feedback on page 207

Stock is held for several reasons:

1   Convenience: having items available as and when required without the disruption and nuisance of making special arrangements.
2   Reserves: for fluctuations in sales demand and/or production schedules.
3   Planning mistakes: including over-ordering and so on.
4   Protection: against forecasting errors, inaccurate records and/or unforeseen events (such as supplier failure).

Stock is therefore an essential part of the production. However, there are drawbacks to carrying stock, including:

1   The costs of storage and handling.
2   Tying up working capital.
3   Cost of insurance and the risks of damage.
4   Potential for depreciation in value.

Because of the need to hold reserve quantities but the costs of doing so, the following constructive approaches to stock reduction have been developed:

•   arranging suppliers to deliver on-time, just-in-time to a tightly managed schedule

15

- reducing orders to the most economic quantities
- improving production forecasts
- employing electronic management information systems (such as electronic point of sale (EPOS)) to replenish stock only when items are sold or consumed
- operating flexible approaches to stock levels (such as dynamic buffering) so that stock levels expand or contract in line with market conditions and customer demand
- asking suppliers/distributors to hold stock instead (also called 'vendor managed inventory').

Buying for production is different from buying to replenish stock. Buying for production requires direct links with the production schedules and an accurate feed of demand forecasting. This allows for accurate planning and demand schedules to be communicated to key suppliers. The emphasis is on maintaining a steady *flow* of supply to the operations, as well as getting the right quality and cost. It also requires robust supply chain management to ensure the risks of disruption are minimised.

Where production is not continuous, either in batches or by project, the concept remains the same but, instead of maintaining steady flow, purchasing needs to ensure delivery and lead times meet with the order requirements for production.

Buying for stock does not need the same level of sophistication, although the focus still needs to be on quality and cost. Stock controllers need to monitor supplies and storage to ensure that efficient quantities are ordered at the right time to replenish depleting stock levels. Over-ordering can lead to expensive storage problems, whereas under-ordering can become inefficient and over-administrative.

Further reading on the issues of order quantities and stock control can be found in the chapter on getting the right quantity in Bailey et al (2005).

Self-assessment question 15.4

List the main differences between buying for stock and buying for production.

Feedback on page 207

15.5 Perishable goods

Learning activity 15.5

From your own workplace, identify any purchase items that are perishable over time. In what ways do these items need to be purchased and stored differently to non-perishable items?

Feedback on page 208

The above learning activity outlines several examples of key perishable items, but there are many more. A perishable item is one that will degrade, degenerate or spoil over time. As the quality of the product diminishes, so does its value and its utility, until it reaches a state of no practical use. This might be defined by a specific quality standard, or by a specific timescale. Once this target has been passed, the product cannot be used for its intended purpose: it has to be discarded, unless it can be renewed or used for some other useful purpose.

Because of the perishable nature of these products, the manner in which they are transported and stored becomes a critical element of the purchasing decision. If the transportation and/or storage are managed poorly, then the goods may perish at a quicker rate, leaving the buyer open to greater risk.

These risks are particularly pertinent in the food production industries, where food products need to adhere to strict quality standards. The use of shelf-lives and 'best before' dates is essential, as is the quality control of goods inwards. Many food producers and retailers now use robust pre-qualification and inspection processes on the suppliers' premises to ensure that quality can be maintained. They back this up with rigorous goods inwards quality control to ensure that only products of suitable quality are accepted on-site.

Once on-site, storage of perishable items is an essential consideration. If this is not managed properly, the rate of perishing will be expedited, possibly leading to higher levels of waste and disposal costs.

Given the nature of perishable goods, the impetus for stockless purchasing and vendor managed inventory has increased considerably in recent years.

Other considerations are required for non-food products. For example the Control of Substances Hazardous to Health (COSHH) regulations require a register of all hazardous substances that are kept on-site (including chemicals) to be maintained. Where these substances are perishable and potentially need disposal, a safe procedure is required to fulfil this need.

Self-assessment question 15.5

In what ways can purchasing influence and improve the supply of perishable goods?

Feedback on page 208

Revision question

Now try the revision question for this session on page 282.

Summary

This study session has segmented purchases by the direct or indirect contribution they make to the organisation's primary tasks. You have studied the contributions that purchasing can make either directly to the production and operations process, or indirectly to supporting the organisation's overheads and infrastructure. This session has also looked at some of the specific requirements of buying commodities and perishable items, as well as the differences of buying for production and buying for stock.

The next study session considers a different form of segmentation: by product and service.

Suggested further reading

You could read the relevant sections of Bailey et al (2005), Buckley (1996), Lysons and Farrington (2006) and Porter (1985).

Feedback on learning activities and self-assessment questions

Feedback on learning activity 15.1

Direct purchases will include raw materials, components, parts, sub-assemblies, commodities, goods for resale and subcontract customer-facing services, and so on.

Indirect purchases will include marketing, information technology (IT), professional services, property and facilities, maintenance and repairs, and so on.

Feedback on self-assessment question 15.1

Indirect purchasing refers to the procurement of all goods and services that are required to support an organisation operate, but excludes those required specifically for the production of the organisation's primary goods/services.

An example from insurance is that indirect purchasing includes all the general ledger expenses required to support the insurance company, whereas direct purchasing refers purely to the insurance claims supply chain.

Another example from the automotive industry is that indirect purchasing includes all the support expenditure to maintain the car assembler's business, whereas direct purchasing refers to the procurement of parts, components and sub-assemblies required to assemble the finished car.

Feedback on learning activity 15.2

Commodities include: aluminium, cocoa, coffee, copper, cotton, gas oil, gold, grains, lead, nickel, rubber, silver, soya beans, tin and wool.

In essence, each of these commodity items represent a form of raw material: that is an item that has either been extracted from the ground or grown in its pure state. These products are used as basic ingredients and materials to manufacture many other items of value.

15

Feedback on self-assessment question 15.2

These will include:

1 Political and socio-economic factors in the market.
2 Harvest yields as a result of weather and natural events.
3 Global economic factors such as recession and/or inflation.
4 Currency fluctuations.
5 Trading tariffs and geo-political trade barriers.

Feedback on learning activity 15.3

The contribution of purchasing could be any of the following:

- reduction in costs of direct purchases and lower unit costs of production
- reduction of overheads (for indirect purchasing)
- third-party risk mitigation and management
- improved quality of purchased products and services
- improved lead delivery times
- improved third-party supplier performance.

Feedback on self-assessment question 15.3

Indirect purchases relate to goods and services that are bought from secondary and support supply chains which help the organisation meet their objectives, but which are not part of the operations process themselves. Examples include HR, professional services, legal, marketing and facilities.

Indirect purchases form part of an organisation's overhead costs, with staff costs, rates and tax. Purchasing can reduce the overheads through better management and procurement of third-party indirect expenditure. It can also help educate and advise the rest of the business on the best way of controlling spend with third parties.

Feedback on learning activity 15.4

Items of stock could include:

- key ingredients, spares, components and parts
- maintenance spares
- fuel
- stationery
- marketing and promotional items
- IT peripherals
- cleaning materials
- safety items.

Stock is usually held on fast-moving items that, if they ran out, would seriously disrupt the day-to-day operations of the organisation. The stock is held in limited quantities to keep the cost of storage to a minimum.

Feedback on self-assessment question 15.4

Both buying for stock and buying for production require a focus on quality and cost. However, there are significant differences regarding the planning,

15

logistics and delivery scheduling. Buying for production requires deliveries to meet the production schedule: this can be as a *flow* for continuous production, or in specific deliveries for projects and/or batch production. Buying for stock requires monitoring stock levels and purchasing on demand as the levels deplete.

Feedback on learning activity 15.5

Perishable items could include:

- foodstuffs and ingredients
- chemicals
- fuel
- printing toner cartridges
- some building materials (including resins, paint and some cementitious products).

As the remaining text of this section outlines, perishable items need special storage requirements and closer control on delivery. They also need monitoring while in storage to ensure that their shelf-life does not become exceeded.

Feedback on self-assessment question 15.5

Purchasing needs to buy at the right price, time, quantity, quality and place. For perishable goods, not only is the quality and cost an important issue for purchasing to consider, but so is the delivery and transportation standards.

By exercising appropriate pre-qualification and quality control methods, purchasing can minimise the deterioration of perishable goods. Efficient stockless purchasing methods and vendor managed inventory can also contribute to reducing the added cost of storing perishable items.

Segmentation: products and services

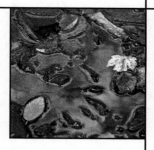

Introduction

Continuing the theme of segmentation, this study session compares and contrasts the essential differences between a product and a service. You will review a series of services that organisations typically purchase, as well as studying the key aspects of specifying and purchasing services. The final section of this study session considers the emerging role of managed service providers.

Session learning objectives

After completing this session you should be able to:

16.1 Compare and contrast the key characteristics of products and services.
16.2 Describe a range of services that most organisations typically purchase.
16.3 Outline the key requirements when specifying a service to be purchased.
16.4 Describe how 'managed services' operate and assess their relative merits from a purchasing perspective.

Unit content coverage

This study session covers the following topics from the official CIPS unit content document:

Statements of practice

- Identify the procurement cycle as it applies to a variety of different organisations and contexts.
- Recognise the transferability of the fundamental principles of purchase and supply management.
- Appraise the need for different approaches to purchasing in differing organisations and contexts.
- Recognise good practice procurement processes and consider how they can be adapted and transferred to other contexts.

Learning objective

2.4 Analyse the differences between purchasing services as opposed to purchasing goods.
- Key differences between a product and a service
- A typical range of services: legal, professional, human resources, advertising and media, facilities management, IT, maintenance repair and operations (MRO) and finance
- Key requirements when specifying a service to be purchased
- Operation and merits of managed services
- Managing service level agreements

16

Prior knowledge

Study sessions 8 – 12 should be covered before this and ideally study session 15 as well

Resources

Access to the internet is preferable, but not essential. You may also wish to access a library for further reading and additional studies, but this is neither compulsory nor essential.

Timing

You should set aside about 4 hours to read and complete this session, including learning activities, self-assessment questions, the suggested further reading (if any) and the revision question.

16.1 Products and service.

What is a service?

Services are difficult to define because of their intangible nature: they cannot be touched or picked up or transported anywhere, yet they have a significant impact on the organisation and its activities that they are provided to.

In 1995, the Centre for Advanced Purchasing Studies in the United States published research that suggested 54% of the third-party expenditure in large organisations was on services (Fearon and Bales, 1995). The trend towards services has increased in more recent years, especially with the growth and popularity of outsourcing.

Learning activity 16.1

Compare and contrast a range of products and services purchased by your own organisation and identify three generic distinctions between a product and a service.

Feedback on page 219

Products and services differ in several ways:

Table 16.1

Services	Products
<ul><li>An activity or process</li><li>Intangible</li><li>Service is produced and consumed simultaneously</li><li>Consumers participate in production</li></ul>	<ul><li>A physical object</li><li>Tangible</li><li>Separation of production and consumption</li><li>Customer may or may not participate in production</li><li>Can be stored</li></ul>

(continued on next page)

16

Table 16.1 (continued)

Services	Products
• Heterogeneous • Perishable (cannot be stored)	

Source: Lysons & Farrington (2005)

In short, there four key distinctions:

1 **Tangibility**: products are tangible, services are intangible.
2 **Separability**: products can be separated from their supplier, services cannot.
3 **Homogeneity**: products are uniform, while services vary at each delivery.
4 **Perishability**: services perish immediately on delivery, products do not.

There are, however, other distinctions:

• Products are relatively easy to specify, because of their tangible nature. However, services are harder to prescribe because of their intangible and heterogeneous nature.
• Products are relatively easy to standardise because production techniques can be mechanised. However, services require a higher level of human involvement and interaction and therefore delivery will differ according to the skill and application of the people involved.
• Buyers can inspect and fully analyse a product before making the purchase, but this is not the case for services.
• Service standards are harder to guarantee.
• Cost analysis (and therefore negotiation) is easier to undertake with products because of their tangible and homogenous nature. Evaluating the cost and the value of a service is more complex.

This said, purchasing services and products still has many similarities: they are not two completely separate activities. For example, the following principles still apply:

1 Services can be segmented, just like any product.
2 Services are bought using the same process steps of the purchasing life cycle.
3 Service spend can still be aggregated.
4 Services can be specified and costed.
5 Services can be measures and assessed.
6 Services suppliers can be rated and/or pre-qualified.

16

Self-assessment question 16.1

Identify four key considerations when purchasing from a service provider.

Feedback on page 219

16.2 Types of service

The purpose of this session is to provide an overview of some of the different types of service that are typically bought by organisations.

Feedback on page 219

Table 16.2 provides a summary description of the main types of service bought by most organisations. There are many other services and specialist activities to add to this list, but these cover the main types.

Table 16.2 Types of service

Service	Description
Audit	Provides check and control service on internal operations by performing independent review (often using external third-party experts). Particularly used as part of corporate governance.
Catering	Provides food and culinary services to staff within organisations. Many organisations now buy-in this service from external third-party specialists.
Cleaning	Provides sanitary, welfare and maintenance to the organisation's premises: part of health and safety practices.
Consultancy	Very broad market that includes wide range of professional advisory services including: strategy, merger and acquisition, change management, business process engineering, project management, outsourcing and organisational development services.
Energy	Includes provision of electricity, gas and oil supplies for lighting, heating and operational plant.
Facilities management	This is an umbrella term referring to any or all services delivered to help manage the organisation's premises. Can include building maintenance, catering, cleaning, security, room reservation and reception services.
Finance and accounting	Includes financial consulting, accountancy, taxation advice, actuarial and financial management advisory services. More recently referred to as 'non-audit' services.
HR services	Range of services relating to the organisational structure, culture and staff. Includes services such as organisational design, payroll, staff benefits, executive compensation, pensions and other staff related schemes.
Legal	Includes range of legislative services such as litigation, claims and disputes, corporate governance, company secretariat, as well

(continued on next page)

16

Table 16.2 *(continued)*

Service	Description
	as commercial and contractual advisory services.
Maintenance	Provides the essential upkeep and repair of the organisation's capital assets, including premises and essential operational plant.
Marketing and advertising	Includes a range of creative design and fulfilment services, such as: branding, market research, creative design, media, public relations and promotion.
Recruitment	Including both permanent and temporary labour fulfilment.
Security	Provision of security services for organisations' staff, premises and assets.
Telecommunications	Data, voice and networking services through cable and mobile technology.
Training	Includes learning and people development activities, including education, training, tuition and coaching through a variety of media.

It is possible to segment these services just like any other purchase. For example, Lysons and Farrington (2005) describe the Hadfield's segmentation of services that are typically purchased by a bank (see figure 16.1):

Figure 16.1: Hadfield's segmentation of services typically purchased by a bank

	Less importance	Greater importance
High-cost services	• Travel • Temporary labour • Construction • PC maintenance	• IT consultancy • Security • Cash operations • Cheque and credit card processing
Low-cost services	• Floristry • Landscaping • Janitorial services • Dry cleaning	• Training • IT hardware maintenance • Mail services • Voice and data network services

Source: adapted from Lysons and Farrington (2005)

Self-assessment question 16.2

Explain why purchasing services is becoming increasingly important in recent times.

Feedback on page 219

16

16.3 Specifying and purchasing services

In previous sections, we have observed the growing importance of buying services and also the greater complexity than purchasing products or goods.

In many ways the principle of specifying and purchasing services is no different to that of products. In essence, the same purchasing life cycle exists for services and products albeit that, because there are specific differences between a product and a service, some of the key stages need to be adapted figure 16.2:

Figure 16.2: purchasing life cycle for services

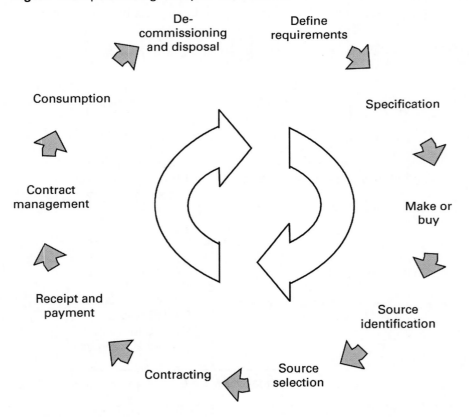

Stage 1: Define requirements

The life cycle starts with the initial identification and definition of need. The business has a requirement and a purchase is required to fulfil it. This represents the initial demand for the service and purchasing has a significant role to play in helping the business define and prioritise the requirements.

Stage 2: Specification

The specification represents the documented statement of requirements. It is the formalisation of the initial need into a technical document that may contain any of the following: a process, a set of technical/quality standards, a methodology or purely a set of deliverables. The specification is used by suppliers to price the need and to check that their service meets the correct technical requirements. Purchasing plays an important role in helping develop the specification by giving critical supply market information and advising on the cost implications of certain specified requirements. This critical stage in purchasing a service is detailed further, below.

Stage 3: Make or buy

The 'make or buy' decision is a critical choice requiring a good understanding of the requirements as well as that of the relative competencies of the market and the organisation. The 'make' decision involves the organisation proceeding to fulfil the need internally through its own internal service provision, whereas the 'buy' decision requires the organisation to purchase from a third party.

Stage 4: Source identification

This stage involves searching and analysing the supply market: it is about identifying suitable and appropriate sources of supply that will fulfil the acceptance criteria of the requirements. This may involve advertising for suitable expressions of interest (such as the *Official Journal of the European Union* for public sector procurement) or other forms of pre-qualification exercise. The purpose is to establish a cadre of suitably qualified and compliant suppliers with which to create a competitive bidding scenario. As expressions of interest are received, so it is purchasing's role to help the business appraise each potential supplier for their suitability.

Stage 5: Source selection

Selecting the source involves identifying the preferred supplier to supply the services required. This may involve inviting the pre-qualified group of suppliers to tender or alternatively requesting proposals from a small number of carefully selected suppliers. A predetermined set of 'order winning criteria' needs to be established to assess the suppliers' propositions. This will involve a range of criteria – not just cost – including: service, quality, innovation, delivery and performance. For service provision, buyers will be looking for confidence that the provider has appropriate experience of delivering this service (or similar) from elsewhere. This may require identifying and examining references from other clients.

Stage 6: Contracting

Stage 7: Receipt and payment

Stage 8: Contract management

These three stages do not differ, whether purchasing services or products. Refer to the purchasing life cycle description in study session 9 for further details.

16

Stage 9: Consumption

Consumption of services takes place at the point of delivery and forms an essential part of the contract.

Stage 10: De-commissioning and disposal

Unlike products, services are fully consumed at the point of delivery and there is therefore no need to 'de-commission' or 'dispose'. This stage is therefore irrelevant for purchasing services.

Specifying services

There are many different names for the specification document required to purchase services. These include: scope of works, statement of requirements, performance specification and a statement of work.

The US Institute of Supply Management defines a statement of work as 'a statement outlining the specific services a contractor is expected to perform, generally indicating the type, level and quality of service as well as the time schedule required'.

Here is a list of the typical contents that need to be included in a scope of works/statement of requirements document:

- Description of the service required, including the objective that needs to be fulfilled.
- Outline of what elements of work are included and excluded in the general 'scope' so that clarity is maintained.
- Detailed description of the deliverables: what, when, where and how they are required, including any specific quality or technical standards.
- Specific conditions that should be fulfilled, including specific standards, methodologies or procedures, as well as specific experience or expertise required of the people involved. This might include a detailed design or a process flow chart, if the service methodology is to be prescribed by the client.
- Timescales: overall deadlines and a breakdown of key milestones.
- The service levels required, including specific measures for each element of service delivery.
- Costings: a description of how the cost of the service is to be broken down into quantifiable components and paid for.

In summary, the specification of the service needs to contain sufficient unambiguous information to allow the supplier to know exactly what needs to be delivered and how the service should be priced.

Self-assessment question 16.3

Identify the key evaluation criteria when assessing a supplier's offer to provide a service.

Feedback on page 220

16.4 Managed services

Managed Services is a relatively new term that applies to a particular method of structuring complex supply chains. In effect, the managed service provider takes on the role of a supply management 'agency' provider by managing the multitude of suppliers in a market and delivering an integrated service/solution to the customer organisation. As a result, the customer organisation has just one interface to manage – with the managed service provider – instead of multiple supplier relationships. The managed service provider is engaged because of the expertise in the given market; they provide the expert management that the customer organisation is unable to fulfil.

There are many examples of this type of arrangement in place. For example, a facilities management company manages all the separate contracts (with cleaners, caterers, security, maintenance and energy providers) on behalf of the customer organisation.

Learning activity 16.4

From the supply-base to your own workplace (or that of an organisation with which you are familiar) identify a managed service provider. Draw a schematic of the supply chain as it exists.

Feedback on page 220

Managed Services are not new – but the terminology has only recently become widespread. In the construction industry, for example, the practice has been in place for decades, where clients have engaged management contractors and prime contractors to manage the contractors and specialist subcontractors and deliver a consolidated construction service. This is illustrated in the figure 16.3:

Figure 16.3: Managed services in the construction industry

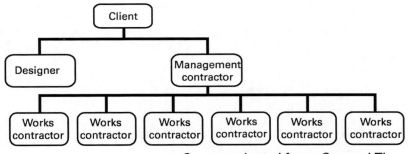

Source: adapted from: Cox and Thompson (1998)

Cox and Thompson (1998) describe the role of the management contractor as one who '…only carries out a management function while the works contractors perform the actual construction operations'. In essence they are describing the function of a managed service provider. They list the tasks of the management contractor as follows:

- programming
- resource allocation

16

217

- logistics
- packaging of works
- contract administration
- liaison with other specialist suppliers
- management and quality control.

In effect, if the management contractor did not provide its service, the client would have to manage all the individual works contractors itself. For some clients, this is not practical as they do not possess the technical knowledge or skills to manage the supply market.

Other examples of managed services include:

- maintenance, repair and operations
- IT (systems integration and outsourced service providers)
- telecoms (voice, data, networking and call centre operations)
- training
- recruitment (permanent and temporary labour)
- marketing (creative, media and fulfilment)
- print (creative design and fulfilment).

Table 16.3 outlines the advantages and disadvantages of managed services.

Table 16.3 the advantages and disadvantages of managed services

Advantages	Disadvantages
1 Uses the expertise of the managed service provider to integrate the multiple suppliers more efficiently (therefore saving both time and cost).	1 Adds extra cost for the management fee.
	2 Tendency to duplicate some aspects of management and administration.
2 More help and advice available for technical issues.	3 Client is one layer removed from the supply market and therefore risks losing market knowledge and expertise.
3 Simpler lines of responsibility (making less).	
4 Devolves responsibility to those most competent to manage it.	4 Managed service provider's liability is often limited to professional negligence.
5 Fewer contractual claims and disputes with suppliers.	5 Client has less control on the process.

Self-assessment question 16.4

Give an example of a 'managed service' and explain how it operates.

Feedback on page 220

Revision question

Now try the revision question for this session on page 282.

Summary

This study session has reviewed the essential differences between a product and a service, as another means of critically segmenting supply. You have reviewed a series of services that an organisation typically purchases, as well as studying the key aspects of specifying and purchasing services. The final section of this study session considered the emerging role of managed service providers.

The next study session continues the theme of segmentation by looking at the essential characteristics of capital versus operational expenditure.

Suggested further reading

You could read the relevant sections of Bailey et al (2005), Fearon and Bales (1995) and Lysons and Farrington (2006).

Feedback on learning activities and self-assessment questions

Feedback on learning activity 16.1

There are several distinctions that can be made, here are some examples:

1   Products are tangible, but services are intangible;
2   Products can be stored and resold, but services cannot be stored or resold;
3   Products can be transported, but services are consumed at the point of delivery;
4   Products are relatively easy to standardised, uniform and repeatable; but services are far harder to achieve this.

Feedback on self-assessment question 16.1

The key considerations need to address some of the risks involved in purchasing services and, in particular, where they differ from products. Specifically these should be:

1   Checking that the service provider can deliver against the service specification.
2   Ensuring all elements of the service are costed transparently.
3   Checking that the service provider uses appropriate processes and standards to standardise (as much as possible) the delivery of the services.
4   The service provider has demonstrable experience of delivering the same service elsewhere.

Feedback on learning activity 16.2

You can use this list as a useful reference point in your studies and your revision. Most organisations buy at least some of the following services: cleaning, energy, telecommunications, security, marketing and advertising, legal, finance and accounting, consultancy, training and human resources (HR) services.

Feedback on self-assessment question 16.2

As noted in the introduction to section 16.1, services account for more than 50% of most large organisations' purchases. This proportion is

16

increasing as more and more organisations outsource business processes. Every outsourced service provider supplies a service and, as the popularity and take-up of business process outsourcing continues to increase, so will the significance of purchasing services.

In addition, many goods and products are now being marketed with a 'service-wrap'. This comprises a range of ancillary services that are included 'free of charge' when a product is purchased. Examples included helpdesks, tutor support, warranties, insurance, extended guarantees and maintenance contracts. While many organisations are offering these additional services as an added-value source of differentiation, they clearly add to the growth of the service industry.

Feedback on learning activity 16.3

There are several ways of specifying services that differentiate themselves from products. These include the use of a scope of works, a statement of requirements and a service level agreement. Other aspects might include specific ways of costing, timing and/or paying for services.

Feedback on self-assessment question 16.3

The key evaluation criteria when assessing service providers will include:

1 Compliance to the statement of works
2 Competence to deliver the service
3 Experience of previously similar services
4 The price and its breakdown
5 Financial stability of the service provider.

Because of the intangible nature of services, many of the above criteria (with the exception of price) are qualitative assessments requiring evaluative measures rather quantification.

Feedback on learning activity 16.4

Not every organisation has managed service providers, but there are several possible solutions. In the event that you had difficulty identifying a managed service provider, read the remaining text in this section to check your understanding.

The schematic will show multiple suppliers in a market supplying to a single supplier [the managed service provider] which, in turn, supplies the customer organisation.

Feedback on self-assessment question 16.4

Several examples were provided in the text including facilities management, construction, IT and telecoms, training, recruitment, maintenance repair and operations, marketing and print.

Managed service providers take on the role of a supply management 'agency' provider by managing the multitude of suppliers in a market and delivering

16

an integrated service/solution to the customer organisation. As a result, the customer organisation has just one interface to manage – with the managed service provider – instead of multiple supplier relationships. The managed service provider is engaged because of the expertise in the given market; they provide the expert management that the customer organisation is unable to fulfil.

16

Segmentation: capital and operational expenditure

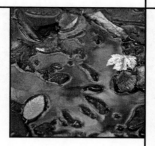

Introduction

This study session concludes your examination of different forms of purchasing segmentation, in which you will consider the basic difference between capital and operational expenditure. Capital items differ from operational purchases because of the complexity of needing to raise investment capital. This study session describes the essential differences between these two types of spend and looks in detail at how investment expenditure is appraised and sourced. Given the fact that most capital goods are large, complex and enduring items of expenditure, the need to understand whole-life costs and the net present value of future expense will also be considered.

Session learning objectives

After completing this session you should be able to:

17.1 With appropriate examples, describe the essential differences between capital and operational expenditure.
17.2 Explain the sources of funding for capital and operational expenditure.
17.3 With examples, explain the concept of whole-life costing.

Unit content coverage

This study session covers the following topics from the official CIPS unit specification:

Statements of practice

- Identify the procurement cycle as it applies to a variety of different organisations and contexts.
- Recognise the transferability of the fundamental principles of purchase and supply management.
- Appraise the need for different approaches to purchasing in differing organisations and contexts.
- Recognise good practice procurement processes and consider how they can be adapted and transferred to other contexts.

Learning objective

2.5 Analyse and explain purchasing and financing capital expenditure items.
- Key differences between operational and capital expenditure
- A range of capital expenditure (CAPEX) items

17

- Financing considerations, including benefit/cost analysis (BCA), investment, return on investment (ROI), break-even, post project appraisal (PPA) and whole-life costing
- Public and private funding initiatives including private finance initiative (PFI), public private partnership (PPP), build-own-operate-transfer (BOOT)
- A simple budgeting cycle
- Economic factors of financing including inflation and interest rates

Prior knowledge

Study sessions 8 – 12 should be covered before this and ideally study sessions 15 and 16 as well.

Resources

Access to the internet is preferable, but not essential. You may also wish to access a library for further reading and additional studies, but this is neither compulsory nor essential.

Timing

You should set aside about 3 hours to read and complete this session, including learning activities, self-assessment questions, the suggested further reading (if any) and the revision question.

17.1 Capital and operational expenditure

Learning activity 17.1

Write a list of capital expenditure items bought by your organisation or an organisation with which you are familiar. What distinguishes them from other expenditure?

Feedback on page 231

In general terms, organisations have two forms of external expenditure: operational expenditure (sometimes abbreviated to OPEX) and capital expenditure (sometimes abbreviated to CAPEX). The distinction forms another critical approach to segmenting supply, and an important one for purchasing functions who need to manage their organisation's spend appropriately.

This distinction is financial and driven by different approaches to financial management. There are however important differences from a purchasing perspective too.

Operational expenditure (OPEX)

Operational expenditure is referred to as 'revenue expenditure' in some financial circles. It relates to day-to-day spend that the organisation needs to perform its everyday operations. It includes most direct and indirect expenditure, as well as most products and services. The term revenue expenditure is used because of the source of funds used to pay for the items: that is, the money comes directly from the revenue of the organisation. Operational expenditure is usually budgeted for on annual budget lines because the spend is regular and/or standardised.

Examples of operational expenditure include: raw materials, professional services, energy, training, marketing, travel, facilities management and maintenance.

Capital expenditure (CAPEX)

Capital expenditure is sometimes referred to as 'investment expenditure' because it is based on the opposite principles to OPEX. In general they are bespoke one-off items that have been custom-made for the client. They are designed, developed and delivered by specialist contractors and in general tend to be high value items, which form part of the company's asset base.

Because of the high value to the organisation – and the fact they form part of the organisation's asset base – they require specific capital investment to purchase; that is, they are not purchased from the everyday operational budgets. Once the investment has been made, the capital asset is handed over to the organisation and added to the balance sheet.

As a general rule, capital expenditure items are regularly serviced and maintained to sustain their value to the company and limit the effects of depreciation. The maintenance is operational expenditure, while the original capital purchase is capital expenditure.

Examples include premises, plant, machinery, heavy equipment, hardware systems and/or infrastructure.

Purchasing (CAPEX and OPEX)

Table 17.1 shows some of the typical differences between purchasing capital and operational expenditure.

Table 17.1 Some of the typical differences between purchasing capital and operational expenditure

Operational expenditure	Capital expenditure
1 Usually the responsibility for the purchase of OPEX is within purchasing's remit: purchasing takes the lead role in the acquisition process.	1 Often the responsibility of other functional areas, such as production or engineering.
2 Paid for from everyday operational budgets that are reviewed and adjusted on an annual basis.	2 Purchasing provides support rather than lead role.
	3 Financing the expenditure is an important dimension: the item is an investment for the organisation.
3 Usually 'standardised' (off the shelf) products or services.	4 Rarely standardised items (unless heavy plant items such as cranes, lifts, pumps and so on)

(continued on next page)

17

225

Table 17.1 *(continued)*

Operational expenditure	Capital expenditure
4 Often paid for in full once delivered.	therefore design and development relatively easy to separate.
5 Items are consumed rather than retained.	5 Often paid for in stages.
6 Little residual value (unless stockpiled).	6 Value is transferred to the balance sheet as an asset.
7 Does not require regular servicing and maintenance.	7 Servicing and maintenance required to sustain the asset's value.

Bailey et al (2005) claim the following list of responsibilities for purchasing's contribution to the acquisition of capital equipment:

- location of sources
- vetting of suppliers
- negotiating
- cost–benefit analyses
- life-cycle costing
- advice on residual values
- organisation of product trials
- establishment of total supply cost
- lease/hire/buy comparison
- contract drafting
- contract management
- provisioning of support materials
- coordination of procurement team.

For further study on the specifics of purchasing capital expenditure items, refer to the chapter on Capital Goods within the recommended text (Bailey et al 2005).

Self-assessment question 17.1

Compare and contrast the key aspects operational and capital expenditure.

Feedback on page 231

17.2 Funding capital expenditure

Learning activity 17.2

Compare and contrast the sources of funding for capital and operational expenditure in your own workplace.

Feedback on page 231

In previous study sessions, you have studied the ways in which purchases are funded and, in particular, the budgeting process that occurs (refer to study session 6). Although this is relatively straightforward for operational expenditure, the process of funding capital goods is more complex, as was shown in section 17.17 of this study guide.

To fund capital expenditure, the following considerations need to be made:

1   How much will the item cost?
2   What is the benefit of having the item?
3   Is there financial justification?
4   When will we receive financial pay-back?
5   What sources of funding are there?
6   Are there any alternative sources of the same benefit?

These first three questions are relatively straightforward. In study session 6 you considered the key components of a business case for investment. The full cost of acquiring the item needs to be calculated and offset against the benefits that it will bring. This process forms part of the feasibility study and comprises the benefit–cost analysis. The benefits need to consider both the tangible and intangible value to the organisation. If the benefits outweigh the costs, then there is financial justification for the investment.

Pay-back period

The pay-back period refers to the length of time needed to recoup the costs of the initial financial outlay: in other words, the time it takes for the newly acquired capital item to make money. In effect this is the time taken for the initial investment to be recovered by the annual inflow of benefits, which is why it is also referred to as the **recovery period**. During the recovery period, the acquisition has not been paid back its initial cash outlay and therefore is operating at a 'loss' for the organisation. However, once the recovery period has expired, the acquisition breaks even and starts to return profits: in effect, the item has been paid for and so all further benefits are 'profits'. Figure 17. illustrates these terms simply.

Figure 17.1: Pay-back period and profits

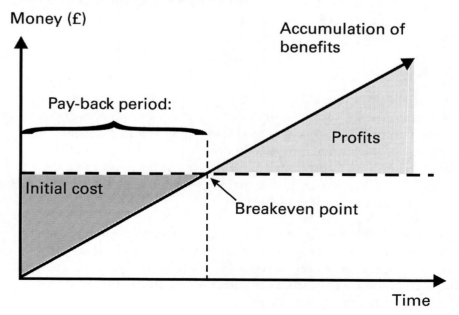

The advantage of the pay-back period method is that accountants and investors know when their purchase will begin to recoup value for the organisation (that is, the breakeven point illustrated in figure 17.1). However, pay-back period is now seen as a one-dimensional approach to appraising financial investment. Its major shortcoming is that it does not take into account the cash flows beyond the initial recovery period and therefore fails to measure the profitability of an investment. This failing is a major oversight, as there is no effective means of identifying the true value of a capital item using this approach.

Financial analysts prefer to use the **discounted cash flow** methods for capital budgeting (namely the internal rate of return and the net present value methods). These methods require the full impact of the costs and the benefits to be accrued over the total life of the asset. The value of the asset is then discounted (at the internal rate of return), so that any future money is adjusted back into today's equivalent worth. This accounts the effects for inflation and the cost of finance in future years. The full worth of the asset is expressed as the **net present value**.

Sources of funding

There are several sources of funding available to organisations investing in capital purchases:

- internal reserves
- loans from financial institutions (for example banks or venture capitalists)
- rights issue (selling of more shares in the company, although this is rarer), for private sector only
- private finance initiative, for public sector
- public private partnership, for public sector.

Alternative options

Given the complexity and expense of purchasing and funding capital expenditure, many organisations explore alternative sourcing options. The two most common alternatives are:

1 Hire.
2 Leasing.

Hiring capital items is the most common approach and is often used for smaller movable items, such as equipment and plant. Examples include excavators, pumps and trailers, amongst many other readily accessible and standard items. The customer pays an hourly, daily, weekly or monthly charge and enters into a rental agreement which, in effect, 'borrows' the item from its owner in return for the charges. Obviously, bespoke items and/or fixed infrastructure is not available for hire.

Leasing is slightly different in that a financial transaction is often required, where the item is leased for a fixed term. Depending on the terms of the lease agreement, the lessee may be required to service and maintain the item. Leasing is common for larger items of capital expenditure such as office suites, warehouses, vehicles and aircraft.

17

With both hiring and leasing, the ownership of the item is retained by the original owner – the asset is not transferred onto the customer's balance sheet – the customer is merely paying for the right to possess and use.

Self-assessment question 17.2

Outline the key funding considerations for investment projects

Feedback on page 231

17.3 Whole-life costing

The concept of whole-life costing is simple: it relates to the total costs incurred by an organisation in sourcing, owning, maintaining and disposing of an item. In short, the full cost of cradle-to-grave ownership.

In general capital expenditure items have large whole-life costs than operational expenditure items because of their longer shelf-life.

Learning activity 17.3

Identify an item of capital expenditure in an organisation with which you are familiar and list all of the costs that have been (and will be) incurred in its lifetime.

Feedback on page 232

Earlier in this study guide, the issue of buying on price alone. The above exercise demonstrates this risk clearly, in that there are many other components affecting the total costs of the goods. In section 9.4, the following 'iceberg' diagram (figure 17.2) (adapted from Bailey et al 2005) was used to illustrate this point.

Figure 17.2: Costs associated with the acquisition of a product or service

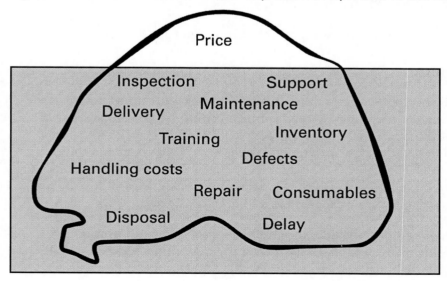

17

To calculate the full effect of whole-life costs, any costs that will be incurred in the future need to be re-calculated into today's equivalent value. This was discussed in the previous section and is referred to **net present value**.

In effect, money spent now costs more than money spent in the future, because of inflationary rises and missed financial investment opportunities. For example, if some capital equipment needed to be serviced at a cost of £10,000, it would be more advantageous to pay for the service next year than this year (assuming the service was non-essential and did not effect performance). To calculate the value of paying costs in the future rather than now, the sum of money needs to be **discounted**.

Discounting is a complex arithmetical process, requiring the analyst to know:

1 the cost
2 which year it will be incurred (that is paid for)
3 the agreed discount rate.

Discount rates vary depending on several economic factors, such as the cost of finance, inflation and other accounting indices. Basically, the higher the discount rate, the less future costs are actually worth.

Many organisations set their own discount rates at specific levels, either to encourage investment or discourage expenditure (depending on the financial policies). For more about discounting and the net present value of capital goods, refer to the recommended text (Bailey et al 2005).

Self-assessment question 17.3

What component costs would you include when calculating the whole-life cost of a commercial vehicle?

Feedback on page 232

Revision question

Now try the revision question for this session on page 282.

Summary

Capital expenditure items differ from operational purchases because of the complexity of needing to raise investment capital. This study session has described the essential differences between these two types of spend and looked in detail at how investment expenditure is appraised and sourced. Given the fact that most capital goods are large, complex and enduring items of expenditure, the need to understand whole-life costs and the net present value of future expense has also been considered.

The study session concludes the examination of different forms of purchasing segmentation. In the next study session, the issues of purchasing across international borders are reviewed.

Suggested further reading

You could read the relevant sections of Bailey et al (2005).

Feedback on learning activities and self-assessment questions

Feedback on learning activity 17.1

Capital items could include: premises, plant, machinery, heavy equipment, hardware systems and/or infrastructure.

In general they are bespoke one-off items that have been custom-made for the client. They are designed, developed and delivered by specialist contractors and in general tend to be high value items, which form part of the company's asset base. As such they often have regular servicing or maintenance to sustain their value.

Feedback on self-assessment question 17.1

Operational expenditure relates to day-to-day spend that the organisation needs to carry out its everyday operations. The source of funds used to pay for the spend comes directly from the revenue of the organisation. Operational expenditure is usually budgeted for on annual budget lines because the spend is regular and/or standardised.

Capital expenditure is based on the opposite principles to OPEX. In general they are bespoke one-off items that have been custom-made for the client. They are designed, developed and delivered by specialist contractors and in general tend to be high-value items, which form part of the company's asset base. As a general rule, capital expenditure items are regularly serviced and maintained to sustain their value to the company and limit the effects of depreciation.

Feedback on learning activity 17.2

Operational expenditure is paid for directly from the revenue of the organisation. It is usually budgeted for on annual budget lines because the spend is regular and/or standard.

Capital expenditure requires specific capital investment to make the purchase; that is, the items are not purchased from everyday operational budgets. Once the investment has been made, the capital asset is handed over to the organisation and added to the balance sheet.

Feedback on self-assessment question 17.2

The main funding considerations for investment projects include:

- How much will the item cost?
- What is the benefit of having the item?
- Is there financial justification?
- When will we receive financial pay-back?

17

- What sources of funding are there?
- Are there any alternative sources of the same benefit?

Feedback on learning activity 17.3

As well as the actual price of the goods, costs could include any of the following:

- costs of sourcing and contracting supplier
- financing charges (if applicable)
- depreciation
- costs of commissioning/implementation (including training)
- testing costs (if applicable)
- operational costs (energy, resourcing, consumables and so on)
- servicing and support
- insurance and warranties (where relevant)
- maintenance
- repair
- de-commissioning
- disposal.

Feedback on self-assessment question 17.3

As well as the price of the commercial vehicle itself, the whole-life costs need to consider the financing charge, road tax (if applicable), fuel efficiency, servicing, training of drivers/operatives and maintenance. The costs of acquisition should also be considered, as well as the costs of disposal.

International perspectives

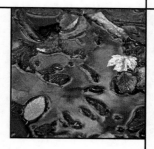

'Successful buying overseas can only be achieved through complete professionalism.'
Alan Branch (2001)

Introduction

This study session reviews some of the key aspects associated with purchasing goods and services across international borders. In particular it looks at the macro-environmental drivers behind globalisation and also the work of organisations such as the World Trade Organization to liberalise international trade. More specifically it focuses on some of the key considerations when sourcing from foreign markets, as well as the role of international standards. Finally, it reviews the contemporary theme of offshoring from a purchasing perspective.

Session learning objectives

After completing this session you should be able to:

18.1 Using appropriate examples, describe international trade regions/zones and international trading agreements. analyse their impact on global trade.

18.2 Identify the key driving forces behind globalisation and describe its influence on world trade.

18.3 Identify the key considerations when purchasing from another country.

18.4 Using examples, discuss the impact of international standards on the purchase of goods and services.

18.5 Appraise the relative merits of offshoring.

Unit content coverage

This study session covers the following topics from the official CIPS unit content document:

Statements of practice

- Identify the procurement cycle as it applies to a variety of different organisations and contexts.
- Recognise the transferability of the fundamental principles of purchase and supply management.
- Appraise the need for different approaches to purchasing in differing organisations and contexts.
- Recognise good practice procurement processes and consider how they can be adapted and transferred to other contexts.
- Compare the diverse legal and regulatory environments in which procurement activity takes place.

18

Learning objective

2.6 Analyse and evaluate the drivers for international purchasing, factors and organisations that affect international trade and the impact on the purchasing function.
- Key drivers for globalisation and standardisation
- The organisations which affect international trade including the World Trade Organization, World Bank, International Chamber of Commerce and European Union
- International trade zones, tariffs and international trading agreements
- Modes of transport and shipping regulations
- Incoterms
- Reasons for sourcing internationally, including market expansion and competitiveness
- Key considerations when sourcing from another country
- Impact of international standards
- Relative merits of offshoring

Prior knowledge

You should read study sessions 1 – 17 as general background knowledge.

Resources

Access to the internet access will be helpful to complete the learning activities in this study session. You may also wish to access a library for further reading and additional studies, but this is not essential.

Timing

You should set aside about 5½ hours to read and complete this session, including learning activities, self-assessment questions, the suggested further reading (if any) and the revision question.

18.1 International trade

Learning activity 18.1

Using the internet, research the background of the World Trade Organization (WTO) (http://www.wto.org) to identify the following:

- the purpose/mission of the WTO.
- the benefits of liberal trade, according to the WTO.

Feedback on page 246

18

Organisations, such as the WTO, aim to free-up world trade from trade barriers on a global scale. On a regional scale, groups of countries or trade blocs have also been trying to lower trade barriers between them and stimulate regional trade. Increasingly, the trade creation effect of regional cooperation is being viewed as an important cause of economic growth.

What is a trade bloc?

There are several different types of trade bloc:

1 **Free trade areas**: such as the North American Free Trade Area (NAFTA), the Asia Pacific Economic Cooperation (APEC) and the Common Market for Eastern and Southern Africa (COMESA). Sovereign countries belonging to the free trade area, trade freely among themselves but have individual trade barriers with countries outside the free trade area.
2 **Customs unions**: such as the European Union, where individual countries combine their custom and trade policies and are no longer fully autonomous in their ability to select their own policy. These areas employ a common external tariff to all imports outside the customs union, but no tariff between those within the union.
3 **Common market**: this trading bloc is a customs union that has, in addition, the free movement of factors of production, such as labour or capital, between its member countries. One example of this is Mercosur in South America.
4 **Economic union**: this is a form of customs union where the level of integration is further developed and member countries adopt common economic policies, such as the Common Agricultural Policy in the European Union. They also may have fixed exchange rates or even be further integrated with a single common currency.

What are trade barriers?

There are many different forms of trade barrier but, put simply, they refer to financial levies, charges and/or penalties that are added to imported goods resulting in a higher cost for the buyer. The effect of trade barriers is to make foreign imports less competitive (because they cost more) and therefore protect domestic industry. This is another form of **protectionism**, discussed in study session 2.

A further form of trade barrier is that of the 'quota': a restriction on the quantity of goods that can be imported from a country. This has the effect of limiting production (because the market demand is curbed) and therefore prevents markets from being flooded with inexpensive foreign produce.

Other forms of trade barrier include the operation of 'intervention prices' where trading blocs fix a minimum price threshold for goods. The presence of this de minimus pricing serves to protect the welfare of domestic producers.

As an example, Cox et al (2002) describe the European Union's quota system for sugar imports as follows: 'Each Member State is allocated an A

18

quota and a B quota, which it must then distribute between its processors. The difference between the A and B quotas relates to a system of production levies that the processors must pay to help finance the cost of disposing of any surplus production. Quota A sugar incurs a levy of around 2%. The quota B levy is much higher, usually in the order of 38%'. They go on to describe how recent WTO trade negotiations (the Uruguay round) have changed the rules for sugar imports and that this is having the effect of reducing the degree of protection enjoyed by EU sugar producers. They conclude that, as a result, the survival of the sugar import merchants has been guaranteed, albeit at the increasingly vulnerability of domestic production.

Liberalisation of trade

There are three governing economic principles supporting 'free' [unrestricted] trade:

1   The **static price effect** suggests that, in the short-term, suppliers hold to their prices and the lowest-price bidder in an open international market wins the contract.
2   The **competition effect** suggests that, in the medium term, competition will begin to increase as other suppliers begin to push down their prices and become more competitive as a result of losing out to the static pricing effect. This lowers markets pricing and offers greater efficiency for the public purse.
3   The **restructuring effect** suggests that, in the longer term, there is a fundamental restructuring within key industrial sectors dominated by government purchasing. This results in inefficient suppliers exiting the market, while efficient suppliers gain market share therefore being able to offer greater economies of scale.

These economic principles helped to support the establishment of the EU public procurement directives, with a view to:

1   Ending national preferences for public sector and utility contract awards.
2   Assisting with the removal artificial trade barriers.
3   Encouraging greater cross-border trade within member states.
4   Increasing the competitiveness of domestic markets and industries.

World Trade Organization (WTO)

Most of the gains that have been achieved globally in terms of the lowering of trade barriers since World War II are attributable to the multilateral negotiations in the framework of the General Agreement on Tariffs and Trade (GATT) – which has now been subsumed by the WTO.

The WTO is based on the economic principle of the **most favoured nation** (MFN) : that is, that no member of the agreement should give preferential treatment or concessions to another member, without extending the same treatment to all other members. Or, in other words, all members of the agreement should receive the same level of preferential treatment, without prejudice.

The WTO does not discourage regional/preferential free trade agreements, so long as they represent complete (not partial) removal of trade barriers for member countries. On this basis, trade agreements such as NAFTA and the EU are allowed, even though they act as exceptions to the MFN principle.

The advantage of the multilateral process of negotiations facilitated by the WTO is that it allows the opportunity for extensive dialogue and, once agreed, the simultaneous and uniformly implemented lowering of trade barriers among all WTO members. The objective is that, once lowered, the barriers remain permanently lowered.

Table 18.1 gives an overview of the WTO.

Table 18.1 Overview of the WTO

Location: Geneva, Switzerland

Established: 1 January 1995

Created by: Uruguay Round negotiations (1986–94)

Membership: 149 countries (on 11 December 2005)

Budget: 175 million Swiss francs for 2006

Secretariat staff: 635

Head: Pascal Lamy (Director-General)

Functions:

- Administering WTO trade agreements
- Forum for trade negotiations
- Handling trade disputes
- Monitoring national trade policies
- Technical assistance and training for developing countries
- Cooperation with other international organisations

Source: WTO website

Although this is admirable, it does make for extremely lengthy debate between governments. However, the WTO states that there are 10 advantages of this form of discussion and agreement:

1. The system promotes peace among members.
2. Trade disputes are handled in an constructive environment.
3. Standard rules make life easier for all.
4. Freer trade reduces the cost of living.
5. Freer trade provides more choice of products and quality.
6. Trade raises incomes.
7. Trade stimulates economic growth.
8. The basic principles make life more efficient.

18

9   Governments are shielded from lobbying by citizens.
10 The system encourages good government.

For further information on these benefits and the work of the WTO in general, refer to the WTO website: http://www.wto.org.

Self-assessment question 18.1

What are some of the main disadvantages of restricted trade?

Feedback on page 247

18.2 Globalisation

Learning activity 18.2

List three main factors supporting the globalisation of commerce.

Feedback on page 247

One framework for describing the external macro-environment is the PESTEL framework, which accounts for the following environmental factors table 18.2:

Table 18.2 Environmental factors in the PESTEL framework

Political factors:	Includes government stability, taxation policies, foreign trade regulations and social welfare.
Economic factors:	Business cycles, economic trends, interest rates, inflation policy, unemployment and disposable income.
Sociocultural factors:	Population demographics, income distribution, social mobility, lifestyles, attitudes to work and leisure, consumerism, education and cultural issues.
Technological factors:	Research and development, innovation, diffusion, obsolescence, convergence and connectivity
Ecological and environmental factors:	Environmental protection, sustainability, recycling and disposal, energy consumption and biodiversity.
Legislative and regulatory frameworks:	Case and statute, jurisdiction, health and safety, product liability and regulation.

Globalisation refers to the increasing spread of international trade and commerce.

Yip (2003) identifies four key drivers of change that impact on different aspects of globalisation as follows, which are shown in table 18.3:

Table 18.3 Four key drivers of change that impact on different aspects of globalisation

Types of globalisation	Drivers of change
Market globalisation	Similar customer needs. Global customers. Transferable marketing.
Cost globalisation	Scale economies. Sourcing efficiencies. Country-specific costs. High product development costs.
Globalisation of competition	Interdependence. Global competitors. High exports/imports.
Globalisation of government policies	Trade policies. Technical standards. Host government policies.

Source: adapted from Yip (2003)

Self-assessment question 18.2

Using the PESTEL framework, describe the key drivers for change in international trade.

Feedback on page 247

18.3 International purchasing

Learning activity 18.3

In an organisation with which you familiar (either your own workplace or one of your regular suppliers), analyse some of the goods and services that are purchased internationally. List three reasons why they are sourced from foreign markets rather than domestically.

Feedback on page 248

There are many reasons why organisations purchase goods and services from other countries and, in many ways, the purchasing process (life cycle) is no different. This section explores some of the additional considerations that a buyer needs to make when purchasing internationally.

In essence, buyers purchase from foreign markets because it gives them a larger market to source from. The principle of **comparative advantage** applies: that is, the relative differences in competitiveness between the

18

markets in any given countries, making it more attractive to source from a foreign country.

Typical comparative advantages that some countries may have are as follows:

- cheaper sources of labour
- higher skilled labour
- more efficient infrastructure
- greater access to specific raw materials.

Although it may be easier to source from local suppliers who speak the same language and are of the same culture, there are many reasons why international trading is more preferable:

The goods may not be available in the domestic market and it is therefore more beneficial to trade directly with foreign producers than through merchants and importers. One example of this is commodity products that are grown and/or extracted in other countries.

Sourcing from foreign markets gives access to a broader range of technological innovation: for example finished goods from southeast Asia or software development skills from India.

There may be insufficient capacity in the domestic market to produce the quantities required, therefore requiring the buyer to find other markets.

Strategic reasons (such as security of supply) may require the buyer to source from another market, particularly if the domestic market is volatile.

Comparative advantage of some countries may give them a lower cost of production, therefore making their products cost less.

Finally, there may be **countertrade** agreements (see below), requiring the buyer to source goods from one particular foreign market in order to sell-in their own products.

There are several specific considerations that need to be worked through when sourcing internationally. These include:

1   **Communication issues**: this will include language and cultural barriers, as well as different time zones and different approaches to international trade. Technical terminology may also differ from country to country.
2   **Currency exchange**: most currencies are readily convertible from one to another, but there is often a bigger issue associated with the fluctuation in exchange rates. This is particularly an issue if there is a long time delay between agreement of the price and its payment. Even simple items may have a lead time of 60–90 days and, in some economies, this could represent a major change in the cost.
3   **Payment**: transfer of funds internationally can cause issues in itself, particularly as most clearing banks will charge additional fees for such a service. This may require financial services such telegraphic transfer, mail transfer and/or banker's drafts. The net effect is to increase the complexity and cost of each payment transaction and, in some cases, the time taken to receive it.

4   **Legislative frameworks** and regulatory frameworks:: will clearly differ from one country to another and therefore the jurisdiction of the governing law. While many purchase contracts will state which governing law applies, if a 'battle of the forms' issue arises the jurisdiction may pass to the supplier's country. This in turn may have significant bearing on the conditions of contract. Because of this, the International Chamber of Commerce has published its *International Commercial Terms*, known more commonly as **Incoterms** (refer to next section).

5   **Transportation**: international trade may require any or all of the five basic modes of transport (road, rail, air, water and pipeline). Given the distance, cost and, at times, complex logistics involved in trading internationally, transportation becomes a significant factor in the sourcing decision.

6   **Customs**: countries' import and export procedures can be considerably administrative and time-consuming. This administration is essential for countries to police their international borders effectively, but can be very costly and, at times, bureaucratic for foreign trade. This requires specific local knowledge and careful planning to be successful.

7   **Countertrade**: as mentioned, countertrade can form one of the main reasons for sourcing goods from a foreign country. In effect, countertrade is a form of reciprocal trading which is designed to help increase the sales of products in another country. The importer (seller) agrees with its buyer that it shall buy an equivalent amount of goods under a separate agreement. Because the agreements balance each other, there is no net exchange of money, therefore reducing the complexity of the transaction. The countertrade may be made on a variety of political and economic grounds, sometimes with government intervention.

For further study on this subject, you are recommended to read the chapter on Buying Internationally in Bailey et al (2005).

Self-assessment question 18.3

List five potential advantages and disadvantages of sourcing goods from a foreign country.

Feedback on page 248

18.4 International standards

Learning activity 18.4

Using the internet, access the website for the International Organization for Standardization (http://www.iso.org), to identify the drivers behind developing international standards.

Feedback on page 249

18

International technical standards

If there were no standards, we would soon notice. Standards make an enormous contribution to most aspects of our lives, although very often, that contribution is invisible. It is when there is an absence of standards that their importance is brought home. For example, as purchasers or users of products, we soon notice when they turn out to be of poor quality, do not fit, are incompatible with equipment we already have, are unreliable or dangerous. When products meet our expectations, we tend to take this for granted. We are usually unaware of the role played by standards in raising levels of quality, safety, reliability, efficiency and interchangeability, as well as in providing such benefits at an economical cost.

The ISO is the world's largest developer of standards. Although ISO's principal activity is the development of technical standards, ISO standards also have important economic and social repercussions. ISO standards make a positive difference, not just to engineers and manufacturers for whom they solve basic problems in production and distribution, but to society as a whole.

The International Standards that ISO develops are very useful. They are useful to industrial and business organisations of all types, to governments and other regulatory bodies, to trade officials, to conformity assessment professionals, to suppliers and customers of products and services in both public and private sectors, and, ultimately, to people in general in their roles as consumers and end users.

ISO standards contribute to making the development, manufacturing and supply of products and services more efficient, safer and cleaner. They make trade between countries easier and fairer. They provide governments with a technical base for health, safety and environmental legislation. They aid in transferring technology to developing countries. ISO standards also serve to safeguard consumers, and users in general, of products and services, as well as to make their lives simpler.

When things go well – for example, when systems, machinery and devices work well and safely – then it is because they conform to standards. And the organisation responsible for many thousands of the standards which benefit society worldwide is ISO.

Although the ISO has published over 15,000 international standards, currently there are two main standards in the ISO family:

ISO 9000(ISO): quality management systems

ISO 14000(ISO): environmental management systems.

The ISO 9000 and ISO 14000 families are among ISO's most widely known standards ever. ISO 9000 is concerned with 'quality management'. This means what the organisation does to enhance customer satisfaction by meeting customer and applicable regulatory requirements and continually to improve its performance in this regard. ISO 14000 is primarily concerned with 'environmental management'. This concerns what the organisation does to minimise harmful effects on the environment caused by its activities, and continually to improve its environmental performance.

ISO – together with the International Electrotechnical Commission (IEC) and the International Telecommunication Union (ITU) – has built a strategic partnership with the WTO with the common goal of promoting a free and fair global trading system. The political agreements reached within the framework of the WTO require underpinning by technical agreements. ISO, IEC and ITU, as the three principal organisations in international standardisation, have the complementary scopes, the framework, the expertise and the experience to provide this technical support for the growth of the global market.

International Commercial Terms

As mentioned in the previous section of this study session, the International Chamber of Commerce has published a set of international commercial terms (referred to as **Incoterms**). They have been designed in an attempt to establish a standardised language for buyers and sellers who are conducting international business, although not all of them have been universally accepted.

Table 18.5 provides a summary of the key terms.

Table 18.5 Summary of Incoterms

Term	Description	Transport mode
EXW	Ex-Works	All modes
FCA	Free Carrier (named place)	All modes
FAS	Free Alongside Ship	Water
FOB	Free On Board	Water
CFR	Cost And Freight	Water
CIF	Cost, Insurance And Freight	Water
CPT	Carriage Paid To (named place)	All modes
CIP	Carriage, Insurance Paid To (named place)	All modes
DAF	Delivered At Frontier (named place)	Land
DES	Delivered Ex-Ship	Water
DEQ	Delivered Ex-Quay	Water
DDU	Delivered Duty Unpaid (named place)	All modes
DDP	Delivered Duty Paid (named place)	All modes

Source: Bailey et al (2005)

For further information about Incoterms and a full description of their meaning, refer to Bailey et al (2005).

18

18.5 Offshoring

In earlier sections of this study session the comparative advantage of different countries was discussed. Organisations will source from international markets where the labour is cheaper, materials are more plentiful and production is more efficient. In some instances these advantages coincide to make the country's economy ideal for low-cost production and inward foreign investment. As such these economies are referred to as **low-cost countries** (LCCs).

Governments of LCCs often provide tax advantages for multi-national countries to invest production facilities in the country, thus enabling them to take advantage of the low cost labour force. For the country, this is also attractive in bringing employment, skills and investment into the local economy.

Organisations considering taking advantage of these benefits have two choices: they can move their production facilities into the country (just like any other relocation, albeit in a foreign country) or they can outsource their operations to a local provider in the country.

Outsourcing business processes and production operations to service providers in LCCs is referred to as **offshoring**. Typically, LCCs include India, China, Eastern Europe, Mexico and South America, all of which are now providing offshoring services to multinational corporations from Western Europe and North America.

Learning activity 18.5

Case study:

Jenny Budding is the IT Manager for a privately owned company of financial advisers in Yorkshire. The company employs 74 staff, over half of whom are qualified financial advisers who need to be serviced with reliable mobile communication technology to be effective in their job.

Owing to a small accident, Jenny's mobile phone is damaged the day before an important meeting with a supplier in Henley-on-Thames. Jenny knows that the mobile phone carrier operates a 24 hour helpline and that, with their help, she should be able to pick up a replacement phone from a local store in Henley immediately before or after her meeting.

When Jenny calls the helpline she has to wait in an automatic queuing system for over five minutes. When the operator answers the call, Jenny has

(continued on next page)

18

Learning activity 18.5 *(continued)*

difficulty explaining the situation and has to repeat herself several times. There is an awkward time delay between speaking and being heard at the other end and there is also a lot of background noise from other operators. Jenny also has a little difficulty understanding the operator's accent.

Jenny wants to know if there is a suitable mobile phone shop in Henley. The operator has not heard of Henley and asks which county it is in, but Jenny is not sure. Jenny is placed on hold for what appears to be a very long time, until another operator comes on the line when Jenny is asked to repeat her situation from the beginning.

Halfway through the conversation the phone line goes dead for no apparent reason and Jenny realises that if she wants the replacement phone she needs to repeat the process all over again.

Given that Jenny selected the company's mobile phone carrier on the basis of the most competitive deal, how will her experience of this situation influence her views when she comes to renew the contract?

Feedback on page 249

Offshoring is one of the current popular business trends of the US and Western Europe. In effect, business activities are outsourced from the organisation and transferred to a low-cost service provider based in an LCC. The benefits for the outsourcer are as follows:

- lower costs of production
- lower overheads and maintenance costs
- lower headcount
- less working capital tied up in fixed assets
- greater opportunity to focus on value-adding core competencies.

The arguments in favour of offshoring are very similar to those of outsourcing: only the business case is often considerably more compelling. Typical savings can range from 30% to 85% on some products.

The case study above showed some of the perceived risks of offshoring. Not all offshoring experiences these issues, but they are relatively common:

- potential language and communication barriers
- mismatch of cultures and working lifestyles
- high turnover of staff
- low rapport between customer and provider
- outage and connectivity failures
- time delays in speech (applies to call centre operations)
- shortage of key skills
- lack of flexibility to change or adapt agreed processes.

One of the biggest concerns when considering offshoring is the control of intellectual property and commercially sensitive information. A combination of the geographical distance and the cultural gap can undermine the security with which sensitive material is kept. In recent years there have been some examples where intellectual property has been copied

18

within the LCC, resulting in an alternative producer setting up a low-cost competitor.

Many of these risks have led to offshoring being given a bad name – for many of the reasons outlined in the case study learning activity. Indeed, some organisations (for example the Alliance & Leicester bank) now promote the fact that they will not offshore their operations, as part of their drive to attract and retain customer loyalty.

The net effect of these benefits and risks is that organisations need to be very careful about which business processes they choose to offshore. The manufacturing boom of southern Asia has demonstrated that LCCs can produce excellent quality goods for a fraction of the cost of that produced in Western Europe. However, customer-facing operations (such as call centres) will face all the issues outlined. Only the most excellent of language skills and communications technology can ensure customer engagement and rapport is successful over the telephone.

Self-assessment question 18.5

List the main purchasing considerations required when offshoring.

Feedback on page 249

Revision question

Now try the revision question for this session on page 282.

Summary

This study session has reviewed some of the key aspects associated with purchasing goods and services across international borders. In particular it has looked at some of the macro-environmental drivers behind globalisation and also the work of organisations such as the WTO to liberalise international trade. More specifically it has focused on some of the key considerations when sourcing from foreign markets, as well as the role of international standards. Finally, it has reviewed the contemporary theme of offshoring from a purchasing perspective.

Suggested further reading

You could read the relevant sections of Bailey et al (2005) and Branch (2001).

Feedback on learning activities and self-assessment questions

Feedback on learning activity 18.1

The WTO's mission is to improve the welfare of the peoples of its member countries, through establishing an international negotiating forum for governments with the aim of lowering barriers to trade.

18

According to the WTO: 'liberal trade policies — policies that allow the unrestricted flow of goods and services — sharpen competition, motivate innovation and breed success. They multiply the rewards that result from producing the best products, with the best design, at the best price.' Or, in other words, the WTO believes that liberal trade creates economic growth and is therefore beneficial for all.

Feedback on self-assessment question 18.1

Where an economic region or country imposes trade barriers, in effect it is restricting itself to opportunities of international trade. Although on the face of it, this is an attempt to protect its domestic markets, in reality the effect is to reduce and stifle competition.

Here is a list of potential drawbacks:

- domestic markets remain uncompetitive
- domestic innovation is stifled
- the country/region does not benefit from better products and/or lower prices
- foreign countries and regions are likely to impose countervailing measures (that is, to mirror the trade barriers imposed)
- foreign markets remain inaccessible for domestic producers
- domestic markets are restricted to trading only within their borders
- citizens are prone to higher prices and less consumer choice
- economic growth is stunted
- the cost of living is increased.

Feedback on learning activity 18.2

These could be any of the following:

- freer trade and fewer trade restrictions
- growth of information technology and communications
- growth of global media
- increase in international travel opportunities
- increasing international competition
- inception of regional currencies, such as the euro
- improved education
- growth of international standards
- growth of international legislative frameworks
- easier foreign currency exchange
- growth of international logistics networks and capabilities.

Feedback on self-assessment question 18.2

Table 18.4

Political factors	Increase in international travel opportunities. Inception of regional currencies, such as the Euro. Freer trade and fewer trade restrictions. Easier foreign currency exchange.
Economic factors	Increasing international competition.

(continued on next page)

18

Table 18.4 *(continued)*

	Inception of regional currencies, such as the Euro. Freer trade and fewer trade restrictions. Easier foreign currency exchange. Growth of international logistics networks and capabilities.
Sociocultural factors	Growth of global media. Increase in international travel opportunities. Improved education.
Technological factors	Growth of information technology and communications. Growth of global media. Growth of international standards. Growth of international logistics networks and capabilities.
Ecological and environmental factors	Growth of international standards. Improved education.
Legislative and regulatory factors and regulatory frameworks:	Growth of international legislative frameworks. Freer trade and fewer trade restrictions.

Feedback on learning activity 18.3

Reasons for sourcing internationally rather than from domestic markets may include:

- goods can be produced for less cost (because of cheap labour and/or efficient manufacturing capabilities)
- the foreign market may have a better source of the raw material
- the foreign market may have specially skilled labour
- international trade agreements (such as countertrade) may require sourcing internationally
- the foreign market may have more innovative products
- there may be insufficient capacity in the domestic market
- each of these reasons may be sufficient to source from foreign markets, or it may be a combination of all of these reasons which drives an organisation to look beyond its domestic market.

Feedback on self-assessment question 18.3

Advantages include:

1 Cheaper goods.
2 Better manufacturing.
3 More market capacity.
4 Better skills.
5 Bigger market.

Disadvantages include:

1 High transportation costs.
2 Risks of currency fluctuation.

18

3   Countertrade issues.
4   Payment problems.
5   Customs issues.

Feedback on learning activity 18.4

The ISO states that its standards help support:

- facilitation of global trade
- improvement of quality, safety, security, environmental and consumer protection
- global dissemination of technologies and good practices.

Feedback on self-assessment question 18.4

International standardisation is attractive for purchasers for the following reasons:

- provides a common language and product description for commerce
- gives confidence that the purchase will conform to a given quality standard
- allows for simplified cost analysis
- ensures known safety standards
- reduces risk of poor workmanship
- easier to inspect and test for compliance
- simplifies the transaction.

Feedback on learning activity 18.5

Although this case study is fictitious, it easily relates to many commonly experienced scenarios of offshored call centres. Jenny has recognised the attempts by the mobile carrier to lower its cost base and offshore some of its business processes (in this case the helpdesk activities) and as a result it has provided her with a competitive deal in the past. However, this particular level of service is unacceptable and will clearly have a negative impact when she comes to review the contract. The experience may help Jenny to avoid purchasing on price alone in the future.

Feedback on self-assessment question 18.5

The main purchasing considerations when offshoring will include all those involved in any other form of international purchasing (that is communications, currency, payment, legislation, transport, customs and countertrade) as well as some of the following specific issues:

- culture and language barriers
- labour supply (skills, training and turnover)
- technology
- flexibility in the contract for changes.

18

Internal supply

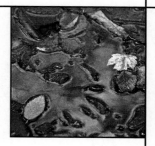

Introduction

This study session reviews the role of internal service providers and, in particular, contrasts the dynamics required to manage performance effectively with those of the external market. One of the most significant issues is that of limited competitive leverage, restricting buyers to a monopoly supply: this is considered in detail.

The study session will review which services are offered internally and consider their merits in relation to an organisation's core competencies. It will also review value chain analysis techniques for identifying the cost and added value of internal function, as well as considering the role and merits of shared service units.

> '...An over-zealous use of [internal] market mechanisms can lead to dysfunctional competition and legalistic contracting, destroying cultures of collaboration and relationships.'
> **Johnson et al (2005)**

Session learning objectives

After completing this session you should be able to:

19.1 Appraise the relative merits of internal versus external supply.
19.2 Using an appropriate theoretical model, describe an internal supply/ value chain.
19.3 Using relevant examples, describe the role of shared service units and outline appropriate measures for ensuring their effectiveness.

Unit content coverage

This study session covers the following topics from the official CIPS unit content document:

Statements of practice

- Identify the procurement cycle as it applies to a variety of different organisations and contexts.
- Recognise the transferability of the fundamental principles of purchase and supply management.
- Appraise the need for different approaches to purchasing in differing organisations and contexts.
- Recognise good practice procurement processes and consider how they can be adapted and transferred to other contexts.

Learning objective

2.2 Identify and explain different methods of purchasing

19

- Classification of supply chains, tiered supply, managed services and the role of an agent
- The purchasing cycle, its key stages and its relative transferability
- Importance of cross-functional teams, varying cross-functional requirements and the impact of this on purchases
- Methods of purchase:
  - Spot-buying and one-off purchases
  - Long-term supply relationships
  - Framework agreements and call-off arrangements
  - Projects: how scoped, purchased and paid for
  - Low value orders including use of purchasing-cards
  - Typical purchase-to-pay (P2P) methods
- Merits of competitive tendering: the key stages, appraisal and evaluation of tenders, and merits of e-tendering
- Good practice and its application to purchasing including benchmarking
- Consumables
- Call-off orders

Prior knowledge

An understanding of study sessions 1 – 7 would provide useful background reading.

Resources

Access to the internet access is preferable, but not essential. You may also wish to access a library for further reading and additional studies, but this is neither compulsory nor essential.

Timing

You should set aside about 4 hours to read and complete this session, including learning activities, self-assessment questions, the suggested further reading (if any) and the revision question.

19.1 Internal and External supply

Learning activity 19.1

From your own workplace (or an organisation with which you are familiar) identify five different functional areas that provide services through internal supply chains.

Feedback on page 262

19

Internal and external supply

Internal supply refers to a service and/or an activity that is provided by an internal function of the organisation, as opposed to a third-party supplier. An example could be the internal print and reprographics team within an organisation. In this example, there are alternative providers in the external market, but the organisation has elected to provide the service from within its own boundaries. This is often referred to as **insourcing**, although the correct meaning of this term is the process by which an external activity is brought in-house.

In theory, organisations do not need large functional departments: virtually every business service and activity can be bought-in from the external market. However, some of the driving factors that compel organisations to provide an internal service are as follows:

- high regular volume, thus securing demand
- scarce resources in the external supply market
- internal costs can be cheaper than the external market
- transaction costs are minimal (no value-added tax, for example)
- high levels of skill and complexity require specialists to be secured
- high levels of confidentiality and market value require the activity to be kept in-house
- keeping the activity in-house maintains control on quality
- the activity is a major source of competitive advantage which needs to be kept in-house.

In 1994, business strategy gurus Gary Hamel and CK Prahalad published their concept of competitive advantage in the modern marketplace based on the control of the **core competencies** of a firm. They argued that firms need to focus on managing and leveraging these resources as the over-riding determinants of success, at the expense of all other functions and activities. The core competence theory became one of the main drivers behind outsourcing, with the view that, if an internal activity is not core, then it should be outsourced.

Hamel and Prahalad (1994) define a core competence as '…a bundle of skills and technologies that enables a company to provide a particular benefit to customers'. Here are their three prerequisites of core competencies:

- **Customer value**: they should 'add value' in the eyes of the customer.
- **Competitor differentiation**: they should be scarce [rare, unique and of value in the market] and difficult to imitate, thus helping the organisation to differentiate itself from others.
- **Extendibility**: they need to be flexible and adaptive to the future needs of the organisation.

The core competence theory flew directly in the face of the concepts of mass production and economies of scale. Although a lot of outsourcing theory has been based on Hamel and Prahalad's work, many organisations still maintain 'non-core' activities in-house. This can be for any of the aforementioned reasons, or simply for reasons of inertia (that is the fact that

19

the sunk and switching costs of outsourcing an internal business process are unviable, even when compared with the benefits of outsourcing).

Internal supply management

Managing internal supply can be fraught with difficulty and political complexity. In reality, however, the process is very similar to that required to manage external supply, albeit with different dynamics at play.

The principal difference between internal and external supply is that of market competition. While external providers are constantly required to compete in the market for their market share, internal providers do not face these threats. In most cases, the organisation dictates that, where an internal service provider exists, the organisation must employ its services.

There are several positive implications of sourcing from an internal service provider and these include:

- Low costs of transaction (no tendering costs, limited contractual costs, no sales/value-added taxes).
- Known entity (the internal provider is an established and known entity of business colleagues).
- Long-term relationship (the internal provider cannot be switched to another supplier and therefore long-term relationships are developed).
- Same culture and values (the internal provider, being part of the same organisation, shares the culture and values: in effect, it is working for the same organisational goals).
- No profit drivers (the internal provider is not set up to make a profit from the rest of the organisation, and therefore is free to focus on providing an efficient service).

So, given all these benefits, why do many organisations experience issues sourcing from internal service providers? The answer lies in the potential drawbacks associated with sourcing from a 'locked-in' supplier over whom there is little or no competitive leverage. These drawbacks include:

- little or no competitive leverage to improve service standards, efficiency and costs
- complacency on the part of the supplier (for reasons of 'lock-in')
- inefficiency on the part of the service provider (because little or no competition)
- little innovation or drive for improvement (again due to a lack of competitive market forces)
- no scale (the internal provider only supplies one customer)
- no experience from elsewhere and therefore all innovation and improvement occurs at limited pace.

In effect, internal service providers are monopoly suppliers supplying to monopsony buyers. There are no effective competitive market conditions and the supplier is locked-in. As a result of these conditions, it is understandable why many organisations find outsourcing an attractive proposition.

19

Self-assessment question 19.1

Appraise the relative merits of sourcing internally rather than externally.

Feedback on page 262

19.2 Value chain

Within any organisation there is a natural hierarchy of functions. As discussed in the previous section, some functions are set up to support the existence of others, whereas other functions are seen as the principal 'value-adding' functions of the organisation.

Every functional activity has a cost associated with it. This includes the staff costs and their associated overheads, such as premises and infrastructure. In addition, each function adds 'value' by bringing a benefit or service to the organisation, which can also be expressed in financial terms. Where a function adds more value in relation to its costs, it is said to be value-adding.

The calculation of added value is a complex procedure, simply because many of the benefits of a function are intangible and therefore difficult to quantify. An internal analysis of an organisation's functional activities will be able to determine which functions add greater value than others, and those that add the most cost.

Learning activity 19.2

From your own workplace (or an organisation with which you are familiar) identify the cost and added value of the purchasing function.

Feedback on page 262

The following diagram outlines the 'value chain' model developed by Michael Porter, which was first introduced in study session 15 to help distinguish between direct and indirect purchases in the organisation. The value chain provides a basic analytical framework for organisations to identify where individual business functions add value and costs to their overall operations.

In effect, there are two types of supply chain in the organisation. The primary supply chain flows from left to right through the organisation and involves the organisation taking in bought goods and services (inward logistics), transforming them through a value-adding operations process and then selling them onwards (through outbound logistics). The secondary/

19

support supply chains feed the organisation and shown beneath the primary supply chain. As well as the internal functions shown (procurement, human resources, technology and infrastructure), they include all the support goods and services required to run the organisation.

It is the secondary/support functions that provide an internal supply service to the rest of the organisation (as shown in figure 19.1).

Figure 19.1: The 'value chain' model

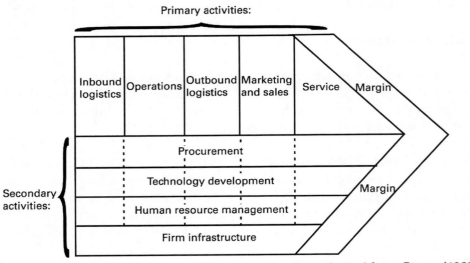

Source: adapted from Porter (1985)

The value chain is a valuable mapping tool used to identify the key financial aspects of each functional activity in the organisation. This provides useful information on each activity and business process. The cost of the activity is compared with the degree of value-add that is given to the end product or service. This can also be compared with the asset base of the organisation to analyse productivity and the return on capital employed.

Porter's value chain is an important strategic analysis tool for the purchasing and supply profession for several reasons:

1   Procurement is identified as a key support activity for the organisation. It is considered to be an essential process for acquiring goods and services to input into the primary activities.
2   Analysing the relative cost and value-add of each activity quickly identifies which activities and business processes are not efficient or effectively carried out. This type of analysis can act as a precursor to outsourcing activities if better services or processes can be found in the external market.
3   Porter used the value chain to link organisations in the supply chain and to analyse the relative costs and value-add of each respective tier. This is called the **Value Network** and provides purchasers with a very powerful value analysis of the supply chain. Refer to Johnson et al (2005) or Porter (1985) for further study in this area.

Table 19.1 outlines an example of value chain analysis taken from the sandwich and coffee retailer Prêt à Manger in the late 1990s.

Table 19.1 Value chain analysis for Prêt à Manger

Firm infrastructure	4%	3%
HR management	3%	1%
Technology	3%	3%
Procurement	3%	<1%
Inbound logistics	<1%	8%
Operations	65%	18%
Outbound logistics	<1%	5%
Marketing and sales	14%	64%
Service	<1%	<1%

Source: adapted from Shepherd 1998

The value chain analysis above is highly informative. For example, it highlights the high costs of production relative to other functions (65% of operational costs). This means that a store's profit margin is likely to be extremely sensitive to any fluctuation in forecast levels. If, for example, a store over-produces its number of sandwiches by 10% or 20% and is unable to sell this excess, then the store incurs a considerable loss in that day's takings (in this case, either –6.5% or –13% respectively).

In this example, the value chain has also been used to illustrate the spread of capital assets. The breakdown shows where Prêt à Manger's working capital is tied up and its heavy investment in sales and marketing (at 64% of asset-base, which includes its high-street retail outlet locations).

Self-assessment question 19.2

In what ways could value chain analysis help support a decision to outsource?

Feedback on page 263

19.3 Shared service units

Learning activity 19.3

With the help of local library or internet resources, define a shared (SSU) service unit and identify an example of one in operation.

Feedback on page 263

The concept of shared services is gaining popularity among multi-location multi-product/service businesses. Under such an operating environment, various common activities are managed by a specific function/business unit for the whole business (in other words, all the operating units).

This is not to be confused with centralisation, because there is no concentration of power in one department. Under a scenario of shared

19

services, individual business units maintain their independence and autonomy while handing over some of the work to be done by specialised internal providers within the organisation. This arrangement could also be viewed as a form of outsourcing, but instead of providing the job to an outside firm, it is allocated to a specialist provider within the business.

The concept of shared services is gaining popularity not only with large multi-national firms; increasingly, large government departments and local government agencies are also moving in this direction.

The main aims of moving into a shared services environment are to:

- enhance corporate value
- focus on partner service and support
- liberate business and operating units to allow them to focus on the strategic aspects of their operations
- transfer business units' non-core activities into shared service units
- create a motivated team that provides consistent, reliable and cost-effective support
- lower costs and raise service levels
- make the best use of investments in technology
- focus on continuous improvement
- harmonise and standardise common business processes to reduce duplication
- maximise the effects of economies of scale.

Surveys on working practices have revealed that the top four reasons for establishing a shared service unit are:

1   better service quality, accuracy and timeliness
2   standardisation of business processes
3   optimisation of working capital
4   reduction in general administrative costs.

Surveys of industry working practices have also indicated the areas that are more commonly managed under a shared services environment. These comprise:

- accounts payable and receivable
- general ledger
- payroll
- financial analysis and reporting
- human resource reporting (compensation and benefits)
- procurement strategy and negotiations
- tax services
- IT development
- legal services
- production planning
- sales forecasting
- print and reprographics.

Traditionally, however, shared services have been concentrated mainly in finance and accounts areas. More recently the trend has been to extend beyond these administrative functions to include other business process activities.

Managing SSUs

Managing the performance of shared service units can be difficult, particularly if there is no competitive leverage to take the business elsewhere. Intra-organisational trading agreements are often established, which operate in similar ways to contracts. However, without financial penalties and the rights of determination and exit, there is still very little effective management control on the out-turning performance of an SSU.

Effective management requires all the standard performance measurement tools (such as key performance indicators, service level agreements and management information reporting), as well as effective stakeholder engagement and escalation. The ultimate threat of determination may not be a viable negotiation tool, but management credibility for the senior manager responsible for the SSU is an emotive issue for improving and maintaining effective performance.

Where an SSU repeatedly fails to deliver, the organisation may elect to review these services in the external market. If the review proves positive, this may lead to outsourcing the business process to a third-party provider, especially given the fact that few SSUs operate core competencies for the organisation.

Self-assessment question 19.3

Identify a list of performance management tools for managing SSUs.

Feedback on page 263

Revision question

Now try the revision question for this session on page 283.

Summary

This study session has reviewed the role of internal service providers and, in particular, contrasted the dynamics required to manage performance effectively with that of the external market. One of the most significant issues is that of limited competitive leverage, restricting buyers to a monopoly supply.

The study session has reviewed which services are offered internally and considered their merits in relation to an organisation's core competencies. It has reviewed techniques for analysing value chains for identifying the cost and added value of internal functions, as well as considering the role and merits of shared service units.

19

The next and final study session of this study guide looks at some of the wider aspects of organisational dynamics and market transactions and, as such, concludes your study of purchasing contexts.

Suggested further reading

You could read the relevant sections of Bailey et al (2005), Johnson et al (2005), Lysons and Farrington (2006) and Porter (1985).

Feedback on learning activities and self-assessment questions

Feedback on learning activity 19.1

There are several functions that provide services through internal supply chains, including:

- human resources (recruitment, staff services and so on)
- learning and development (training and development opportunities)
- IT (provision of technology and networking solutions)
- maintenance (routine maintenance, servicing and minor repairs)
- legal (provision of legal advice and services)
- finance (provision of financial accounting and management)
- purchasing (management and support of third-party expenditure).

Feedback on self-assessment question 19.1

The advantages of sourcing from an internal service provider include:

- low costs of transaction
- supplier is a known entity
- the buyer automatically benefits from a long term relationship
- the buyer and supplier share the same culture and values
- there are no profit drivers requiring one party to make a profitable return from the other.

The potential disadvantages of sourcing from an internal service provider include:

- little or no competitive leverage to improve service standards, efficiency and costs
- complacency on the part of the internal service provider
- inefficiency on the part of the internal service provider
- little innovation or drive for improvement
- no scale to offer the buyer economies and efficiency
- no experience from elsewhere and therefore innovation and improvement occurs at a limited pace.

Feedback on learning activity 19.2

This learning activity demonstrates the difficulty and complexity of calculating the true costs and added value of a functional activity, irrespective of which function is under review.

The costs of a function may be expressed simply as the annual budget, providing there is full recognition of the overhead costs that the function incurs. These will include cross-charges for other support functions (such as HR, finance, legal and so on), as well as other expenses including premises, taxation and infrastructure (such as IT, telecommunications and relevant software licensing). Where the budget does not cover these elements, it does not reflect its true cost of operation.

The added value of a purchasing function is too often reduced to an expression of the cost savings that purchasing activities generate. Although this is an easy financial measure to assess, there are many other benefits of purchasing, including risk mitigation, supply management and regulatory compliance.

Feedback on self-assessment question 19.2

Porter's value chain makes a useful internal comparison of the costs and added value of each functional activity and business process. Where the added value outweighs the cost, there is a potential for a core competence. However, where the costs far outweigh the added value the organisation may wish to consider a market review of the activity to check whether there is a more competitive offering in the external market.

Value chain analysis can help support decisions to outsource by demonstrating that an internal business process is not cost effective or that it adds relative little added value. In either of these cases, the propensity to outsource is increased.

Feedback on learning activity 19.3

Shared services refer to internal services that are provided by one function to a number of others within the organisation. The services offered are shared by each recipient business unit, with the internal service provider's operating unit being referred to as a shared service unit (SSU).

There are many examples of SSUs in large multi-national corporations. For example, many retail banks form an SSU for processing payments. Intelligent Processing Solutions Limited (iPSL) is one of the UK's leading outsourced providers of cheque clearance and payments processing services operating as an SSU for leading financial institutions. It occupies approximately 67% of the UK market share in cheque clearing and comprises a joint venture between Unisys, Barclays, Lloyds TSB and HSBC.

Feedback on self-assessment question 19.3

These could include:

- balanced business scorecard
- key performance indicators
- service level agreements
- management information and reporting
- benchmarking
- conflict resolution schemes and escalation routes.

Transactional activities

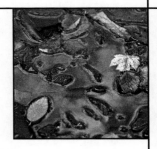

Introduction

This is the concluding study session of this CIPS study guide. In it you will study specific issues associated with organisational transactions and, in particular, the context they set for purchasing. You will review major activities such as mergers and acquisitions and study the work of the Competition Commission in maintaining the competitiveness of the UK economy. You will also review the strategic contribution that purchasing can play in supporting mergers and acquisitions, as well as the merits of consortium purchasing.

'It's not news to anyone that few acquisitions actually benefit the shareholders of the acquiring company...'
Hamel and Prahalad (1994)

Session learning objectives

After completing this session you should be able to:

20.1 Describe the principal organisational transactions.
20.2 Outline the role of the Competition Commission.
20.3 Describe the strategic and operational roles purchasing can play to support mergers and acquisitions.
20.4 Appraise the relative merits of consortium buying.

Unit content coverage

This study session covers the following topics from the official CIPS unit content document:

Statement of practice

- Identify the procurement cycle as it applies to a variety of different organisations and contexts.
- Recognise the transferability of the fundamental principles of purchase and supply management.
- Appraise the need for different approaches to purchasing in differing organisations and contexts.
- Recognise good practice procurement processes and consider how they can be adapted and transferred to other contexts.
- Compare the diverse legal and regulatory environments in which the procurement activity takes place.

Learning objective

1.2 Appraise the different types of private sector organisations and the differing demands that they place on those managing the provision of goods and services including:
- Different forms, including limited companies, plcs and limited liability partnerships

- Formation and cessation of private sector firms
- Regulation of private sector and impact on purchasing
- Impact of profit motive on purchasing activities
- Transactional activity such as mergers and acquisitions (M&A) together with role of the Competition Commission
- Specific types of private sector organisations and influences on purchasing function:
  - Manufacturing
  - Engineering
  - Fast moving consumer goods (FMCG)
  - Retail
  - Technology
  - Services

Prior knowledge

You need to cover study sessions 1 – 5 to fulfil the background requirements for this session but, as this represents the concluding study session of this guide, it will be helpful to conclude your studies with this specific study session.

Resources

Access to the internet is preferable, but not essential. You may also wish to access a library for further reading and additional studies, but this is neither compulsory nor essential.

Timing

You should set aside about 4½ hours to read and complete this session, including learning activities, self-assessment questions, the suggested further reading (if any) and the revision question.

20.1 Organisational transactions

The term 'transactional activity' takes on a completely different meaning at the level of corporate strategy. For purchasing, a transaction usually refers to the commercial exchange associated with acquiring goods and services (in terms of the contract and payment). In corporate strategy, transactions refer to the acquisition: (or disposal) of corporate resources, namely through acquisition and/or merger.

Learning activity 20.1

Using the internet, identify a current acquisition or merger: that is being discussed in the financial news (try www.ft.com for example). Having completed your research into the subject, prepare a list of the perceived

(continued on next page)

advantages and disadvantages with the acquisition/merger that are being discussed.

Feedback on page 276

There are three principal forms of organisational transaction:

1 **Acquisition**: where the owners of a company decide to buy the ownership of another, thereby integrating the newly bought company into the existing to form a single entity. An example is the acquisition of the UK mobile phone company O2 by the Spanish telecommunications company Telefónica in late 2005.
2 **Merger**: where the owners of two separate companies agree to integrate their resources and form a single entity. An example is the formation of the insurer CGU by the merging of Commercial Union and General Accident in 1998. CGU subsequently merged with Norwich Union in 2000 to form Aviva.
3 **Strategic alliance** (or joint venture): where the owners of two separate companies agree to establish a long-term strategic relationship but still keep their separate entities, such as Renault and Nissan. Some joint ventures form a separate (third) entity for the specific operation of the agreement. For example, PSA Peugeot-Citroën has several joint ventures with other automotive manufacturers for the development and production of its range of cars. One example is TPCA in the Czech Republic, which is a joint venture between Toyota and PSA Peugeot-Citroën.

There are many different motives driving a strategy to acquire or merge with another corporate entity. Without doubt, acquisition and/or mergers are large complex activities involving considerable change and transformation. The degree of change is fundamental, comprising significant investment in terms of time, money and resources. Given this, there have to be compelling reasons to proceed with such a strategy.

Johnson et al (2005) describe three potential motives for acquisition and merger:

1 environmental change
2 capability motives
3 expectation of shareholders.

A change in the macro-environmental conditions can lead a company to decide it needs to acquire (or merge) to keep abreast of the changing situation. This could include:

- **Speed to market**: where an industry is rapidly developing through innovation or new entrants, companies will acquire and/or merge to keep up with developments and/or acquire the skills required to be successful in the future.
- **Competition**: some markets are difficult to enter because the level of competition is high and there are existing barriers to entry. Acquisition allows a company to enter the market by buying its place in the competition.

- **Deregulation**: has been a major driving force behind many merger and acquisitions (particularly utilities) as the operating regulations and barriers to entry have been removed, thus allowing new entrants in.

Capability motives include:

- **Exploitation of core competencies**: where the acquiring company takes control and ownership of key resources and skills required to innovate, make profit and succeed in specific markets.
- **Cost efficiency**: where the acquisition or merger creates economies of scale and synergy by reducing duplicated resources and making the operations more efficient and cost effective.
- **Learning**: where the acquirer takes ownership of another company to learn the secrets of its success and/or to take quick control of its innovation. In effect the acquisition is a far quicker and more effective means of developing these competencies.
- **Access to customers**: an acquisition or merger gives instant access to new and different customer groups and markets.

Finally, expectations of shareholders drive acquisition by:

- **Growth**: shareholders demand increasing growth in terms of value and return on investment for their shareholding. This is particularly so for institutional investors such as banks and insurance companies.
- **Speculation**: the acquisition/merger boosts initial share prices and allows speculative share dealing to make a quick return on their investments in the short term.

Self-assessment question 20.1

Explain why competitors might agree to merge.

Feedback on page 277

20.2 Competition Commission

Learning activity 20.2

Using internet resources, identify the purpose and role of the UK's Competition Commission (you may find http://www.competition-commission.org.uk useful).

Feedback on page 277

The competitive nature of markets has been discussed in detail in study session 8 of this guide. One of the key factors reducing the competitiveness of markets is that of consolidation. Market consolidation occurs where competitors merge and/or there are a significant number of acquisitions – thus reducing the overall number of market players.

20

One of the key risks of market consolidation is the emergence of oligopolies, cartels and/or monopolies – thus reducing the competitiveness and undermining public interest. From a government perspective this risks the health of the domestic economy and the interest/wealth of consumers. In the UK, public bodies such as the Office of Fair Trading and the Competition Commission have been established by the government to monitor such dynamics.

The Competition Commission is an independent public body established by the Competition Act 1998, replacing the Monopolies and Mergers Commission on 1 April 1999.

The Commission conducts in-depth inquiries into acquisitions, mergers, markets and the regulation of the major regulated industries. Every inquiry is undertaken in response to a reference made to it by another authority: usually by the Office of Fair Trading (OFT) but in certain circumstances the Secretary of State for Trade and Industry, or by the regulators under sector-specific legislative provisions relating to regulated industries. The Commission has no power to conduct inquiries on its own initiative.

The Enterprise Act 2002 introduces a new regime for the assessment of mergers and markets in the UK. Under the legislation which the Act replaces, the Commission used to determine whether matters were against the public interest. The public interest test has been replaced by tests focused specifically on competition issues. The new regime also differs from the previous regime where the Commission's power in relation to remedies was only to make recommendations to the Secretary of State.

The Commission consists of 'members', who are supported by staff. The Chairman of the Commission is also a member of the Commission and chairs the Council (the strategic management board). The Council also includes the Deputy Chairmen, the Chief Executive, and two non-executive Commission members appointed to the Council.

Members are appointed by the Secretary of State for Trade and Industry for an eight year term following an open competition. They are appointed for their individual experience, ability and diversity of background, not as representatives of particular organisations, interests or political parties. There are usually about 50 members and, except for the Chairman, they work part-time. There are also specialist panels for specific industries such as utilities, telecommunications, water and newspapers. The utilities panel is the specialist panel for gas and electricity inquiries.

UK government stance on competition

The UK government is committed to promoting competition in the economy by improving the UK's productivity performance and making markets work well for consumers, so as to achieve prosperity for all. The White Paper on Competition in 2001 set out the government's vision for the Competition Commission as a world-class competition authority.

The Competition Commission's contribution

The Competition Commission is an executive non-departmental public body that is independent from government, though wholly funded by the

20

Department for Trade and Industry (DTI). The detailed Management Statement and Financial Memorandum for the Competition Commission are published on the Competition Commission's web site (http://www.competition-commission.org.uk, Competition Commission).

In aiming to become a 'world-class' competition authority, the Competition Commission's activities contribute:

- to an increase in the level of competition in the UK economy
- to the UK's economic performance and productivity in the international economy, where competitive pressures are becoming increasingly global.

The Competition Commission's contribution also makes markets work for consumers. In many cases consumers will benefit from:

- lower prices
- a wider range of choice
- more innovation
- higher quality products and services.

Responsibilities

The DTI has responsibilities for setting the overall policy and legal framework for competition and consumer issues in the UK and for negotiating in the European Union and increasingly internationally. The Secretary of State is responsible specifically for the appointment of Members of the Competition Commission, for the provision and monitoring of its funding and for assessing the Commission's contribution towards the overall DTI targets.

The Competition Commission has statutory powers and responsibilities covering competition issues. It conducts in-depth inquiries into acquisitions, mergers and markets. It makes decisions against the competition tests set out in the Enterprise Act 2002 and, in the event of adverse findings, it decides on appropriate remedies. It also investigates references on the regulated sectors of the economy.

Referrals to the Competition Commission

The Commission may receive references from the Office of Fair Trading or from sector regulators having concurrent powers if they have: 'reasonable grounds for suspecting that any feature, or combination of features, of a market in the United Kingdom for goods and services prevents, restricts or distorts competition in connection with the supply or acquisition of any goods and services in the United Kingdom or a part of the United Kingdom'.

A 'feature' of a market is taken as referring to:

1   the structure of the market concerned or any aspect of that structure;
2   any conduct (whether or not in the market concerned) of one or more than one person who supplies or acquires goods or services in the market concerned; or

20

270

3   any conduct relating to the market concerned of customers of any person who supplies or acquires goods or services.

Like its predecessor, the Competition Commission has the right to invoke penalties and/or a moratorium on the progress of a merger, if market activities are construed as being uncompetitive.

Self-assessment question 20.2

Explain the ways in which restricted competition can cause supply risks and issues

Feedback on page 277

20.3 Mergers and acquisitions

Learning activity 20.3

Imagine you are the purchasing manager responsible for the purchasing function of an organisation which is about to go through a merger. Table 20.1 shows a comparison of your own supply base with that of the counterpart you will be merging with.

Table 20.1

Your supply base	Supply base of merging company
3 suppliers of IT equipment (£2.7m)	2 suppliers of IT equipment (£2.4m)
1 facilities management supplier (£1.4m)	1 facilities management supplier (£1.3m)
2 media-buying agencies (£0.7m)	4 creative agencies (£0.9m)
1 fleet management company (£0.8m)	No fleet management
1 print supplier (£0.4m)	3 print suppliers (£0.6m)
1 travel management company (£0.6m)	1 travel management company (£0.8m)

Describe what opportunities there are for synergy if the merger goes ahead.

Feedback on page 277

Figure 20.1: The main stages in an acquisition or merger

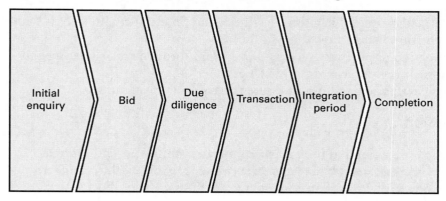

It is extremely rare for purchasing and supply functions to be involved in the merger and acquisition process before the bid has been agreed. This is usually because of the extreme caution that companies place on these activities, where, for confidentiality, only a handful of key personnel in the company have any knowledge of the intention to acquire or merge.

Although it may be inspirational to believe that purchasing staff have appropriate and transferable commercial skills for the acquisition of corporate entities, this is an optimistic view of purchasing's remit and capabilities.

There are, however, two key areas in the transaction process where purchasing and supply can contribute value effectively:

1   the period of due diligence
2   the integration period.

Due diligence

Due diligence is the name given to the period leading up to the finalisation of the transaction, where in-depth investigations, audits, reviews and analyses are undertaken to ensure that an appropriate commercial exchange takes place. Due diligence can last anything from four weeks up to three months, or sometimes even longer for larger and more complex deals. During this period, some of the following activities take place:

- financial analysis to check the accuracy of the accounts and the ledger(s)
- contract review to analyse the value/risk associated with potential transfer of third-party contracts (on both the buy-side and the sell-side), including licensing and rights to use issues
- customer review to analyse the existing customer base and its loyalty
- governance to check for appropriate legislative, regulatory and procedural frameworks
- review and valuation of key assets and capital items
- assessment of the goodwill and other intangible assets in the company
- estimation of potential synergies achievable as result of the transaction
- market analysis to ensure correct valuation
- initial integration planning to assess timescales for integration, key risks and potential dependencies.

Purchasing is able to make a significant contribution to due diligence through supporting the following activities:

1   contract analysis of key risks, liabilities and financial commitments with major suppliers;
2   evaluation of potential synergy and savings through amalgamating and rationalising the shared supply base;
3   stock evaluation and risk assessment across the organisation.

Integration

Once the transaction has been finalised most organisations enter into a period of integration. This is where the two entities physically 'merge' to become one legal entity. Some integration periods are very short (just a few weeks), whereas other integration periods can take 9–12 months to complete. If the merger or acquisition needs to be ratified by a regulator or by government, then the integration period can take even longer. For example, when Barclays Bank plc acquired The Woolwich plc, the deal had to be passed by statute in the House of Commons (the Barclays Group Reorganisation Bill). Legislation of this nature takes a long time, as MPs need to be satisfied that the needs of customers and the general public have been taken into consideration fairly and appropriately.

In effect, the integration period comprises a major organisational transformation, as new functions are established and/or re-organised to accommodate the merged entity. The integration is managed in much the same way as a large change programme, with a dedicated project team, sponsorship and governance.

Typically, the following activities can take place during an integration project:

- departments and functions are amalgamated, often leading to staff having to apply for new or shared positions and sometimes leading to redundancies
- some business activities are terminated
- some staff are re-located and premises sold-off
- staff are re-trained
- some capital assets are stripped and sold-off to raise cash to support other integration activities
- considerable communication is required to maintain effective operational performance within the company, as well as maintaining customer and shareholder confidence
- products and services are reviewed, consolidated and sometimes divested
- the new entity is sometimes re-named or re-branded (particularly after a merger)
- corporate strategy of the newly merged entity is re-evaluated and developed
- new governance, policies and procedures are adopted
- third-party commitments are reviewed and contracts terminated or assigned to the new entity
- rights of third parties (such as licensing and rights to use (RTU) for software and other protected assets) are reviewed and any commercial issues resolved with the third parties concerned
- the supply-base is consolidated and rationalised.

Purchasing can make a significant contribution to the integration period in the following ways:

1   Many integration projects are run by third-party management consultants who are engaged to deliver the anticipated synergy benefits. Purchasing can help by establishing an effective services agreement with the consultancy.
2   The supply base rationalisation project can contribute significant savings through economies of scale. This is usually managed in a series of workstreams, where each workstream relates to a specific commodity or market category of spend.

20

3   All licensing and RTU issues need resolving quickly and efficiently to reduce the commercial exposure of the company.
4   Third-party contracts need reviewing and, where necessary, terminating.
5   Third-party suppliers need accurate and regular communication about the changes, particularly if the changes affect the accounting teams, the address of the company and/or the change of name.

In addition, the purchasing functions of the two former entities need to be reviewed and rationalised, wherever practically possible so that the third-party expenditure needs of the new single entity are satisfied effectively.

Self-assessment question 20.3

Describe the potential benefits purchasing can bring to an organisational merger.

Feedback on page 278

20.4 Consortium buying

Learning activity 20.4

Using an internet search engine, identify an example of consortium buying in either the public or private sector. Describe the activities and purchases that are shared.

Feedback on page 278

Lysons and Farrington (2006) define purchasing consortia as follows:

'A collaborative arrangement under which two or more organisations combine their requirements for a specified range of goods and services to gain price, design, supply availability and assurance benefits from greater volumes of purchases'.

Put simply, a purchasing consortium is an organisational entity that aggregates demand on behalf of its members with the objective of gaining the benefits of purchasing with scale.

Purchasing consortia cover a wide range of industries including both the private, public and not-for-profit sectors (including universities and libraries). The principle behind consortia is that if the group acts as a single unit, then it will have greater purchasing power in many of the supply markets, thus creating greater benefit than each of the members acting on their own.

20

Advantages of purchasing consortia

There are many advantages of purchasing consortia, including:

- All members have the opportunity of benefiting from larger economies of scale, thus increasing efficiency and reducing the costs of transactions.
- Members can share skills and resources and therefore have a greater access to product and/or market expertise.
- Search, pre-qualification and selection costs are reduced as the duplication is eradicated across all member organisations.
- Bulk purchasing allows members to enjoy the benefits of greater leverage in their respective markets – thus increasing cost savings and quality/ service levels.
- Risks are reduced because of the greater purchasing power of the consortium.

Disadvantages of purchasing consortia

- Compliance can become a major issue, as all members have the rights of veto if they do not want to purchase the agreed specification.
- Non-compliance leads to disaggregation of spend and reduced purchasing power, therefore negating one of the major benefits of the consortium.
- Reaching agreement on the method of purchase, the specification and the pre-qualification/selection criteria usually requires considerably more administrative effort because of the need to ensure buy-in from all parties before proceeding.
- The agreed specifications tend to be for standardised products only and therefore tailored or specialist goods are unlikely to be purchased through consortia.
- In the event of supplier failure and/or contract breach, non-affected members of the consortium are unwilling to assume the liabilities of others.
- Some consortia are prohibited under EU provisions (see next paragraph).
- Some suppliers are less attracted to supplying to consortia as they view this type of account as difficult to do business with because of the slow business decisions and the multiple points of purchase.

Consortia in the EU

Some forms of consortia can be viewed as being prohibited by EU legislation. For example, Article 85(1) of the EEC Treaty states that:

'… all agreements, decisions and concerted practices (hereafter referred to as agreements) which have as their object or effect the prevention, restriction or distortion of competition within the common market are prohibited as incompatible with the common market… this applies, however, only if such agreements affect trade between Member States'.

In general, however, the EU welcomes cooperation among small- and medium-sized enterprises where '…such cooperation enables them to work

20

more efficiently and increase their productivity and competitiveness in a larger market'.

Self-assessment question 20.4

Compare and contrast the relative merits of supplying a consortium from the perspective of a supplier.

Feedback on page 278

Revision question

Now try the revision question for this session on page 283.

Summary

This is the concluding study session of this CIPS study guide. In it you have studied specific issues associated with organisational transactions and, in particular, the context they set for purchasing. You have studied major activities such as mergers and acquisitions and reviewed the work of the Competition Commission in maintaining the competitiveness of the UK economy. You have also reviewed the contribution that purchasing can play in supporting mergers and acquisitions, as well as the merits of consortium purchasing.

Suggested further reading

You could read the relevant sections of Johnson et al (2005) and Lysons and Farrington (2006).

Feedback on learning activities and self-assessment questions

Feedback on learning activity 20.1

There are many examples of acquisitions and mergers occurring in the news at any given time. If you select a large or high profile acquisition/merger, you will find plenty of discussion in the media to formulate a list of advantages and disadvantages. These could include:

Perceived advantages:

- strengthens market position by consolidating market share
- increases market value of company
- economies of scale and synergy between merged entities
- increased access to customer groups
- acquisition of skills, competencies and innovation
- increase in assets of company
- support strategic direction of company.

Perceived disadvantages:

- time consuming
- costly
- wrong strategy
- too complex to merge successfully
- loss of focus
- inappropriate use of shareholder's capital
- dilution of brand.

Feedback on self-assessment question 20.1

Competitors will agree to merge if they see this strategy as providing mutual advantage for their companies and respective shareholders. This may typically occur in mature or saturated markets where merging is seen as an effective means to secure additional market share and the resulting economies of scale this produces. In merging, the two companies are recognising the fact that they can operate and perform better as a single unit, rather than as two separate entities. This could be as the result of shared resources, complementary skills/assets and/or cross-utilisation of market experience and customers.

Feedback on learning activity 20.2

The Competition Commission aims to contribute to an increase in the level of competition in the UK economy and to contribute to the UK's economic performance and productivity in the international economy, where competitive pressures are becoming increasingly global.

Its role is to monitor the competitiveness of markets within the UK economy after referral from either the Office of Fair Trading or the government.

Feedback on self-assessment question 20.2

Restricted competition can give an unbalanced position of dominance to a supply market which in turn can lead to:

- price increases
- reduced quality and/or service levels
- stifled innovation
- potential security of supply issues.

Feedback on learning activity 20.3

Synergy may exist where the supply base of the two former organisations appears to provide the same goods and services. In this case, the IT equipment, facilities management, print and travel management suppliers appear to be duplicated. Through spend aggregation and supply base rationalisation there are opportunities for synergy. The synergy will be in the form of increased discounts for larger volumes of business and reduced administrative effort in managing multiple suppliers.

Feedback on self-assessment question 20.3

Purchasing can offer specific commercial advice during the period of due diligence through:

- contract analysis of key risks, liabilities and financial commitments with major suppliers
- evaluation of potential synergy and savings through amalgamating and rationalising the shared supply base
- stock evaluation and risk assessment across the organisation.

Purchasing also contributes during the integration period with the following commercial activities:

- establishing an effective services agreement with the management consultancy responsible for the integration project
- rationalising the supply base to contribute significant savings through economies of scale
- resolving all licensing and RTU issues quickly and efficiently to reduce the commercial exposure of the company
- reviewing third-party contracts and, where necessary, terminating.
- communicating accurately and regularly with third-party suppliers about the changes, particularly if the changes affect the accounting teams, the address of the company and/or the change of name.

In addition, purchasing can contribute its own benefits by eliminating any duplication in the merged purchasing functions.

Feedback on learning activity 20.4

There are several examples of consortium buying in existence in the UK, including the nine Regional Centres of Excellence that support local authority purchasing in the public sector (refer to Regional Centres of Excellence: http://www.rcoe.gov.uk). The local authorities pool together their demand for goods and services to aggregate volume and offer larger contracts for suppliers. They also pool purchasing resources for managing the tender and contract award processes, to be administratively efficient.

Feedback on self-assessment question 20.4

A supplier will view a consortium as having the following potential advantages:

- larger volume of business than approaching the individual members
- an opportunity to 'lock-out' rival competitors
- a single contract, therefore more cost efficient
- an opportunity to get 'in' with a wide range of clients.

Conversely, the supplier will view a consortium as having the following potential disadvantages:

- slow and bureaucratic decision-making
- multiple points of sale, making the business administratively burdensome

- compliance to the contract from members may be an issue, therefore volumes and commitments are uncertain
- difficult to do business with.

Revision questions

Revision question for study session 2

Evaluate three forms of private sector enterprise.

Feedback on page 285

Revision question for study session 3

Classify the main ways in which market sectors are grouped and distinguished.

Feedback on page 285

Revision question for study session 4

Explain why the public sector is regulated and what role the regulator plays.

Feedback on page 285

Revision question for study session 6

Describe the principal components of a business case for investment.

Feedback on page 286

Revision question for study session 7

Appraise the relative merits of 'part-time' purchasing.

Feedback on page 287

Revision question for study session 8

Classify Harland's four types of supply chain and review the utility of such a model.

Feedback on page 287

Revision question for study session 9

Evaluate the merits of purchasing on price alone.

Feedback on page 287

Revision question for study session 10

Define what is meant by the term 'purchase-to-pay (P2P) process' and review the benefits of implementing a professional P2P process in an organisation.

Feedback on page 288

Revision question for study session 11

Appraise the relative merits of competitive tendering.

Feedback on page 288

Revision question for study session 13

Discuss the ways in which purchasing activities can directly impact the customer.

Feedback on page 288

Revision question for study session 14

Evaluate the benefits for consumers of an organisation ensuring its key suppliers comply with its corporate social responsibility (CSR) policy.

Feedback on page 289

Revision question for study session 15

Discriminate between buying for production and buying for stock, using appropriate examples to illustrate your answers.

Feedback on page 289

Revision question for study session 16

Appraise the advantages and disadvantages of engaging a managed service provider to manage part of the supply base.

Feedback on page 290

Revision question for study session 17

Discuss the ways in which purchasing contributes to the acquisition and maintenance of capital items.

Feedback on page 290

Revision question for study session 18

Evaluate the benefits of liberalised international trade from a purchasing perspective.

Feedback on page 290

Revision question for study session 19

Discuss the relative benefits of supplying services internally rather than sourcing from the external market.

Feedback on page 291

Revision question for study session 20

Explain the input a purchasing manager can give during a merger or acquisition.

Feedback on page 291

Feedback on revision questions

Feedback on revision question for study session 2

Sole traders are private sector companies with a single owner. They are easy to establish and incur very low administration fees. The owner has significant degrees of freedom to run the business how they wish to, while remaining wholly responsible for the activities and therefore benefiting from all the profits received. However, the business is also wholly reliant on the owner for funding and resources, which, at times, can be restrictive. Business loans have to be guaranteed by personal loans and all the financial responsibilities and liabilities lie directly with the owner.

Partnerships are similar to sole traders in that they remain unincorporated. They are owned by two or more people (called partners), each with their own stake in the business. The partners share the financial responsibilities, making it easier to raise finance and the spread of risk and liability are easier. Partnerships can, however, be relatively bureaucratic and slow in decision-making because of the number of partners involved; and there is considerably less freedom than a sole trader because of the need to consult all partners.

Limited liability companies refer to privately owned companies that have been formally registered and incorporated as a separate legal entity. This means the owners' liability towards losses is limited to the extent to which they have invested in the company. It also means that the company is required to submit annual accounting reports for public scrutiny. Private limited companies remain 'closed' to other investors, whereas public limited companies trade on the stock exchange to raise investment share capital, but potentially risking changes in ownership. Limited companies require a greater degree of administration and accountability than unincorporated companies.

Feedback on revision question for study session 3

Market sectors are classified by ownership and control (such as public or private ownership), by size (such as small–medium enterprises) and by business activity (such as primary, secondary or tertiary sectors).

Classifying businesses helps to distinguish between different types of organisation for analytical and comparative purposes.

Feedback on revision question for study session 4

The public sector is regulated for several reasons predominantly associated with protecting the interests of public welfare and the national economy.

While there is little need to protect consumers from excess profiteering in the public sector, the role of the regulator is to ensure probity, value for money and good practice.

Typical roles of a public sector regulator might include:

- setting standards of good practice including consumer protection, safe practices, quality standards and service levels
- handling complaints from the public about any matters concerning the industry, the market, the service or specific organisations
- monitoring and auditing the activities of organisations within the market including compliance to standards and service levels
- receiving and reviewing regular organisational reports and returns regarding the organisation's performance
- communicating and promoting the work of the market to maintain consumer confidence
- regulating practice and issuing warnings, controls and levies for repeated non-compliant practice
- reporting to the government
- closure of non-performing operations (such as a school or hospital).

While regulation provides security and protection for the public interest, it also comes at a cost to the government and taxpaying public. The cost includes additional administrative burdens and slower decision-making on aspects of policy and direction. There is also the challenge of who regulates the regulators.

Feedback on revision question for study session 6

Typically business cases will include:

- An outline of the project, its rationale and the need it will fulfil.
- A detailed breakdown of the costs of the project in terms of design, construction, operation, maintenance and ultimate disposal.
- A detailed review of the tangible benefits of the project and its return on investment.
- Details of any other intangible benefits.
- An investment schedule detailing when the capital investment is required and over what time period.
- A calculation to show how and when the money will be paid back, including an outline of when the project will break even (or in other words have paid for itself).
- Details of all financing calculations, particularly where future money has needed to be discounted to present values.
- A description of any assumptions that have had to be made in forming the business case.
- An overview of any risks, dependencies and issues – including contingency plans where the risks are significant or potentially disruptive.
- A high level summary of the next steps and required actions to initiate the project.

Feedback on revision question for study session 7

Part-time purchasing refers to purchasing activities that are carried out by staff from non-purchasing functions as an additional part of their day-to-day operational roles.

The disadvantages associated with 'part-time' purchasing concern the potential lack of professional spend management. There are concerns about inconsistency with policy, lack of full effectiveness and potential exposure to commercial risks. Furthermore, where the organisation has specific policies regarding purchasing ethics, contact with suppliers and/or tendering rules and procedures there is a risk that these may not be adhered to. Given the nature of the 'part-time' term, there is also a risk that the full amount of time cannot be given to the purchasing activity, especially where members of staff have other full-time responsibilities to fulfil.

Conversely, however, part-time purchasing can demonstrate an effective means of spreading purchasing responsibilities throughout the organisation. It can also utilise the technical skills and knowledge base of other functions where purchasing does not have that capability.

Feedback on revision question for study session 8

Supply chains by their nature are difficult to define. Professor Christine Harland classified the following four types of supply chain:

1   The internal supply chain: where there is an internal process of supply within a single organisational entity
2   The dyadic supply chain: where the supply chain is characterised by an exchange between two organisations (typically the buyer and the supplier)
3   The external supply chain: where there is a passage of goods and added-value process through a series of organisations from one to another
4   The network: where there are complex tiers and associations of organisations supplying one another interactively.

This model helps to classify supply chains from an organisational perspective in a simple conceptual manner. However, this classification does not adequately describe or analyse the process of activities that transform the raw materials to finished goods for the end consumer. The model does not distinguish between added-value activities: it simply defines who within the supply chain does what.

Feedback on revision question for study session 9

Price is the most visible and tangible cost when buying any goods or services, but it is not the only cost associated with purchasing. Other costs include: delivery, maintenance, support, inspection, training, warranties, insurance, repair, disposal and so on. These costs combine with the price to form the total acquisition cost.

The risk of purchasing on price alone is that all other costs are ignored. Price is an insufficient indicator of the overall cost and by focusing on price alone, other business requirements (such as service, quality and/or delivery) can be overlooked.

Feedback on revision question for study session 10

Purchase-to-pay (P2P) refers to the end-to-end process for procuring and paying for goods and services, starting with the initial requisition and ending with the order fulfilled and paid for.

It is important to implement professional P2P processes to allow staff across the organisation to procure goods and services efficiently, effectively and without due commercial risk. Professional P2P processes include e-catalogues, purchasing cards and Purchase Order systems. By making the processes easy to use, they encourage staff to follow the correct procedures, which in turn prevents non-compliant spend. Commercial risk is minimised if staff comply with professional P2P processes as purchases can be covered by standard terms and conditions, policy is adhered to and the potential for fraud is reduced.

Feedback on revision question for study session 11

Competitive tendering is used to provide a structured and controlled competitive enquiry process within a supply market. Tenders provide a consistent method of sharing commercial information with a select group of potential suppliers, while also providing a consistent and 'fair' approach to receiving competitive bids.

Criticisms against tendering have included the administrative effort required to manage the tender process and the time it takes. Some critics argue that competitive tendering removes the opportunity for supplier innovation and creativity, therefore reducing the bidding process to a price war. Although there is some merit in these criticisms, it usually depends on how the tender process has been structured and used by the buyer.

Feedback on revision question for study session 13

Every activity within an organisation has an impact on the customer: it may not be direct (as in marketing, production or customer services) but most activities are systemic. Purchasing will therefore definitely have indirect impact on the customer, sometimes direct.

Here are four examples of ways in which purchasing may have direct impact on the customer:

- Purchasing buys goods for resale: that is, products that are passed on immediately to the customer without any changes. Examples include retail such as branded goods in supermarkets and DIY stores.
- Purchasing sources goods and services to support a 'value-added services' customer offering. This usually takes the form of a 'product wrap': typically a range of additional products and services made

available to customers if they buy the principal product. Examples include credit cards and professional subscription memberships.

- Purchasing sources product warranties and/or insurances for the customer from specialist service providers. Examples will include maintenance care cover for electrical goods.
- Purchasing gets invited to be involved in a supply chain audit or development programme, which includes the participation of customers and suppliers within the supply chain.

Feedback on revision question for study session 14

The benefits of having a robust CSR policy and ensuring that all suppliers are complying with the organisation's standards – especially those who produce goods for resale – are significant for several reasons:

1 The reputation and branding of the organisation are enhanced.
2 Consumers have greater confidence in the values of the organisation and/or product.
3 Consumers have a stronger loyalty and affinity to the brand.
4 There is less likelihood of a lawsuit or public media event causing reputational damage.
5 There are commercial benefits in adopting environmentally sustainable practices such as recycling.
6 The organisation can be viewed as an 'employer of choice'.
7 Suppliers recognise that the organisation will not tolerate unacceptable practices.

Conversely, if CSR is not taken into consideration adequately, the potential risks are considerable.

Feedback on revision question for study session 15

Buying for production is different than buying to replenish stock. Buying for production requires direct links with production schedules and an accurate feed of demand forecasting: an example is the purchase and supply of engine blocks for an automotive assembler.

Buying for production requires accurate planning and the demand schedules to be communicated to key suppliers. The emphasis is on maintaining a steady *flow* of supply to the operations, as well as getting the right quality and cost. It also requires robust supply chain management to ensure the risks of disruption are minimised.

Where production is not continuous, either in batches or by project, the concept remains the same but, instead of maintaining steady flow, purchasing needs to ensure delivery and lead times meet with the order requirements for production.

Buying for stock does not need the same level of sophistication, although the focus still needs to be on quality and cost. An example of buying for stock is the purchase of pulverised fuel ash for a concrete batching plant.

Stock controllers need to monitor supplies and storage to ensure that efficient quantities are ordered at the right time to replenish depleting stock levels. Over-ordering can lead to expensive storage problems, whilst under-ordering can become inefficient and over-administrative.

Feedback on revision question for study session 16

Managed services use the expertise of the principal supplier to engage and manage the supply base effectively and efficiently, thus saving time and expense for the lead organisation. Managed service providers can provide help and assistance with key technical issues and there often fewer supplier claims and disputes as a result. Operating a managed service gives the lead organisation simpler lines of responsibility and devolves responsibility to those most competent to manage it.

However, managed services can add extra management layers and costs to the supply base, while having a tendency to duplicate some of the management and administration. The managed service provider removes the client one hierarchy further away from the supply base, often meaning that the client has less control on the process and loses market/technical knowledge over time.

Feedback on revision question for study session 17

Capital items usually require investment expenditure to be purchased, because of the significant sums of money involved. As such, many capital items are purchased by technical specialists, such as engineers or chartered surveyors.

Purchasing contributes to both the acquisition and maintenance of capital items through helping identify sources of supply and pre-qualifying potential suppliers. Purchasing can support the development of the cost/benefit analysis, developing specifications and life-cycle costing. It can also help lower costs through negotiation with suppliers and managing their contracts effectively.

Feedback on revision question for study session 18

Where an economic region or country imposes trade barriers, in effect it is restricting itself to opportunities for international trade. Although on the face of it, this is an attempt to protect its domestic markets, in reality the effect is to reduce and stifle competition.

From a purchasing perspective, here is a list of the advantages of liberalised international trade:

- international markets are competitive
- market innovation is encouraged
- there are wider opportunities to source better products and/or lower prices
- there is greater access to specialist markets

- supplies of scarce materials and commodities are more secure
- overheads and the cost of production are reduced.

Feedback on revision question for study session 19

Some of the benefits available to organisations for sourcing internally are as follows:

- high regular volume, thus securing demand
- if resources in the external supply market are scarce it benefits having an internal supply
- internal costs can be cheaper than the external market
- transaction costs are minimal (no value-added tax, for example)
- if high levels of skill and complexity are required and specialists need to be secured, then this can be assured through internal service provision and employment of the specialists
- where high levels of confidentiality and market value require significant control, the activity is most secure if kept in-house
- keeping the activity in-house maintains control on quality.

Feedback on revision question for study session 20

It is extremely rare for purchasing and supply functions to be involved in the merger and acquisition process before the bid has been agreed. This is usually because of the extreme caution that companies place on these activities, where, for confidentiality, only a handful of key personnel in the company have any knowledge of the intention to acquire or merge.

Although it may be inspirational to believe that purchasing staff have appropriate and transferable commercial skills for the acquisition of corporate entities, this is an optimistic view of purchasing's remit and capabilities.

Purchasing can offer specific commercial advice during the period of due diligence through:

- contract analysis of key risks, liabilities and financial commitments with major suppliers
- evaluation of potential synergy and savings through amalgamating and rationalising the shared supply base
- stock evaluation and risk assessment across the organisation.

Purchasing also contributes during the integration period with the following commercial activities:

- establishing an effective services agreement with the management consultancy responsible for the integration project
- rationalising the supply base to contribute significant savings through economies of scale
- resolving all licensing and rights to use issues quickly and efficiently to reduce the commercial exposure of the company
- reviewing third party contracts and, where necessary, terminating

- communicating accurately and regularly with third party suppliers about the changes, particularly if the changes affect the accounting teams, the address of the company and/or the change of name.

In addition, purchasing can contribute its own benefits by eliminating any duplication in the merged purchasing functions.

References and bibliography

This section contains a complete A-Z listing of all publications, materials or websites referred to in this course book. Books, articles and research are listed under the first author's (or in some cases the editor's) surname. Where no author name has been given, the publication is listed under the name of the organisation that published it. Websites are listed under the name of the organisation providing the website.

Bailey, P, D Farmer, D Jessop and D Jones (2005) *Purchasing Principles and Management*, 9th edition, FT Prentice Hall, Harlow.

Branch, AE (2001) *International Purchasing and Management*, Thomson Learning, London.

Buckley, J (1996) *Guide to World Commodity Markets*, 7th edition, Kogan Page, London.

CIPS (1998) *Purchasing Policies & Procedures*, Chartered Institute of Purchasing & Supply, Easton (ISBN 1-86124-003-1).

Cox, AW (1993) *Public Procurement in the EC, Volume 1: The Single Market Rules and the Enforcement Regime After 1992*, Earlsgate Press, Boston UK.

Cox, A (1997) *Business Success*, Earlsgate Press, Boston UK – with particular reference to the chapter referring to critical supply chain assets.

Cox, A and I Thompson (1998) *Contracting for Business Success*, Thomas Telford, London.

Cox, A, P Ireland et al (2002) *Supply Chains, Markets and Power*, Routledge, London.

Daft, RL (2003) *Organization Theory and Design,* 8th edition. Belmont: South-Western/Thomson Learning

Dobler, DW and DN Burt (1996) *Purchasing and Supply Management*, 6th edition, McGraw-Hill, New York. (Note: this edition has been superseded by several follow-on titles by the same authors, although the text is still relevant for purchasing studies.)

Ford D, LE Gadde, H Håkansson, A Lungren, I Snehota, P Turnbull and D Wilson (1998) *Managing Business Relationships*, John Wiley, New York.

Fearon HE and WA Bales (1995) *Purchasing of Non-traditional Goods and Services*, Center for Advanced Purchasing Studies, Tempe, Arizona.

Furlong, P and A Cox (1995) *The European Union at the Cross-Roads*, Earlsgate Press, Boston UK.

Handy, C (1999) *Understanding Organizations*, 4th edition, Penguin, London.

Hines, P (1994) *Creating World Class Suppliers: Unlocking Mutual Competitive Advantage*, Pitman Publishing, London.

Johnson, G, K Scholes and R Whittington (2005) *Exploring Corporate Strategy*, 7th edition, FT Prentice Hall, Harlow.

Lamming, R (1993) *Beyond Partnership*, Prentice Hall, New York.

Lamming, R and AW Cox (1995) *Strategic Procurement Management in the 1990s: Concepts and Cases*, Earlsgate Press, Boston UK.

Lysons, K and B Farrington (2006) *Purchasing and Supply Chain Management*, 7th edition, FT Prentice Hall, Harlow.

Mullins, LJ (2005) *Management and Organisational Behaviour*, 7th edition, FT Prentice Hall, Harlow.

Oakland, JS (1993) *Total Quality Management*, Butterworth-Heinemann

Porter, ME (1980) *Competitive Strategy: techniques for analyzing industries and competitors*, Macmillan Publishing Co Inc, New York.

Porter, ME (1985) *Competitive Advantage*, Free Press, New York.

Raftery, J (1991) *Principles of Building Economics*, Blackwell, Oxford.

Slack, N, S Chambers, C Harland, R Johnston and A Harrison (1998) *Operations Management*, 2nd edition, FT Pitman Publishing, London.

Womack JP, DT Jones and D Roos (1990) *The Machine that Changed the World*, Rawson Associates, New York.

Index